Troubling educational cultures in the Nordic countries

the Tufnell Press,
London,
United Kingdom
www.tufnellpress.co.uk
email contact@tufnellpress.co.uk

British Library Cataloguing-in-Publication Data
A catalogue record for this book is
available from the British Library

paperback ISBN	*1872767591*
ISBN-13	*978-1-872767-59-8*
Kindle	*978-1-872767-64-2*

Printed in England and U.S.A. by Lightning Source

Troubling educational cultures in the Nordic countries

edited by
Touko Vaahtera, Anna-Maija Niemi, Sirpa Lappalainen
and Dennis Beach

The Ethnography and Education book series aims to publish a range of authored and edited collections including both substantive research projects and methodological texts and in particular we hope to include recent PhDs. Our priority is for ethnographies that prioritise the experiences and perspectives of those involved and that also reflect a sociological perspective with international significance. We are particularly interested in those ethnographies that explicate and challenge the effects of educational policies and practices and interrogate and develop theories about educational structures, policies and experiences. We value ethnographic methodology that involves long-term engagement with those studied in order to understand their cultures, that use multiple methods of generating data and that recognise the centrality of the researcher in the research process.

www.ethnographyandeducation.org

The editors welcome substantive proposals that seek to:

explicate and challenge the effects of educational policies and practices and
interrogate and develop theories about educational structures, policies and experiences,
highlight the agency of educational actors,
provide accounts of how the everyday practices of those engaged in education and instrumental in social reproduction.

Details of recent titles in this series can be found at the end of this book

Contents

Introduction

Troubling educational cultures in the Nordic Countries: Introduction

Touko Vaahtera, Anna-Maija Niemi, Sirpa Lappalainen and Dennis Beach

Let's make trouble!

In her book, *School trouble: identity, power and politics in education,* Deborah Youdell (2011) calls researchers and educators to be *trouble makers,* who contest the normative assumptions that frame, for example, notions of gender, sexuality, ethnicity, ability, learning and behaviour in the context of education. From the point of view of a non-Nordic audience it might look as if there is very little to *trouble* in Nordic countries, which score well in terms of formal equality of opportunity in education. Still educational inequalities related to economic, social and cultural dimensions have remained; young people of working class, ethnic minority or special education background tend to end up in culturally less-valued educational routes more often than white middle class youth (e.g. Dovemark and Beach, 2016, Berhanu, 2016a, 2016b; Niemi and Mietola, 2017; Rinne, 2012) and higher education and especially the economically most rewarding and culturally appreciated fields, such as medicine and law are still accessible mostly for well-to-do families (e.g. Beach and Puaca, 2014; Nori, 2011). Moreover, the most recent aims for tightening policies towards all groups dependent on any kind of social services or support signal decreasing solidarity towards less privileged people. For example, the Nordic Countries elaborate their immigration policy aiming to take care that they are not more tempting to asylum seekers than their neighbouring countries.

The authors of this book have taken the *call for troubling* seriously and are enthusiastic in applying it to the Nordic context. As we were troubed about the concept *troubling* in the title of the this book, we decided to start by exploring that particular concept and how the articles in the book are related to it. First of all, we do not view trouble as something that needs to be resolved, but rather something that challenges how particular categories exist without being in the need of troubling. Thus, rather than resolve the trouble we seek to *make* some trouble. Here we are inspired by Judith Butler's idea of gender trouble concerning the need to contest normative assumptions about gender and sexuality. *Gender trouble* for Butler is a process that reshapes norms that produce heterosexuality and two opposite sexes as natural and real. Along these lines, the trouble we put forward in this book seeks to contest the normative assumptions that frame notions of ability, ethnicity, learning and behaviour in the context of education. For Butler (1999/1990; 1993a), gender trouble is an inevitable process that happens when the illusion of heterosexual hegemony (Butler, 1993a) is disputed just through the existence of various bodies which do not conform (or which rather accidentally fail to conform) to the order that the heterosexual hegemony wants to maintain. Thus, almost everyone troubles heterosexual hegemony in some sense. Robert McRuer's (2006) reading of a critically queer version of gender trouble (see Butler, 1993b), however, emphasises intentionality.

From the perspective of cultural studies, Robert McRuer (2006) suggests that the *critically queer* version of gender trouble does not merely imply that the maintaining of heterosexual hegemony can only fail. Rather, it emphasises various forms of collective work that actively challenge the normative notions of bodies and sexualities. In this version of gender trouble, people who actively resist heteronormativity (in spite of their sexual identities) engender gender trouble. Following McRuer (2006), we want to trouble educational cultures in the critically queer sense of gender trouble. In this respect, we highlight the importance of the methodological perspective of cultural studies. Cultural studies aims to articulate social circumstances in a way that it enables less-familiar articulations to emerge and the political nature of everyday life to become evident (e.g. Morley and Chen, 1996). It highlights that there are struggles of the understandings of everyday life. This means that we pay attention to how we conceptualise phenomena, such as globalisation, gender, sexuality or for example learning, and how our conceptualisations are connected with our political aims.

While various agents intentionally reshape norms they cannot control how their work functions and is later interpreted. A viewpoint that resists closures and emphasises effects rather than fixed meanings is at the core of the methodology of cultural studies (e.g. Morley and Chen, 1996). In addition, when this book focuses on educational cultures, we also want to underscore the ways that education can engender surprising effects because it changes its subjects. As Kevin Kumashiro (2002: 8) claims we cannot control what students learn. Moreover, we cannot control how students will use what they have learned. To trouble educational cultures means that we acknowledge the unexpected nature of education and learning. We also acknowledge that education can be troubled also by those who are not considered to be formal authorities of educational practices. In this book, this means, for example, queer youth who seek to challenge heteronormativity in schools (Taavetti in this book) and pupils who aim at taking over a pedagogisised school yard for free play and wandering (Rönnlund in this book).

As well as problematising dominant ways of making sense troubling education means commitment to seek paths to critical thinking and more progressive pedagogical practices. Jón Ingvar Kjaran and Ingólfur Ásgeir Jóhannesson consider the processes of challenging heteronormativity in classrooms and how the National Curriculum Guide can be used to put forward countercultural knowledges of sexuality. Kjaran and Jóhannesson show that even a formal school can sometimes be a queer counterpublic. Drawing on postcolonial theorisations that challenge still existing colonial reasoning, Pia Mikander demonstrates how discourse analysis makes visible unequal global power relations, hence having the potential to shake euro-centric worldviews in social sciences teaching. Riikka Taavetti explores in her chapter what kinds of forms of resistance queer students imagine. Taavetti asks, how could the heteronormative culture of schools be challenged from the perspective of queer students? Her analysis shows that young queer students correct and criticise their teachers and even imagine ways to support adult queers. In all these three chapters educational settings emerge as sites that contest taken-for-granted positions of learners.

Troubling culture

What are we talking about when we say the aim is to trouble educational cultures? By *culture* we mean on the one hand various human-made works including literature, architecture, films, and different cultural texts of different genres. On the other hand, drawing on Raymond Williams (1961), we understand the term culture in a wider way. For Williams (1961: 41), 'culture is a description of a particular way of life, which expresses certain meanings and values not only in art and learning but also in institutions and ordinary behaviour.' This broader definition of culture makes it possible to explore diverse practices of everyday life in educational contexts. It enables a focus on the sites that for some 'are not *culture* at all (ibid.: 42).' This means exploring habits, practices and styles–*ways of life* and *way of making* (de Certeau, 1984) that also appear to be mundane or *low* but express the broader values of society.

We also want to pay attention to how globalisation and globalised networks are present in Nordic societies (see Anthias and Lloyd, 2002: 2). In the first chapter of the book, Dennis Beach makes a synthesis of educational experiences of young men in multi-cultural, multi-ethnic suburbs. Based on extensive meta-ethnographic analysis, he highlights the reasons for potential feelings of alienation of these young men but at the same time emphasises the young men's capacity for creativity and learning. The crucial question is whether the actors in the Swedish education system are able to recognise this potential and put it to work for a safe, equal and democratic society.

The book particularly aims at analysing and troubling educational cultures, their complexity and distinctive meanings given to them. The approach matters because school is crucial in children's and young people's subject formation. It frames how they understand themselves as learners and more broadly as human beings. Moreover, school, when guiding students to follow particular paths has very material effects on young people's future prospects. We cannot talk about a fair and equal education system until school is a place where all students can equally reach a sense of adequacy regardless their various backgrounds, genders, sexual identities or capabilities.

For us, the troubling of educational cultures can be done by unexpected agents too and it can take us in unforeseen directions and while we connect the troubling of educational cultures with the context of anti-oppressive education (Kumashiro, 2002), we still want to leave it open what kind of work troubles education. According to Kumashiro (2002), a process that troubles education can never be finished. It is an ongoing process that seeks to interrogate educational ideas and practices, over and over again, in order to make a more just society possible. Kumashiro claims that if we seek social change that would make less oppressive futures possible, we have to constantly trouble education. In Kumashiro's (2002: 202) terms, this work should 'simultaneously be anti-oppressive in some ways while troubling those very ways of being.'

The title of the book leads a reader to examine and trouble Nordic educational ideals. It explores in detail the cultural practices that emerge from the Nordic educational landscapes, especially in Denmark, Finland, Iceland and Sweden. Equality, social justice and democracy have traditionally been ideas through which Nordic countries have imagined themselves as Nations (see Anderson, 2006). Schooling was seen as crucial in the development of the Nordic welfare state, where everyone was supposed to have equal opportunities regardless of social background, abilities, gender or region of living (Blossing, Imsen and Moos, 2014).

Traditionally, Nordic Countries have had a mainly publicly funded and governed comprehensive schooling system free of charge for pupils. But neo-liberalism with its emphasis on economy, marketisation, new public management and individualism (e.g. Arnesen, Lahelma, Lundahl and Öhrn, 2014; Beach, 2010), have fundamentally shaken the grounds for Nordic self-understanding and ideas of the aims of schooling. How and to what extent this transformation has happened varies among Nordic Countries. The extreme case is that of privatisation in the Swedish education system, which has been argued to be one of the most market oriented education systems in the world (e.g. Hudson, 2011). In Finland, the public attitude towards the selection and free school choice has been somewhat suspicious and one can still strongly question the relevance of the concept of *school market* (Kosunen, 2014). School choice is an urban phenomenon, most probably occurring in ethnically and economically diverse areas (Kosunen, 2014), so leading to the polarisation effect (Ahonen, 2014). Polarisation occurs when particular (in this case middle class, European) ways of life are seen as more favourable and exceptions to them as suspicious. We argue then that it is extremely important to challenge the idea that there exists a particular Nordic way of life particularly at this moment when racism in Nordic Countries takes forms in which cultural diversity is occasionally opposed as if it were something new. So to trouble culture means to challenge the notion of a homogenous Nordic way of life that was pure and uncontaminated in the past. Pia Mikander's chapter calls educators to problematise the cultural explanations that take views of hegemonic groups for granted and leaves others in the margin, for example through silencing, victimising or even demonising practices (see also chapter by Beach).

It has been argued that neo-liberal reasoning pushes a rights-based model of citizenship toward consumer oriented, entrepreneurial and economic subjects (Peters, 2011: 174). However, in Iceland the dramatic economic downfall in 2008 influenced the political climate challenging neo-liberal reasoning (Sigurðardóttir, Guðjónsdóttir, and Karlsdóttir, 2014). Iceland, then, is an example of country, where the trend has recently been towards more inclusive education (ibid., 109). Moreover, by legitimating queer studies as both as a source of teaching as well as course content the current Icelandic curriculum is extremely progressive even in the Nordic context. Students' interviews introduced in Kjaran and Jóhannesson's chapter shows that both policies and practices matter when taken as granted views are troubled.

At the beginning of the neo-liberal turn, Danish educational politics were relatively reluctant to reflect economic policies. However, in the last ten years participatory democracy and the idea of *education for all* have given way to an emphasis on excellence (Rasmussen and Moos, 2014) and the ways that schools have specific profiles. For example health or sports related specialisation is increasing among schools (Otrel-Cass and Kondrup Kristensen in this book). Furthermore, as Kathrin Otrel-Cass and Liv Kondrup Kristensen show in their chapter, in this context there have been attempts to include physical activity into the lessons of general studies and in this way foster the potentialities of students. They show how these attempts can take a form that eventually dismisses the ubiquitous ways embodiment and learning are connected with each other.

Troubling ability

In recent years, many disability studies scholars (McRuer, 2006; Campbell, 2009; Goodley, 2014; Kafer, 2013) have suggested that it is necessary to investigate not only disability but the cultural processes that engender able-bodiedness as the normative ideal that appears to express humanity in the most perfect sense. We suggest that cultural studies in education, too, ought to interrogate ideals of ability. In this sense, following McRuer's (2006) formulation of *ability trouble* we want to make ability trouble in order to reshape the way we tend to think about education. By *ability trouble* we mean intentional and accidental processes that undermine normative notions of disability/able-bodiedness. Ability trouble for us means on the one hand the ways in which various bodies/minds do not conform the norm of able-bodiedness and on the other the conceptualisations of disability rights movements and disability studies that challenge a worldview that assumes able-bodiedness.

We suggest that the educational cultures of school, academia and everyday life consist of many, often unacknowledged, assumptions around ability. This applied to not only mean academic skills but also more mundane skills and abilities. Consider how school shapes the circadian rhythm, controling when students wake up, and when they move and eat. We might suggest that these mundane ways of controlling the bodies of students, let alone the learning of physical skills and the emphasis of good social skills, reflect the ableist ideals of wider society. Ina Juva and Touko Vaahtera pay attention to the ableist dimensions of understandings of social skills in the context of comprehensive schooling. They highlight the contingency of the idea of social skills and argue that when social skills are understood in relation to the labour market, not all forms of sociality can be recognised as socially skilful behaviour.

While the book turns to these daily issues, the ability trouble that we put forward emphasises the various contexts around ability norms, where the ideal of able-bodiedness is reinforced through the practices of education. For example,

Juva and Vaahtera consider what kind of abilities school wants to fortify. We also ask what are students' possibilities for negotiation and resistance. In her detailed micro level classroom analysis in a special education unit (SENU), Yvonne Karlsson examines students' aims to establish their adequacy within school culture, which continuously defines them as problematic.

We explore how students and learners are named and shaped in the practices of education through socially constructed binaries, such as active/passive, competent/poor and disabled/able-bodied (Niemi and Kurki, 2014). In this respect, we ask what kind of specific aims and ideals intertwine with the educational aims that attempt to activate students. Socially constructed binaries often define what is regarded as *normal* being and behaviour, hence some subjectivities and bodies become incompatible– even impossible– with the school's notions of a (desirable) student and a learner. (Niemi and Kurki, 2014; Youdell, 2006; Ashton, 2011; Grue, 2011).

In this book, Rönnlund and Juva and Vaahtera unpack the idea of the active student, showing how the idea of the active student is also a way of controlling students. Juva and Vaahtera analyse how the idea of social skills in the context of schooling reinforces an individualistic idea of social behaviour. In the chapter *Schoolyard cultures,* Maria Rönnlund demonstrates how a schoolyard, often seen a rather irrelevant part of the school, actually enables many pedagogical interventions and is still a place where the aims of the official school can be disputed. Cultural materialists such as Williams (1961, 1977, 1983) and McRuer (2006) understand that culture always includes conflicts. By conflicts we mean disagreements of how cultural categories, concepts and practices can be used and to what ends do particular cultural understandings lead us. In this respect, to trouble culture means that we acknowledge the contingent nature of culture as *a way of life*. Thus, we do not assume that everyone has affinity for the same community and the same cultural products. Furthermore for us, the culture without a conflict of its content seems alarming since such an understanding can lead to a totalising view of culture. On the other hand, the authors of the book also pay attention to how conflicts in regards to culture as a way of life emerge when we note how many cultural practices are exclusive (see Goodley, 2014; Yuval-Davies, 2011; Niemi and Mietola, 2017).

The specificity of ethnographic methodology in cultural studies in education

When the aim is to examine the complexities and nuances of educational cultures, methodologies, that address everyday life of schooling are required. Ethnography, emphasising embodied experiences in a site of interest and the utilisation of various data-production methods as well as analytical strategies, has been recognised as a tool for deeper understanding of how education *works*. There is a strong tradition of educational ethnography, among Nordic researchers of educational sciences, specifically among researchers inspired by cultural, critical, youth, feminist and/or policy studies in education (see e.g. Lahelma, Lappalainen, Mietola and Palmu, 2014; Paju et al., 2014; Gudmundsson, Beach and Vestel, 2013; Gordon, Lahelma and Beach, 2003). Nordic scholars have been influenced mainly by the Anglophone world; drawing both from the British tradition, with sociological interest in relations between structures and agency, and the US tradition in cultural anthropology (Delamont and Atkinson, 1995: Gordon, Holland and Lahelma, 2001). Generations of Nordic educational ethnographers have grown up with Paul Willis's *Learning to labour* learning to understand the school as a site of political, social and cultural struggle, and the way that youth identities are constituted within schools (Dolby and Dimitriadis, 2004: 2). Policy reforms, for example, are not seen as innocent but shaping educational cultures sometimes with unexpected effects.

Kathrin Otrel-Cass and Liv Kontrup Kristensen have conducted micro-level analysis on the effects of the *New Nordic School* reform introduced in Denmark, 2014, with the aim of increasing physical activity into everyday schooling. This policy intervention was justified by referring its positive effects on the learning and health of young people. But in their detailed analysis Otrel-Cass and Kontrup Kristensen show how *learning by moving* does not necessarily improve students' sense of learning and might even lead to new forms of marginalisation by favouring capable embodiment. Here an educational practice that seeks to emphasise an embodied aspect of learning and in that way enable a more complex understanding of being a student, might eventually turn out to strengthen the establishment. Nordic ethnographers have been interested in examining how changes in education politics and policies re-shape educational cultures (e.g. Lunneblad, Odenbring and Hellman, 2016). They might have also been enthusiastic in examining in detail how school cultures turn out to produce and reproduce social, cultural and economic divisions despite a comprehensive schooling system, free of charge education and *goodwill* in developing inclusive practices (e.g. Moldenhawer, 2009; Niemi and Kurki, 2014; Hjélmer and Rosvall, 2016). By combining ethnographic fieldwork with autoethnographic reflections, Jukka Lehtonen pays attention to how practices that seek to intervene in hegemonic understandings fail. Lehtonen analyses the educational outreach work of the Finnish LGBTI[1] rights organisation Seta and suggests that while Seta aims to challenge sexual norms, the way that Seta emphasises the ordinariness of non-heterosexual lives does not challenge the heteronormative culture.

What we think is important in Nordic ethnographic research done in the field of educational sciences is the capacity in producing reflexive and critical insights into the practices of educational institutions, expected to be exemplary in terms of equality and social justice (Beach, 2010). The ethnographic contributions presented in this book opens up diverse viewpoints to analyse and trouble the educational cultures, practices and distinctive meanings given to them by the actors in the field. Yvonne Karlsson's text is an example of ethno-methodological classroom study, in which particular pedagogical practices and situations are analysed closely by attempting to understand, what is happening in those practices and how the participants of the study are positioned in the practices of the classroom.

The starting point of this book project was when the Nordforsk funded Nordic Centre of Excellence (NCoE): Justice through education in the Nordic Countries (JustEd) suggested that researchers affiliated to this center would seek answers to the question, How do systems, cultures and actors in education enable and constrain justice in the context of globalising Nordic welfare states? The authors of this book have focused on cultural processes, examining the blind spots of education systems considered to be the most equal in the world: they have shown that young people who do not fulfil cultural expectations are still relatively easily pushed into the margin; they have highlighted how the pedagogical practices aimed to promote equality might turn out to establish the privileged position of hegemonic majority or even create new forms of marginalisation. However, the potential for counter politics that occurs both in young people and grass root educators has been pointed out. As Kjaran and Jóhanesson's chapter shows, education policy, which does not uncritically give

1. In this book, authors use different versions of this acronym (LGBTI/LGBTIQ). We have deliberately chosen to use different versions because it shows how the acronym is changeable and it emerges in different forms in specific local and social contexts

in to neo-liberal reasoning, can create space for fair, sensitive and intellectually inspiring education.

References

Ahonen, S., (2014) A school for all in Finland, in Blossing, U., Imsen, G. and Moos, L., (eds.) *The Nordic Education Model. 'A school for all' encounters with neo-liberal policy,* Dordrech: Springer, 77-94.

Anderson, B., (2006). *Imagined communities: Reflections on the origin and spread of nationalism*, 3 ed., London: Verso.

Anthias, F. and Lloyd, C., (2002) *Rethinking anti-racisms. From theory to practice*, London & New York: Routledge.

Ashton, J. R., (2011) The CEC professional standards: A Foucauldian genealogy of the re/construction of special education, *International journal of inclusive education,* 15(8): 775-795.

Arnesen, A-L., Lahelma, E., Lundahl, L. and Öhrn, E., (2014) Unfolding the context and the contents: Critical perspectives on contemporary Nordic schooling, in Arnesen, A-L., Lahelma, E., Lundahl, L. and Öhrn, E., (eds.) *Fair and competitive? Critical perspectives on contemporary Nordic schooling*, London: Tufnell Press, 1-19.

Beach, D., (2010) Socialisation and commercialisation in the restructuring of education and health professions in Europe: Questions of global class and gender, *Current sociology*, 58(4): 551-569.

Beach, D. and Puaca, G., (2014) Changing higher education by converging policy-packages: education choices and student identities. *European Journal of Higher Education*, 4(1): 67-79.

Berhanu, G., (2016a) Contemporary Swedish society and education: inequities and challenges, in Beach, D. and Dyson, A., (eds.) *Equity and education in cold climates in Sweden and England*, London: Tufnell Press, 43-59.

Berhanu, G., (2016b) Concepts of equity in Swedish society and education: historical perspectives, in Beach, D. and Dyson, A., (eds.) *Equity and education in cold climates in Sweden and England*, London: Tufnell Press, 27-42.

Blossing, U., Imsen, G. and Moos, L., (2014) Nordic schools in time of change, in Blossing, U., Imsen, G. and Moos, L., (eds.) *The Nordic education model. 'A school for all' encounters with neo-liberal policy,* Dordrech: Springer, 1-14.

Butler, J., (1990) *Gender trouble. Feminism, and the subversion of identity*, 2nd ed., New York: Routledge.

Butler, J., (1993a) *Bodies that matter: On the discursive limits of 'sex'*, New York: Routledge.

Butler, J. (1993b) Critically queer, *GLQ: A journal of lesbian and gay studies*, 1(1): 17-32.

Campbell, F. K., (2009) *Contours of ableism: the production of disability and abledness*, New York: Palgrave Macmillan.

de Certeau, M., (1984) *The practice of everyday life* [Arts de Faire], Rendall, S. (trans.), Berkeley: University of California Press.

Delamont, S. and Atkinson, P., (1995) *Fighting familiarity: Essays on education and ethnography*, Cresskill, New Jersey: Hampton Press.

Dolby, N., and Dimitriadis, G., (2004) *Learning to labour in new times*, London: Routledge.

Dovemark, M. and Beach, D., (2016) From learning to labour to learning to precariarity, *Ethnography & education,* (11)2: 174-188.

Goodley, D., (2014) *Dis/ability studies. Theorising disablism and ableism*, New York: Routledge.

Gordon T., Holland, J. and Lahelma, E., (2001) Ethnographic research in educational settings, in Atkinson, P., Coffey, A., Delamont, S., Lofland, J. and Lofland, L., (eds.) *Handbook of ethnography*, London: SAGE, 188-203.

Gordon T., Lahelma, E. and Beach, D., (2003) Marketisation of democratic education: ethnographic insights, in Beach, D., Gordon, T. and Lahelma, E., (eds.) *Democratic education: Ethnographic challenges,* London: Tufnell Press, 1-9.

Grue, J., (2011) Discourse analysis and disability: Some topics and issues, *Discourse society*, 22 (5): 532-546.

Gudmundsson, G., Beach, D., and Vestel, V., (2013) *Young people and marginalisation: Young people from immigrant families in Scandinavia*, London: Tufnell Press.

Hjélmer, C. and Rosvall, P-Å., (2016) Does social justice count? 'Lived democracy' in mathematics classes in diverse Swedish upper secondary programmes, *Journal of curriculum studies*, published online 24 January 2016: 1-19.

Hudson, C., (2011) Evaluation - and the (not so) softlysoftly approach to governance and its consequences for the compulsory education in the Nordic Countries, *Education inquiry*, 2(4): 671-688.

Kafer, A., (2013) *Feminist, queer, crip*, Bloomington: Indiana University Press.

Kosunen, S., (2014) Reputation and parental logics of action in local school choice space in Finland, *Journal of education policy*, 29(4): 443-466.

Kumashiro, K., (2002) *Troubling education: Queer activism and antioppressive pedagogy*, New York: RoutledgeFalmer.

Lahelma, E., Lappalainen, S., Mietola, R. and Palmu, T., (2014) Discussions that 'tickle our brains': constructing interpretations through multiple ethnographic data-sets, *Ethnography and education,* 9 (1): 51-65.

Lunneblad, J., Odenbring, Y. and Hellman, A., (2016) A strong commitment: conforming a school identity at one compulsory faith school in a disadvantaged area, *Ethnography and education,* published online http://dx.doi.org/10.1080/17457823.2016.1216323, 1-15.

McRuer, R., (2006) *Crip theory: Cultural signs of queerness and disability*, New York: New York University Press.

Mietola, R., Lahelma, E., Lappalainen, S. and Palmu, T., (2005) Johdattelua kohtaamisiin kasvatuksen, koulutuksen ja tutkimuksen kentillä, in Mietola, R., Lahelma, E., Lappalainen, S. and Palmu, T., (eds.) *Kohtaamisia kasvatuksen ja koulutuksen kentillä. Erontekoja ja yhdessä tekemistä,* Turku: Painosalama Oy.

Moldenhawer, B., (2009) *Comparative report on education. Ethnic differences in education and diverging prospects for urban youth in an enlarged Europe*, European Commission's seventh framework programme (FP7/2007-2013).

Morley, D. and Chen, K.-H., (1996) *Stuart Hall: Critical dialogues in cultural studies*, London: Routledge.

Nelson, G., Treichler, P. A., and Grossberg, L., (1992) Cultural studies: An introduction, in Grossberg, L., Nelson, G., and Treichler, P. A., (eds.) *Cultural Studies,* New York: Routledge, 1-22.

Niemi, A.-M. and Kurki, T., (2014) Getting on the right track? Educational choice-making of students with special educational needs in pre-vocational education and training, *Disability & society*, 29(10): 1631-1644.

Niemi, A.-M. and Mietola, R., (2017) Between hopes and possibilities: (Special) educational paths, agency and subjectivities, *Scandinavian journal of disability research*, 19 (3): 218-229.

Nori, H., (2011) *Keille yliopiston portit avautuvat? Tutkimus suomalaisiin yliopistoihin ja eri tieteenaloille valikoitumisesta 2000-luvun alussa*, Thesis (PhD), Univeristy of Turku, Annales Universitatis Turkuensis C 309.

Paju, E., Salo, U.-M., Guttorm, H., Hohti, R., Lappalainen, S., Mietola, R. and Niemi, A.-M., (2014) Feministinen etnografia: Tietämistä ja tutkimista kasvatuksen kentillä, *Sukupuolentutkimus*, 27(4): 30-41.

Peters, M., (2011) *Neoliberalism and after? Education, social policy, and the crisis of western capitalism*, New York, NY: Peter Lang.

Rasmussen, A. and Moos, L., (2014) A school for less than all in Denmark, in Blossing, U., Imsen, G. and Moos, L., (eds.) *The Nordic education model. 'A school for all' encounters with neo-liberal policy,* Dordrech: Springer, 95-113.

Rinne, R., (2012) Koulutetun eliitin erottautuminen [The distinction of the educated elite], in Kettunen, P., and Simola, H., (eds.) *Tiedon ja osaamisen Suomi [Finland a country of knowledge],* Helsinki: Finnish Hisltorical Association, 367-407.

Sigurðardóttir, A. K., Guðjónsdóttir, H. and Karlsdóttir, J., (2014) The development of a school for all in Iceland: Equality, threats and political conditions, in Blossing, U., Imsen, G. and Moos, L., (eds.) *The Nordic education model. 'A school for all' encounters with neo-liberal policy,* Dordrech: Springer, 95-113.

Williams, R., (1961) *The long revolution*, London: Chatto & Windus.

Williams, R., (1983) *Culture & society 1780-1950,* New York: Columbia University Press.

Williams, R., (1977) *Marxism and literature*, Oxford: Oxford University Press.

Youdell, D., (2011) *School trouble: identity, power and politics in education*, Abingdom: Routledge.

Youdell, D., (2006) *Impossible bodies, impossible selves: Exclusions and student subjectivities*, Dordrecht: Springer.

Yuval-Davies, N., (2011) *The politics of belonging: intersectional contestations*, London Sage.

Chapter 1

The learning and creativity of male youth from multi-cultural suburbs

Dennis Beach

This chapter is based on a meta-ethnographic analysis of the learning of groups of multi-ethnic male youth in multi-cultural, multi poverty suburbs in Sweden. These are very special kinds of places. Lindbäck and Sernhede (2013) have described them as places that are both inside and outside of Sweden, at the same time, foreign and alienated; and as territorially stigmatised and isolated islands *outside of Sweden*; yet also placed within this very rich country (Alinia, 2006; Sernhede, 2007; Lindbäck and Sernhede, 2013). To people from outside the Nordic region this might sound very strange. Reflecting characteristics that are broadly attributed to the Nordic region as a whole, Sweden has an internationally iconic reputation for being a fair and highly democratic State with high levels of class and gender parity in terms of education and social inclusion, with open attitudes and policies toward migrants, asylum seekers and recently settled new (trans)-nationals and their children (Gudmundsson, 2013).

The existence of the territorially stigmatised, multi-poverty, multi-ethnic places of exclusion described by Sernhede and others, disrupts and challenges this iconic reputation. It describes areas that in the sense of Wacquant (2008) merge the characteristics of the American ghetto and the European model of marginal peripheries. As expressed in Beach (2017b) they form what Agier (2009) termed *territories of abandonment* for discarded lives (Beach and Sernhede, 2011). Alinia (2006), Borelius (2010), Schwartz (2013), Sernhede (2007), and Öhrn (2012) have each also picked up on these points. Their recognition forms the first starting point for the present chapter which based on a meta-ethnographic investigation, considers certain aspects of education and learning that have been described in ethnographic research for multi-ethnic youth in multi-cultural suburbs on the outskirts of some of Sweden's major cities. The claims about high standards of justice, equity and inclusion are questioned based on this analysis.

The foundational research for a meta-ethnography is ethnographic. This involves two things in particular. The first is to study education *in situ* through repeatable observations and involvement. The second is to de-mystify and de-naturalise what has previously been taken for granted, and to re-theorise education from the bottom up based on long-term engagement and multiple methods of data production. Methods employed,

The direct involvement of the researcher in the everyday life activities of participants;

A focus on the study of educational life in a particular case in depth at a particular site or a strictly limited number of such sites;

The recognition that the researcher is the main research instrument;

High status being given to the accounts of participants' perspectives;

A spiral of data collection, hypothesis building and theory testing;

Examining relationships between macro–and micro-sociological perspectives.

The method of meta-ethnography makes use of the findings from a number of specifically focused ethnographic works as a way to extend their generalisability and claims toward various stakeholders (Eisenhart, 2017; Noblitt and Hare, 1988). It involves cross-case comparative analyses with the intention of producimg broad (but nuanced) generalisations (Borgnakke, 2017; Hernández-Hernández and Sancho Gil, 2017). This means:

(i) Identifying a relevant sample of texts based on their presumed contribution to addressing an important research question;
(ii) Reading these carefully to identify the main concepts;
(iii) Checking the relevance of each concept within the scope of the studies; and
(iv) Synthesising findings and identifying patterns in terms of the cultural processes evident in single ethnographies and making general claims about them.

By being meta-ethnographic the chapter has certain characteristics that are generally considered problematic in conventional ethnographic research (Hernández-Hernández and Sancho Gil, 2017; Kakos and Fritzsche, 2017). One of these is that meta-ethnography only analyses written ethnographic texts and that the contextual features from each of the different studies are generally not considered as such in this analysis. It is only the content and the messages of the different ethnographic accounts that are focused on, not the contexts in which the individual research projects behind them were conducted (Borgnakke, 2017; Kakos and Fritzsche, 2017). For the present chapter this means that I do not actually try to analyse how young people learn in different educational settings. Instead, what I consider, describe and discuss is what different ethnographic research articles, chapters and books have said about this learning and in particular concerning the obvious capabilities to learn that pupils in schools and youth outside so obviously display but that seems to be ignored or downplayed in official policy (Beach, 2017a, 2017b; Hernández-Hernández and Sancho Gil, 2017).

The point here is that pupils from multi-poverty, multi-ethnic suburbs are often identified as being in difficulties with respect to their learning. Indeed in some scenarios they are even said to be unable to learn without special help and salvation kinds of pedagogy (Beach, Dovemark, Schwartz and Öhrn, 2013) and both Beach (2017b), Schwartz (2013) and Hernández-Hernández and Sancho Gil (2017) have described that a veritable education industry has grown up around this discourse of inability. Yet, as they, and also others such as Trondman et al. (2012), Lundberg (2015) and Widigson (2013) point out the pupils in question are far from as hopeless and impossible as they are portrayed.

The present chapter picks up on these points. In doing so it will level a critique at current educational ideologies and practices; particularly in relation to the ways the skills and creativity in learning that are clearly present in relation to children and youth from marginalised areas is ignored and/or downplayed and even at times devalued. It in this way critiques the recently developing discourse about a disparity of educational performance between groups of students defined by socioeconomic status (SES), race/ethnicity and gender that has developed following the poor performance by Sweden on the PISA evaluations. This discourse often highlights middle-class cultural capital along with positive parental involvement and responsibility and pupil motivation and responsibility (Dovemark, 2004; Schwartz, 2013).

Data

The research articles chapters and books analysed in this meta-ethnography include in particular the following articles:

Beach, D., (2017a) Personalisation and the education commodity: a meta-ethnographic analysis, *Ethnography and education*, DOI: 10.1080/17457823.2016.1247738

Beach, D., Dovemark, M., Schwartz, A. and Öhrn, E., (2013) Complexities and contradictions of educational inclusion: A meta-ethnographic analysis, *Nordic Studies in Education*, 33: 254-268.

Beach, D. and Sernhede, O., (2011) From learning to labour to learning for marginality: School segregation in Swedish suburbs, *British Journal of Sociology of Education*, 32: 257-274.

Beach, D. and Sernhede, O., (2012) Learning processes and social mobilisation in a Swedish metropolitan hip-hop collective, *Urban Education*, 47: 939-958.

These articles are in themselves to a degree brought about through a meta-ethnographic research analysis; explicitly so in two of them. Their findings are brought together in the present chapter and new conclusions about the recent discourse concerning education failure and the policies that have been developed to address them are developed. This is in line with meta-ethnography as described by Noblit and Hare (1988), Eisenhart (2017) and others such as Borgnakke (2017), Hernández-Hernández and Sancho Gil (2017) and Kakos and Fritzsche (2017). Meta-ethnographic analyses will often produce synthesising findings that make statements that, although not necessarily present in the individual studies, make relevant claims about their findings (Beach, 2017b; Hernández-Hernández and Sancho Gil, 2017). In the present case these new claims address in particular the creative learning of marginalised youth groups identified in ethnographic research. They address and critique the much publicised discourse in Sweden about a disparity of educational performance between groups of students defined by socioeconomic status, race/ethnicity and gender and the different factors that are suggested to account for the disparity. Educational stereotyping and the concentration of pupils of race from low socio-economic backgrounds in low-achieving, highly segregated housing areas and their schools is given important attention (Beach and Sernhede, 2011, 2012; Beach et al., 2013; Lundberg, 2015) and as described in Beach (2017b) recent socio-economic changes and increased migration have added new dimensions to educational inequalities and the major challenges facing Sweden concerning the possibilities for all its students to obtain an equal education.

The ethnographic texts involved in the present study were identified through broad familiarity with the field in question. They were developed on the basis of previous meta-analyses of ethnographies that were known to me through my involvement in ethnography in the Nordic region and my work with and within a Nordic research network on youth and marginalisation. This search process was also supplemented by a specific search process using items such as [ethnography OR ethnographic] and [migration OR migrant] and [Sweden] and [education OR school]. The data-bases consulted were Scopus and Eric, but Google Scholar and Taylor & Francis Online advanced citation search were also used. An overview of the materials that have been involved is presented in Appendix 1,Table 1. p. 29.

Meta-ethnography is a very particular methodology that is grounded on cross case analyses of extensive *in situ* studies that provide contextualised and detailed participant oriented insider accounts of everyday practices. It makes use of the findings from a collection of specifically focused ethnographies and looks for common patterns in them based on comparative reading and cross-case translations in a search for tendencies that may indicate whether different findings from different places can be interpreted to have important things in common (Beach et al., 2013). It is a form of trans-local and trans-temporal synthesis that tries to move analyses beyond the unique first hand concepts and interpretations of individual investigations from different sites and across cumulative bodies. The intention is to provide a new perspective from reciprocal translations of individual research.

What meta-ethnography involves then, is taking the concepts and findings from individual studies and exploring for possible common elements and plausible grounds for forming examinable lines of argument that eventually can be forged into a common narrative. The lines of argument will derive from interpretations of interpretations and representations from original ethnographic studies but they will not be ethnographic in the original sense of participant oriented and contextually interpretative. Ethnography places great emphasis on participation with and learning from informants through interactions with them in their everyday life, and it puts high premium on this insider perspective. Meta-ethnography is based on comparative cross-case translations from close analytical readings of several related previously published ethnographic studies (Beach et al., 2013). Texts that are not quintessentially ethnographic are also used for juxtaposition but their analysis is not part of the identification and extraction of key concepts or a line of argument form of reasoning. It is a meta-interpretation of ethnographic research.

There is nothing particularly new about this. It is a practice that can be found in the history of humanist approaches to anthropology by Paul Rabinow, George Marcus and others decades ago. The concept of the hermeneutic consistency of interpretations can be raised as a criterion for interpretive quality. This refers to the analysis of separate texts to achieve a coherent explanation of the events, ideas or concepts they name and describe, and it is this that is plainly at play. It means that meta-ethnography involves drawing together the depictions of previously separate ethnographic investigations through a process of reciprocal translation that allows a researcher to speak beyond individual cases, through the generation of interpretations that have, or at least are intended to have, a value and meaning over and above what could be derived from the *post hoc* comparison of discrete case studies alone.

In the hermeneutic sense then there is an attempt at the fusion of horizons of texts and their interpretations in a manner that can be found in a range of academic areas from aesthetics to jurisprudence. In the sense of Gadamer in *Truth and Method* the concept likens the notion of approaching truth by conversation and as an exchange between conversational partners and is determined by the evolving understandings and expressions of the matter at issue and as linguistically mediated.

Results

The main findings from the analysis of the materials gathered will now be presented. This has been organised as a narrative using key themes that are each connected to and derived from research about the educational experiences of young men in multi-cultural, multi-ethnic suburbs. They are (i) Urban segregation, territorial stigma and multi-dimensional poverty, (ii) Contrasting stories of education need and value, and (iii) Youth creativity and learning in migrant intensive suburbs.

Urban segregation, territorial stigma and multi-dimensional poverty

A main problem in relation to race and education experiences in Sweden is the segregation and polarisation of urban spaces, along with the territorial stigmatisation of some of them (Beach et al., 2013), and the feelings of alienation that could develop from this segregation, polarisation and alienation (Lundberg, 2015). Lindbäck and Sernhede (2013) have also discussed these issues. Paraphrasing one of their informants they described things roughly as follows:

> Where we live there are only foreign people/.../No Swedes. It's only about twenty minutes to town but it's like a world away/.../It's poorer for one thing and more crowded, with not a lot to do. When you go someplace with lots Swedes you feel like people are looking at you and you think you don't belong/.../You want to belong but that's not how it feels.

Comments by informants like the one above were linked by Lindbäck and Sernhede to research such as that by Dikec (2007) and Wacquant (2008), where they are said to reflect global tendencies in urban areas that separate and segregate immigrant-dense (racially and ethnically differently composed) housing areas and their citizens from the rest of society and mark them out as being both different and, in some way at least, problematic (also Lundberg, 2015; Schwartz, 2013). These are features that had so far rarely found their way into formal educational policy according to Lindbäck and Sernhede (2013), which was instead all too often based on socially constructed deficit views of other kinds of people and their cultures, rather than considerations of the conditions of global and national inequities within our current social order and how these are represented (Beach, 2017a, 2017b; Bouakaz, 2007; Borelius, 2010; Trondman et al., 2012; Widigson, 2013; Öhrn, 2012). Lunneblad (2006) also made this point, as did Lindbäck and Sernhede (2013) and Schwartz (2013).

There is an historical antecedent to the patterns identified here. As the authors listed above and others have noted, areas such as the ones in question have been associated with poverty and education failure before. Their failings are not new phenomena (Öhrn, 2012). Ethnic background, the location of the home, and social class still constitute fundamental foundations for differential treatment and outcomes in education that are based on a mundane use of language in academic cultures that conceal forms of symbolic violence. These forms of violence are a direct contravention of principles of justice in education, in line with for instance Young (1990). They have been committed against poor people generally, and now recently against people of colour in particular (Lundberg, 2015). Their presence suggests that although education is officially expressed as based on independence and academic neutrality this is an illusion. In practice education is culturally biased and socially reproductive. Academic theses by Anneli Schwartz (2013) and Laid Bouakaz (2007) have gone to significant lengths when investigating these features. They made use of concepts from Pierre Bourdieu, but also Basil Bernstein in the case of Schwartz.

Schwartz's research was based on ethnographic studies of the use of individuating pedagogies that had been specifically selected and adopted for what had been identified as 'failing schools in multi-cultural/multi-ethnic contexts'. The pedagogy was marketed by a national entrepreneur in Schwartz's research, and adopted by the local authority as a 'saviour pedagogy' for what was described as pupils' learning ills and difficulties. However it was characterised by several key contradictions as a pedagogy of achievement and there was the possibility that it was situated within a discourse, which was from the outset (i.e. ideologically and a priori) about what weak pupils from deficient backgrounds need in order to compensate for their inability to learn, due to limitations concerning their home experiences, parental knowledge and individual motivation and language skills (Lundberg, 2015). This negative discourse was a master narrative that determined how the pupils were treated (Schwartz, 2013). It was pushed into the school from the political level of local government according to Schwartz's findings and it positioned the pupils as struggling and unmotivated individuals from difficult migrant intensive areas with educationally uninterested parents who needed a compensatory kind of pedagogy more than others did, in order to learn (Beach et al., 2013). Without the help of a saviour pedagogy they were *written off* as educational subjects and this of course created social strain for some of them in their relationships with education and the schooling processes, within which school statistics ultimately identified them as failing anyway. They were considered to be worth nothing without this saviour pedagogy. As an informant in Trondman et al. (2012) put it you give us everything but I am worth nothing.

However, there was also a second contradiction here according to the research by Bouakaz, Schwartz and Trondman et al., but this time in terms of the ethnographic details their research provided about the pupils and their learning. Rather than being uninterested in their education and its social conditions, and basically unable to learn without special help, the pupils were very conscious of their situation (i.e. they had obviously learned this if nothing else) and they were also clearly aware of what the pedagogy they were being given access to in school signalled about how they and their backgrounds were viewed and valued (Beach and Sernhede, 2012, 2013). But these pupils had also constructed a different discourse of themselves and their chances in school. Lundberg (2015) and Schwartz (2013) have described this well. In this alternative bottom up discourse the pupils were not deficient and unmotivated, but rather capable and interested (Schwartz, 2013; Trondman et al., 2012) and school failure, as it was formally labelled, was said to depend on other things than their inability and the ineffectivity of their teachers (also Beach, 2017a).

Contradictory stories of education need and value

Returning briefly again to the concern of the chapter with the current discourse of a disparity and the different factors that are suggested to account for it, what begins to emerge through the previous section is that there are two sides to this story. One of them seems to derive from reproductions of official knowledge and is used to explain distinctions that are identified in official statistics. It states that schools in multi-cultural migrant intensive suburbs around our major cities are under-attaining and ineffective; as are the teachers in them; because their pupils are unmotivated, have uninterested parents with language difficulties. They are incapable of raising themselves above a very basic level of learning, without the help of special pedagogies that take their specific background and difficulties into consideration according to this discourse (also Schwartz, 2013). This is a story about *damaged* or deficient pupils that–like the white working class in previous decades–can be saved or 'salvaged' and Bouakaz (2007), Grüber (2006), Schwartz (2013) and Lundberg (2015) have all indicated that this is a dominant national and international policy position.[1]

The other story comes from the meta-analysis of the close-up, fine-grained insider informed knowledge generated within ethnographic studies. Based on individual and distinct, separate ethnographic studies, it states that youth from areas like the ones in question here, that is, from migrant intensive multi-poverty suburban areas do not need saving or salvaging in these respects (Grüber, 2006; Schwartz, 2013; Trondman et al., 2012; Widigson, 2013). Instead, as this research also reports, they are motivated learners who are very cooperative and supportive, and neither they nor their teachers and parents are passive observers in the unfolding of predetermined life-chances. Graphic descriptions of how these young people actively appropriate school knowledge as a crucial resource in their life– and learning projects are also provided.

The investigations that are reported from in Sernhede (2007) and Söderman (2007) fit within this second story about the creativity of marginalised youth. Their studies focussed on informal learning amongst young men from suburban areas outside school and as did Bouakaz, Schwartz, Trondman et al. and Widigson, in their research, they identified extensive examples of a strong capacity for advanced learning and communication that is often missed in mainstream education research, and missing from the formal constructions of official education policy (Beach and Sernhede, 2012). Moreover the symbolic creativity and understanding shown by these youths was simply staggering

1 Börjesson (2016) and before that Dovemark (2004) also discuss a string of political texts from the 1990s that lay the foundations for a shift in educational discourse and practice away from equality and collective values to competition, freedom of choice, personal responsibility and private interests and involvement as a foundation for describing learning and accounting for differences in performances. They include texts such as Ds 1991:18; 1992:7; 1993:27; 1994:18; 1994:50; 1994:72; 1994:123; 1995:5; SOU 1988:20; 1990:14; 1990:44; 1992:38; 1992:54; 1995:109; 1995:113; 1996:22; 1997:121.

according to their investigations (also Beach and Sernhede, 2013), which therefore threw out a significant challenge to common representations of these young suburban men as simply and inevitably unmotivated learners and educational failures. Quite the opposite to this, they were very active learners who were clearly able to both learn in school and make this learning useful in their wider life activities, and they also demonstrated recognition of an inherent value in their culture and upbringing as well, together with a commitment to proclaim the virtues of this culture rather than deride it (Öhrn, 2012). As some informants cited in these investigations stated:

> Much of the time we are looked at and talked about as problems at school and as mainly having problems there and at home as well [and] we do have problems in school but not because of our homes or our past. The problem is in the present at least as much as it is the past and it is not just our problem/.../You need to find a way to become something (Ali).

> We try to communicate this to get people we meet to think/.../We are doing a kind of adult education of our time (Enrico).

> Living out here is a bit like being (in) another world/.../We are the blacks of this country. (But) as an immigrant kid from this place you're nobody and that's what the criminal gangs/.../build on (Victor).

> People need to belong/.../ When we make music and perform, we can get in /.../They tried hip-hop in school too [but] it didn't work/.../It didn't feel right (Laslo).

Several things are suggested here. The first is of course that as stated earlier, the young people concerned recognise that they are characterised on the basis of race, place and class identities that are used as explanations for their educational failure. The second is that their creative learning and communication actually contradicts these descriptions (Schwartz, 2013). It expresses that with these young men from the multi-poverty multi-ethnic suburbs as an example, the young people from these areas are not only capable of learning, they also exhibit very advanced forms of learning and communication (Beach, 2017a). This means that it is unlikely that it is their backgrounds that are a problem. Indeed on closer analysis they are of course a value (Widigson, 2013) and neither do they need the help of special kinds of pedagogy to learn. In fact what is really missing is a simple, genuine recognition of (and basic solid support for) their ability and commitment to do so (Beach, 2017b; Beach and Sernhede, 2012, 2013; Bouakaz, 2007; Lundberg, 2015; Trondman et al., 2012). Third, it is important that the content of school knowledge and the learning experiences of the school were not expressed as a waste of time either by the ethnographic portrayals of schooling produced by the ethnographers or in the words of the informants cited in these investigations. On the contrary school learning was 'something that could be useful when integrated into life-wide learning outside or after school'.

Youth creativity and learning in migrant intensive suburbs

The disclosures above about the creative learning ability of youth within their own sub-cultures are of course not new, and indeed educators have been trying to capitalise on things like sport, punk, rock, soul, and other youth cultural forms of expression, as a way to reach out to what are described as in some way 'weak', 'difficult', or unmotivated learners (Beach, 2017b). Instead, as the ethnographic research sensually suggests:

> These pupils are far from as hopeless and impossible as they are portrayed and that this 'hopeless label' is ideologically and politically generated in a way that (perhaps deliberately) localises the difficulties of performance in a particular way, as problems of schools that are both in crisis and in need of extra help due to an over-abundance of deficient pupils from deficient backgrounds and places, who do not speak our language.

The reasons behind these kinds of exclamations about failing schools, teachers and schools in territorially stigmatised suburbs have not been extensively researched as yet. Funding in educational research is now controlled externally and it has not been made available to answer political questions of this kind. There has however been some speculation about what these reasons might be. One of the speculations is that the devaluation of former welfare State education projects is fundamental to the creation of a foundation from which to launch new policies of individual responsibility, private development and personal choice (Beach, 2017a) which it brings us to the next point. That is:

> Although school agents and curriculum planners may often try to do something positive in this situation, to help the young people in their charge (Lundberg, 2015), they can often do so in a counter-productive and contradictory way, either by excluding anything connected to the pupils' background and experiences from the school curriculum (Schwartz, 2013), or by changing school content through including selected aspects of youth culture within it, based on assumptions that one or the other of these things is needed and nothing else will do (Lundberg, 2015).

Developing the curriculum in parts around hip-hop pedagogy has been quite regularly presented as an example of this approach. But as Beach (2017b) and Söderman (2007) note, this kind of pedagogical innovation rarely seems to work as anticipated. As informants have put it, doing things like hip-hop instead of formal school just doesn't feel right, 'as rapping isn't the same in school (and) doing it instead of schoolwork isn't good for us' (Laslo), and as signalled in research by Beach (2017a, 2017b) and others such as Lundberg (2015) and Schwartz (2013), using these kinds of content actually means that access to the kinds of knowledge that are formally valued are denied.

There are good reasons to heed Laslo's words according to the meta-ethnography. Hip-hop pedagogy will not work as a transformative pedagogy and for clearly identified reasons. These are firstly of course that as the details of the ethnographic investigations of schooling experiences amongst migrant pupils in Sweden suggest, the relational and motivational problems with studying, which are targeted in the personalisation of the curriculum through hip-hop and other forms of youth-culture inspired pedagogy, are not among the more significant problems in the first place. It is the current structuring of political discourse about the education needs of the suburbs around deficit understandings about the pupils there that is the problem (Beach et al., 2013), together with the multi-dimensional poverty and negative stereotyping of the places the pupils come from (Borelius, 2010).

Looked at in line with critical hermeneutics and the concept of hermeneutic consistency in the sense of Gadamer, where what is sought is agreement about something based on an exchange that is determined by the evolving understandings and expressions of the matter at issue as linguistically mediated, there are some very clear implications embedded in the statements above concerning what the real problems of education attainment may be. These are described also in theses recently by Lundberg (2015). They are that it is actually the predominant attitude in formal education toward others' values, cultures, beliefs, religion and traditions that are the problem, rather than these traditions and values and similar, in themselves. The understandings about them and the condition of certain neighbourhoods are what is deficit (Bouakaz, 2007; Grüber, 2006). There are also very clear grounds for saying this:

> The young people concerned can learn (Schwartz, 2013; Widigson, 2013).
> School is not experienced by them as hostile (Trondman et al., 2012).
> Their teachers are not unknowledgeable, uninterested or uncaring.
> Relationships between teachers and pupils are generally expressed positively by both parties (Lundberg, 2015).

These are all significant points in the present analysis and it is here where the potential value of what we have learned from ethnography lies (Beach, 2017b). It tells us that creating successful learning and education success is not only (if at all) about breaking down subject matter by forming classroom content around the incorporation of knowledge from the social worlds of youth. It is about using our ethnographic knowledge concerning youth creativity and learning to *inform* rather than concretely *form and fill* schooling practices (Lundberg, 2015; Schwartz, 2013). This double recognition (the double hieroglyph) is important. It implies that although institutionalising things like hip-hop from informal youth culture may set out to enhance cultural relevance, restructure the politics of the classroom, and try to facilitate positive relationships between teachers and students (Beach, 2017a) this new progressivism will not challenge powerful official knowledge, nor will it challenge understandings of suburban youth as inferior learners (Söderman, 2007). It will only deny them formal institutional access to powerful knowledge (Lundberg, 2015; Schwartz, 2013). To reiterate, as remarked by Beach et al. (2013) and Beach (2017b):

> It is not the culture and background of the pupils that is the problem. The problem is instead the history of dominance bourgeois culture in education and society and the way this is incorporated in policy, curricula and forms of assessment.

There are serious inconsistencies in the pedagogical responses to the difficulties migrant youth from multi-poverty suburbs experience in school. This is obvious here. They can be described in terms of the following two points. Firstly, when a particular kind of pedagogy is only used *for them* (Lundberg, 2015), *in their schools* (Schwartz, 2013), it is predicated on and signals back the assumption that the troubles of minority students can be attributed to them, their cultures or backgrounds and their particular schools in the first place, and that it is only by dealing with these deficiencies in some kind of special way that they will be able to learn (Bouakaz, 2007; Öhrn, 2012). Secondly, quite the opposite to this, it is the very presence of things like this special kind of treatment that confirms them as weak learners (Beach, 2017a, 2017b), and it leads to them having their formal rites, rituals and learning possibilities in education determined in a special way. Whether this is through a salvation pedagogical approach or by using youth culturally inspired special pedagogy and content that restricts their access to formal, official and powerful education content is of little importance. Both are equally negative if in different ways to some degree.

Discussion

This chapter has been developed from a meta-ethnographic analysis of research in Sweden following the recently developing discourse about a disparity of educational performance between groups of students defined by socioeconomic status, race/ethnicity and gender that has developed following Sweden's PISA performances recently. This discourse targets quite negatively particular areas, the schools in them and particularly their pupils, who are described in deficit terms and in need of compensatory, sometime termed salvation pedagogies in order to be able to learn productively and become worthy building blocks in a globally connected economically successful knowledge society. In mainstream policy it is not possible to see these areas and the people in them as capable of generating anything truly creative or positive at all without special help. Suburban places and the people in them must be changed through the miracles of saviour pedagogies to avoid the trap of becoming a chronically marginalised *micro-jobbing* disposable labour-power.

The chapter has set out to provide a bottom-up response to this discourse. I have focused particularly on ethnographies about the education and educational experiences of youth in schools in migrant intensive multi-poverty suburbs in Sweden of the kind that are targeted in the discourse. Fourteen book length ethnographic monographs, one book chapter and twelve research articles have provided the main data and have been analysed in detail. The emerging ideas have then been juxtaposed against four previous meta-ethnographic works as well as books, book chapters, and research articles from other Nordic countries and beyond that have explored similar issues.

Official national policy for tackling education inequity and performance differences have been considered in the analysis. These policies are suggested to generally target the lack of middle-class cultural capital, limited parental involvement, language factors and pupil motivation. This is a mismatch with what the ethnographies have identified as a problem which is white middle-class values and curricula together with high concentrations of pupils with migrant backgrounds from low socio-economic backgrounds in low-achieving, highly segregated housing areas and their schools. Multi-dimensional poverty and the presence of territorial stigmatisation have been further themes.

There are several things here that are not all that new. One of them is about the areas in question. As Beach (2017b) and earlier Beach and Lunneblad (2011), Lunneblad (2006) and Lindbäck and Sernhede (2013) suggest, these areas have always had a problem of territorial stigmatisation, although in the past this targeted the white working class rather than the new population in the areas in question, which is increasingly trans-nationalist, migrant and unemployed. Also significant is that material conditions are harsher today. Learning to labour was a norm in school for working-class children in the past and their housing areas and the schools in them had a reasonably high material standard. Today, following the movement of industrial production to cheap labour-zones elsewhere, the reduction in available taxation revenue and the disappearance of commodified labour there is less wealth available and this has contributed to a massive material hollowing out of the neighbourhoods (Beach and Sernhede, 2011, 2013; Borelius, 2010). The introduction of market politics and the concept of free public choice as an arbiter of interest and investment in education has added to these problems. Discourses of cultural deficit now colour the dominant images of the people from these now *work-less* job-zones and under-resourced places.

However, there is one further point to raise here. It concerns the creative responses of the young people from the areas in question, which literally all of the research has described as far more creative and able to learn than objectively portrayed in official educational political discourse, the media and formal school statistics (Beach, 2017b; Beach and Sernhede, 2012, 2013). They were not inevitable intellectual failures and this is a point of optimism if it can be appropriately engaged with (Bouakaz, 2007). The children and youth in the schools were also predominantly positive towards their studies and committed toward doing well, and their teachers recognised and tried to respond to this. Schools were not expressed as a total waste of time or a devaluing experience and pupils were also shown to be able to make use of school knowledge in creative and productive ways, both within schools and in their life projects outside schools as well (Beach, 2017a). School was respected as a positive opportunity and alternative, particularly now that learning to labour is no longer viable. What is more school was not where the youth in question felt most devalued and degraded (Beach et al., 2013). On the contrary they described their schools as relatively safe spaces to meet with friends and do interesting things in (Schwartz, 2013; Trondman et al, 2012). What was more open to question was under what circumstances this creativity and learning may be enacted, informed, further developed and made useful, and in relation to what kinds of projects and interests (Beach, 2017b).

Conclusions

The present meta-ethnography has been developed from ethnographies from research in the poorest suburbs in a rich de-industrialised country. It has synthesised results from these studies that have described how these young people utilised diverse points of view in a life-wide form of integrated, self-sustained, and advanced independent learning. However, it has also made clear that the schooling of these new suburban groups is not unproblematic. There are many problems, but globalisation and the history and contemporary presence of class and racial power and politics, not the culture and backgrounds, or motivation and learning, or language skills of the youth themselves or their parents, are the most important ones. As important are the segregation and concentration of poverty and unemployment in a way that has created very difficult circumstances for a now ethnically other and increasingly socially segregated and economically marginalised lower-class-without-work. At the same time the young people from these areas have not failed to respond in creative ways to this situation. These are important issues. As identified in recent publications by Thomas Piketty, Fazal Rizvi and other critical scholars, there is constant and increasing global social economic and educational inequality today, as capitalist organisations have been freed from the shackles of regulation that were present during the era of a serious communist alternative concerning the organisation of production. Proliferating insecurities for the mass of the global population have resulted from this and trajectories of precariousness now loop back and forth within our new (post)modern global condition. Education is tightly implicated in these processes.

Appendix 1

Table 1 Data

Beach, D., (2017a) Personalisation and the education commodity: a meta-ethnographic analysis, Ethnography and education, DOI: 10.1080/17457823.2016.1247738

Beach, D., Dovemark, M., Schwartz, A. and Öhrn, E., (2013) Complexities and contradictions of educational inclusion: A meta-ethnographic analysis, Nordic Studies in Education, 33: 254-268.

Beach, D. and Sernhede, O., (2011) From learning to labour to learning for marginality: School segregation in Swedish suburbs, British Journal of Sociology of Education, 32: 257-274.

Beach, D. and Sernhede, O., (2012) Learning processes and social mobilisation in a Swedish metropolitan hip-hop collective, Urban Education, 47: 939-958.

Book length works: e·g· monographies and anthologies

Aretun, Å. 2007. *Barns 'växa vilt' och vuxnas vilja att forma: formell och informell socialisation i en muslimsk skola.* Linköping: Linköpings universitet.

Bouakaz, L. 2007. *Parental involvement in school: What promotes and what hinders parental involvement in an urban school.* (PhD thesis) Malmö högskola, Lärarutbildningen.

Bunar, N. 2001. *Skolan mitt i förorten.* Stockholm: Symposion.

Gitz-Johansen, T. 2006. *Den multikulturelle skole: integration og sortering* (1. udgave ed.). Frederiksberg: Roskilde forlag.

Grüber, S. 2006. *Skolan Gör Skillnad: Etnicitet och Institutionell Praktik.* (Linköping Studies in Arts and Science 387). Linköping: Linköpings Universitet, Institutionen för Samhälls- och Välfärdsstudier.

Dovemark, M. 2004. *Ansvar-Flexibilitet-Valrihet: En etnografisk studie om en skola i förändring.* (Göteborg Studies in Educational Science). Göteborg: Acta Universitatis Gothenburgensis.

Jonsson, R. 2007. *Blatte betyder kompis. Om maskulinitet och språkanvändning i en högstadieskola.* Stockholm: Ordfront.

Lundberg, O. 2015. *On cultural racism and school learning: An ethnographic study.* (Göteborg Studies in Educational Science). Göteborg: Acta Universitatis Gothenburgensis.

Lunneblad, J. 2006. *Förskolan och mångfallden.* (Göteborg Studies in Educational Science). Göteborg: Acta Universitatis Gothenburgensis.

Moinian, F. 2007. *Negotiating identities : exploring children's perspectives on themselves and their lives.* Stockholm: Stockholm Institute of Education Press (HLS förlag).

Schwartz, A. 2013. *Pedagogik, plats och prestationer en etnografisk studie om en skola i förorten* (Göteborg Studies in Educational Science). Göteborg: Acta Universitatis Gothenburgensis.

Sernhede, O. 2007. *AlieNation is My Nation. Om Hip hop och unga mäns utanförskap i det Nya Sverige.* Stockholm: Ordfront.

Söderman, J. 2007. *Rapp i käften.* (Studies in Music and Music Education nr 10, Malmö Academy of Music). Lund: Lunds Universitet.

Widigson, M. 2013. *Från miljonprogram till högskoleprogram: plats, agentskap och villkorad valfrihet.* Academic Thesis. Gothenburg: University of Gothenburg.

Book chapters

Lindbäck, J. and O. Sernhede (2013. Divided city - divided school: Upper secondary school students and urban space. In G. Gudmundsson, D. Author and V. Vestel (Eds). *Excluded youth in itself and for itself: Young people from immigrant families in Scandinavia.* London: Tufnell Press.

Journal articles

Andersen, C. 2006. Troubling Ethnicity and Cultural Diversity in Norwegian Preschool. *Journal of Australian Research in Early Childhood Education.* 13, no.1: 3-11.

Andersson, M. 2003. Immigrant youth and the dynamics of marginalization. *Young*, Vol. 11(1): 74-89.

Arnesen, A.L. & Lundahl, L. 2006 Still Social and Democratic? Inclusive Education Policies in the Nordic Welfare States. *Scandinavian Journal of Educational Research*, 50(3): 285-300.

Borelius, U. 2010. Två förorter, *Utbildning & Demokrati* 19: 11-24.

Bunar, N. 2008. If we only had a few more Swedes. *Ungdomsforskning*, 2. 39-44.

Bunar, N. 2008. The Free Schools Riddle: Between traditional social democratic, neo-liberal and multicultural tenets, *Scandinavian Journal of Education Research*, 52: 423-438.

Bunar, N. 2010. Choosing for quality or inequality: current perspectives on the implementation of school choice policy in Sweden. *Journal of Education Policy*, 25: 1-18.

Lunneblad, J. and T. Johansson, 2012. Learning from each other? Multicultural pedagogy, parental education and governance, *Race Ethnicity and Education*, 15:5: 705-723, DOI: 10.1080/13613324.2011.624508.

Schwartz, A. 2013. Pupil Responses to a Saviour Pedagogy: an ethnographic study, *European Educational Research Journal*, 11: 601-608.

Schwartz, A. and E. Öhrn (2012. Fellowship and solidarity? Secondary students' responses to strong classification and framing in education, in W Pink (Ed), *Schools and marginalized youth: an international perspective.* Cresshill, NJ: Hampton Press.

Trondman, M., R. Taha and A. Lund. 2012. For Aïsha: On identity as potentiality, *Identities: Global Studies in Culture and Power*, 19(4), 533-543.

Yang, C-L. 2016. Encounters between the 'oppressed' and the 'oppressor': rethinking Paulo Freire in anti-racist feminist education in Sweden, *Race Ethnicity and Education*, 19(4):, 835-855, DOI: 10.1080/13613324.2014.88542

References

Agier, M., (2009) The ghetto, the hyperghetto and the fragmentation of the world, *International journal of urban and regional research*, 33(3): 854-857.

Alinia, M., (2006) Invandraren, förorten och maktens rumsliga förankring, in Kamali, M., (ed.) *Den segregerade integrationen: Om socialsammanhållning och dess hinder. Rapport av utredningen om makt, integration och strukturell diskriminering*, Stockholm: Regeringen SOU 2006:73: 66-90.

Beach, D., (2017a) Personalisation and the education commodity: a meta-ethnographic analysis, *Ethnography and education,* DOI: 10.1080/17457823.2016.1247738.

Beach, D., (2017b) Whose justice is this! Capitalism, class and education justice and inclusion in the Nordic countries: Race, space and class history, *Educational review,* DOI: org/10.1080/00131911.2017.1288609.

Beach, D., Dovemark, M., Schwartz, A. and Öhrn, E., (2013) Complexities and contradictions of educational inclusion: A meta-ethnographic analysis, *Nordic studies in education,* 33 (2): 254-268.

Beach, D. and Lunneblad, J., (2011) Ethnographic investigations of issues of race in Scandinavian education research, *Ethnography and education*, 6: 29-43.

Beach, D. and Sernhede, O., (2011) From learning to labour to learning for marginality: school segregation and marginalization in Swedish suburbs, *British journal of sociology of education,* 32(2): 257-274.

Beach, D. and Sernhede, O., (2012) Learning processes and social mobilization in a Swedish metropolitan hip-hop collective, *Urban education,* 47(5): 939-958.

Beach, D. and Sernhede, O., (2013) On creativity and resistance in Nordic youth culture on the margins, in Gudmundsson, G., Vestel, V. and Beach, D., (eds.) *Excluded youth in itself and for itself: Young people from immigrant families in Scandinavia*, London: Tufnell, 61-84.

Borelius, U., (2010) Två förorter, *Utbildning and demokrati*, 19: 11-24.

Borgnakke, K., (2017) Meta-ethnography and systematic reviews - linked to the evidence movement and caught in a dilemma, *Ethnography and education,* 12(2): 194-210.

Bouakaz, L. 2007. *Parental involvement in school: What promotes and what hinders parental involvement in an urban school.* (PhD thesis), Malmö högskola.

Börjesson, M., (2016) *Från likvärdighet till marknad: en studie av offentligt och privat inflytande över skolans styrning I svensk utbildningspolitik 1969-1999*, Örebro: Örebro Studies in Education 52.

Dikec, M., (2007) *Badlands of the republic*, Oxford: Blackwell.

Dovemark, M., (2004) *Ansvar-flexibilitet-valfrihet. En etnografisk studie om en skola i förändring*, Thesis (PhD), Göteborgs Universitet.

Ds 1991:18. Vidga brukarinflytandet! En vag till ökad delaktighet och bättre service.

Ds 1992:7. Marknadsorientering av kommunal verksamhet. Konsekvenser och möjligheter.

Ds 1993:27. Alternativa produktionsformer i kommunal verksamhet. Vem utför och på vilka villkor? En rapport utarbetad på uppdrag av Lokaldemokratikommitten.

Ds 1994:18. Agenda 2000. Kompetens och individualisering.

Ds 1994:50. Valfrihetsrevolutionen i praktiken.

Ds 1994:72. Valfrihet inom skolan. Konsekvenser for kostnader, resultat och segregation. Rapport till expertgruppen for studier i offentlig ekonomi.

Ds 1994:123. Vi vill vara med att bestämma. Modeller for medborgarinflytande i statsmiljö och på landet.

Ds 1995:5. Där man inte har något inflytande finns inget personligt ansvar. En översyn av elev - och föräldrainflytandet i skolan.

Eisenhart, M., (2017) A matter of scale: multi-scale ethnographic research on education in the United States, *Ethnography and education,* 12(2): 134-147.

Grüber, S., (2006) *Skolan gör skillnad: Etnicitet och institutionell praktik*, Thesis (PhD), Linköpings Universitet.

Gudmundsson, G., (2013) Introduction: Excluded youth in itself and for itself: Young people from immigrant families in Scandinavia, in Gudmundsson, G., Author, D. and Vestel, V., (eds.) *Youth and marginalisaltion: Young people from immigrant families in Scandinavia* London: Tufnell Press.

Hernández-Hernández, F. and Sancho Gil, J., (2017) Using meta-ethnographic analysis to understand and represent youth's notions and experiences of learning in and out of secondary school, *Ethnography and education,* 12(2): 178-193.

Kakos, M. and Fritzsche, B., (2017) A meta-ethnography of two studies on interactions in schools: reflections on the process of translation, *Ethnography and education,* 12(2): 228-242.

Lindbäck, J. and Sernhede, O., (2013) Divided city - divided school: Upper secondary school students and urban space, in Gudmundsson, G., Author, D. and Vestel, V., (eds.) *Youth and marginalisaltion: Young people from immigrant families in Scandinavia*, London: Tufnell Press.

Lundberg, O., (2015) *On cultural racism and school learning: An ethnographic study*, Göteborgs Universitet.

Lunneblad, J., (2006) *Förskolan och mångfallden*, Thesis (PhD), Göteborgs Universitet.

Noblit, G. W. and Hare, R. D., (1988) *Meta-ethnography: synthesizing qualitative studies*, Newbury Park, California: Sage.

Öhrn, E., (2012) Urban education and segregation: The responses from young people, *European educational research journal*, 11: 45-57.

Schwartz, A., (2013) *Pedagogik, plats och prestationer en etnografisk studie om en skola i förorten*, Thesis (PhD), University of Gothenburg.

Sernhede, O., (2007) *AlieNation is my nation. Om hip hop och unga mäns utanförskap i det Nya Sverige*, Stockholm: Ordfront.

SOU 1988:20. En förändrad ansvarsfördelning och styrning på skolområdet. Betänkande från beredningen om ansvarsfördelning och styrning på skolområdet.

SOU 1990:14. Långtidsutredningen 1990. Bilaga 22. Utbildning for 2000-talet.

SOU 1990:44. Demokrati och makt i Sverige. Maktutredningens huvudrapport.

SOU 1992:38. Fristående skolor. Bidrag och elevavgifter.

SOU 1992:54. Mer for mindre - nya styrformer for barn - och ungdomspolitiken.

SOU 1995:109. Likvärdigutbildning på lika villkor. Slutbetänkande av friskolekommittén.

SOU 1995:113. Fristående gymnasieskolor. Betänkande av Utredningen om fristående gymnasieskolor.

SOU 1996:22. Inflytande på riktigt - Om elevers rätt till inflytande, delaktighet och ansvar. Delbetänkande av Skolkommittén.

SOU 1997:121. Skolfrågor - Om skola i en ny tid. Slutbetänkande av Skolkommittén.

Söderman, J., (2007) *Rapp i käften*, Thesis (PhD), Lunds Universitet.

Trondman, M., Taha, R. and Lund, A., (2012) For Aïsha: On identity as potentiality, *Identities: Global studies in culture and power,* 19: 533-543.

Wacquant, L., *(2008) Urban outcasts: a comparative sociology of advanced marginality, Cambridge: Polity Press.*

Widigson, M., (2013) *Från miljonprogram till högskoleprogram: plats, agentskap och villkorad valfrihet,* Thesis (PhD), University of Gothenburg.

Young, I. M., (1990) *Justice and politics of difference*, Princeton: Princeton University Press.

Chapter 2

The ideal school-yard child: Subjectivity in teachers' representations of educational outdoor space

Maria Rönnlund

Nordic classroom studies have provided rich knowledge about the schooling that takes place in indoor educational practices. Less attention has been paid however to schooling in outdoor educational environments. Such spatial focus is of particular interest because to many children the educational outdoor milieu–like the school-yard–represents a 'free' space in relation to the classroom. From studies in which children are asked their thoughts and opinions, we learn that the school-yard represents a break from teaching and learning and other classroom activities. For many children, the school-yard is understood as a space where they can play and interact freely, and only to a small extent as a space where education takes place (e.g. Alerby, 2003; Norddahl and Einarsdottir, 2015; Thomson, 2007; Villanen and Alerby, 2013). Nevertheless, educative ambitions of various kinds and intensity are and have always been–tied to the school-yard (Larsson, Norlin and Rönnlund, 2017).

Previous research has pointed out the school-yard as a space where the institutional framing of subjectivity is strong (the concept of subjectivity is discussed in the following sections). The school-yard is seen as a disciplinary space governed by adults' perceptions of appropriate behaviour and where individual pupils are moulded into desirable subjects (Bjerrum Nielsen, 2009). Its design, materials, rules, and regulations–both spoken and implicit–convey something about the institution's view of the appropriate schoolchild and contain what has been described as a 'hidden curriculum' (Rosa, 2013; Titman, 1994). In the school-yard, pupils learn lessons about themselves and about life without anyone explicitly teaching them.

This chapter focuses on the teachers' understandings of the school-yard as an arena for schooling. By analysing school-yard project plans written by teachers, the aim of this paper is to contribute to the discussion about schooling in educational contexts outside the classroom. In total, nine project plans from Swedish primary schools have been analysed. The text documents communicate the teachers' understandings of the school-yard as a social and educational space and their ideas about how to improve and develop the school-yard. From these representations it has been possible to distinguish how they understand appropriate pupilness in relation to the school-yard–how teachers understand *the ideal school-yard child*.

The school-yard–a regulated and free space

During break-times in the school-yard, the children are supervised by teachers and are under the regulations of rules that encourage certain behaviours and silence others. In a study of three primary school playgrounds in England, the children were, for example, forbidden to play certain games, carry out particular activities, or enter particular areas, and interviews with the children playing there resulted in a long list of do's and don'ts like *walk slowly, don't play there, don't run, don't scream*, and similar prohibitions (Thomson, 2007). The fostering is sometimes explicit and clear, as in this example, but it can also be implicit and more directed towards children as individual subjects rather than towards regulations. Research on outdoor education highlights the school-yard as an arena for schooling in a more distinct perspective–as a space for teaching and learning. In this field of research, teachers', local authorities', institutions', and organisations' views on the school-yard as a place for learning emerge. The research reflects the central characteristics of learning in outdoor settings–and while many of the studies reflect the school's outdoor milieu and the school surroundings as a learning arena, there are also studies highlighting the outdoors as a source of knowledge (e.g. Fägerstam, 2014). This last perspective applies not least to environmental projects in which teachers use nature and the physical milieu to teach about environmental issues (Carrier, 2009; Tranter and Malone, 2004; Maynard and Waters, 2007).

Teaching, learning, and fostering are not things that children themselves primarily connect to the school-yard. The school-yard is often the only place in the school environment where children are relatively free to choose their activities and with whom to interact and spend time. Because of this, the school-yard is often a highly valued place for pupils. They understand the school-yard as a space where they can exercise free mobility and as a facilitator for social relations–a place where they can play and have fun (Kostenius, 2011; Rönnlund, 2015a; Thomson, 2007; Villanen and Alerby, 2013). At the same time, children seem to appreciate the presence of teachers in the school-yard and the possibility to interact with them (Norddahl and Einarsdottir, 2015). Children interviewed by Villanen and Alerby expressed the importance of social relations with both peers and teachers, emphasising the positive experience of teachers' participation in their play. They also saw the school-yard as a place for learning. However, it was not a learning connected to academic skills and knowledge, but rather learning in terms of practical skills such as climbing a tree or riding a skateboard (Villanen and Alerby, 2013).

Something that stands out from previous research is that the school-yard plays an important role in processing social relations and identity. This applies not least to gender, and the school-yard represents a social space where gender is constantly constructed, reconstructed, and negotiated (Connolly, 2003; Epstein et al., 2001; Evaldsson, 2004, 2005; Fjørtoft et al., 2009; Frosh et al., 2002; Gustafson, 2006; Kofoed, 2008; Reay, 2001; Renold, 2005; Rysst, 2015; Skelton, 2001; Öqvist, 2009). Several studies, many of them from Anglo-Saxon cultures, picture the school-yard as a place that is often segregated in terms of gender (Connolly, 2003; Delamont, 1990; Epstein et al., 2001; Frosh et al., 2002; Renold, 2005; Skelton, 2001; Thorne, 1993). Nordic studies, which are often ethnographic studies in which one or a few playgrounds have been studied at close range, give a similar, but also a more varied, picture than the Anglo-Saxon studies. The school-yard is also reported to be gender segregated in Nordic studies (Bjerrum Nielsen and Rudberg, 1991; Fjørtoft et al., 2009; Kofoed, 2008; Öqvist, 2009), but reported variations (Evaldsson, 2004, 2005; Gustafson, 2009; Rönnlund, 2015a) challenge the traditional and established image of the school-yard as strongly gender segregated. Studies highlighting gender patterns also point at different expectations of how girls and boys should act and behave in different school areas and suggest that girls are expected to be more quiet and quiescent than boys (Gordon et al., 2000).[1]

These and other studies indicate that various activities and multiple social interrelations are at play in outdoor educational milieus and that the school-yard is a social space where children socially are becoming pupils. These studies also indicate that various understandings of the school-yard exist in parallel. In this chapter, the focus will be on the teachers' understandings of the school-yard and, in connection with this, their ideas about ideal subjectivity.

Representations of space and subjectivity

For French philosopher Henri Lefebvre (1991), social space is understood as constantly produced through various interconnected spatial dimensions. He

1 Gordon, Holland and Lahelma (2000) outline their analysis using the concepts of *physical space*, *official space*, and *informal space*.

distinguishes three dimensions in the production of space: representations of space, spatial practice and representational space. The first dimension refers to abstract conceptions of space, such as policymakers', architects', and local authorities' planned spaces. The second dimension refers to physical and routinely perceived everyday space. Finally, the third dimension, the lived space, refers to existential and symbolic space that is both physical and subjective at the same time and that accommodates symbols, experiences, dreams, and emotions. The three dimensions interact in the production of social space. The ways social space is lived and experienced is affected, for example, not only by physical space and design but also by how space is conceptualised by politicians, architects, and others who are in charge of planning institutional spaces (Lefebvre, 1991; see also Rönnlund and Tollefsen, 2016).

In order to analyse school practices, studies of different spatial dimensions and their interactions have previously been performed with a focus on the indoors (e.g. Gordon et al., 2000), and with a focus on the outdoors (e.g. Rönnlund, 2015b). This study focuses on the single spatial dimension of representations of space. The school-yard is understood as a social space loaded with institutional and social intentions and expectations through national and local policy documents and plans of various kinds. While other studies have often looked at representations of space at the national level (e.g. Ulleberg, 2006), this study concentrates on representations at the local school level, and more specifically at local school-yard project plans.

Social space is significant for the process of becoming an individual subject–a *self*. Subjectivity is individual in the sense that it concerns an individual subject, but more importantly, it takes place in social space, and is by these means a social process. Children's subjectivities are for example formed and processed in their daily lives, in school and in the school-yard (Holloway and Valentine, 2000). As a social process it is concerned with normality and deviance–some actions and behaviours are perceived as appropriate, while others are seen as inappropriate. In institutional educational contexts, processing subjectivity refers to a great extent to socially becoming a pupil. Pupilness refers according to Kofoed (2008) to diverse ways of developing and performing situated knowledge of school life and consists of processes of subjectivity concerned with normality. However, normality also works through its opposite, 'by what is perceived as wrongdoing, as the inappropriate' (Kofoed, 2008: 417). Normality, as well as the *wanted*–the ideal–is situated and under constant negotiation in a process in which the subject is both active and acted on (Kofoed, 2008). This study does not explore these processes *per se*. However, exploring teachers' representations of the school-yard–and the ideas of ideal subjectivity embedded in these representations–gives an idea of the social processes of becoming an individual subject–a *self*–and a pupil.

Analysing the project plans

The material used in this study consists of nine school-yard project plans from nine different primary schools in a northern region in Sweden. The project plans were sent in to the organisation Naturskolan in 2012 when they called for schools to apply for financial support in order to improve and develop their school-yards.[2] The text documents, which were collectively authored by groups of teachers at each school, communicated teachers' representations of the school-yard, including their ambitions and expectations with the school-yard, their thoughts about how the school-yard should be used and their ideas about design and equipment.[3]

The analysis, which was mainly inductive, was conducted in two phases. The first phase was aimed at identifying themes in the teachers' descriptions of their present and future school-yard, and to discuss them separately and in relation to each other. The second phase was aimed at identifying how subjectivity emerged in the texts. This part of the analysis was inspired by interpretations of Critical Discourse Analysis (Wodac and Meyer, 2001), and the question that guided this part of the analysis was how ideal subjectivity stood out in the texts and what explicit and implicit assumptions about children were connected to this ideal subjectivity.

The analysis is outlined in five sections. The first three sections cover the identified themes. The fourth section discusses the themes together, and the fifth outlines how ideal subjectivity appeared in the data. In all sections, the results are discussed in relation to previous studies about teachers' and children's understandings and experiences of the school-yard. In the chapter's final section, the results are discussed in relation to schooling at a more general level.

---

2 The Swedish organisation Naturskolan was formed in the early 1980s, initiating activities in schools around the country. Their pedagogical concept is that teaching–as a complement to indoor education–should take place in nature and/or in schools' outdoor environments.

3 The announcement from Naturskolan was not very detailed–schools were encouraged to initiate school-yard projects of various kinds. However, some examples of school-yard project ideas were mentioned, for instance *cultivation and composting*, *art and crafts activities* and *creating spatiality* and *places for talking*.

Space for teaching and learning

One theme in the teachers' representations of the school-yard was teaching and learning. They wrote about and envisioned the school-yard as a space where teaching and learning take place, using expressions such as 'we want to create a learning environment' and space for 'outdoor pedagogical activities'.

Teaching and learning were mainly put forward as collective and coeval activities–the teachers wrote about *gathering* children–and as activities that require a teacher or a pedagogue of some kind. While some plans contained specific details about the pedagogical activities that they had in mind, like *theatre and music performances, gardening,* or *science, mathematics and language teaching,* others did not specify any particular kinds of teaching and/or pedagogical activities.

Another characteristic was that teaching and learning were related to defined physical and geographic spaces. The project plans described intentions to create spots specifically designed for outdoor education–like a *gathering place for outdoor classes, an outdoor classroom, a venue or classroom for teaching classes outdoor,* or *an amphitheatre.*

When the gathering places and outdoor classrooms were described in detail, they often had a design that allowed the children to sit down, like *a grandstand with seating, seating and tables,* or *a sheltered area with seating.* The main pattern was planning for seating about twenty to thirty children, which is the size of an ordinary class:

> We want a place outdoors where we can have a fireplace and seating for approximately twenty children.

By situating learning in specific spots and using the same terminology as for indoor teaching (*classroom, classes,* or similar), teaching and learning in the school-yard turned out to be bound by time and space and only to a small extent as something that takes place all over the school-yard and at any particular time.

Parallel with the idea of creating space for gathering fairly large groups of pupils to sit down together, the plans also contained ideas for creating *places within the place,* i.e. secluded places for small groups of pupils to come together. The ideal seemed to be spatial variation in terms of size and type:

> In close connection to this place we want to build windbreaks that shelter, border, and create places within the place–places for games, discussions, and for working in small groups.

The desire to create small, secluded, and private places for teaching and learning might have been related to a previously reported view of the school-yard as a place with a lot of speed and motion and as a rather messy and noisy place and therefore an unattractive area for teaching (Fägerstam, 2014).[4] A longing for secluded places that offer privacy has also been observed in studies where children's voices are studied. However, children's appreciation of still and calm places does not seem to be linked to the idea of learning academic skills, but rather to a general need for tranquillity and withdrawing. Research indicates that many children wish for and seek out places–and this refers to the entire school environment–where they can spend some time alone or with one or two friends and where they can enjoy intimate, nest like, enclosed, and hidden places. They need places suitable to think and reflect and where they can relax without interruption. For some children, such refuges become important places of attachment or security in times of trouble. Children also use such places to act out dramas or stories (Kostenius, 2011; Norddahl and Einarsdottir, 2015; Rönnlund, 2015a; Änggård, 2012).

Based on the analysis, the teachers thus aimed to transform the outdoor space to be suitable for indoor pedagogy. This included creating spaces–by design and equipment–for governing and controlling pupils but also blocking nature out by for example building shelters against the wind.

Space for physical activities

A second theme in the teachers' representations of the school-yard was physical activity. They envisioned and planned for a school-yard where various physical activities take place:

> We want a variation of activities that together turn the breaks into a joyful moment during the school day.

4 Fägerstam (2014) reports on Swedish junior high school teachers' experiences of an outdoor teaching project and concludes that while the teachers perceived the schoolyard as noisy and unattractive before the start of the project, they believed that it worked quite well as a place for learning both during and after the project.

While some plans only vaguely talked about increased physical activity in the school-yard, others gave more detailed descriptions about how to increase physical activity. In order to achieve a *good outdoor milieu* with increased physical activities, one plan was to build an *adventure course*. There were also smaller-scale plans for how to increase physical activity, like painting the paved ground with squares, circles, and other symbols and thereby attracting children to engage in physical activity and mobility:

> To paint the ground with Twister dots, noughts and crosses, numerical systems and suchlike, as a complement to football squares and hopscotch.

By painting the ground with various symbols and decorations, the teachers wanted to invite the children to take part in different types of games and activities—not just ordinary and common ballgames such as football. Still another idea was to equip the school-yard with various playground materials, like games and sports equipment packed in mobile boxes:

> We want to introduce activity boxes that both children and teachers can use in order to initiate physical activities.

The core idea behind decorating the ground, equipping the school-yard with mobile activity boxes, and building the adventure course was that the children themselves should be active agents in the school-yard. Still, the teachers described themselves as having an important role to motivate the children—teachers needed to actively encourage children to take part in different activities. Taken together, the plans encouraged both spontaneous activities initiated by children and planned activities led by teachers:

> We would like to create an outdoor space where children feel comfortable, a space that stimulates both spontaneous activities and activities that are initiated and governed by adults.

In order to augment teacher-initiated activities, the authors of the project plan cited above presented a program that was meant to increase the number of teachers in the yard during break-time. As a complement to the teachers who were usually present in the school-yard during break time and were in charge of supervising the children, they planned to introduce teachers with a particular responsibility for initiating activities:

> Every break-time shall include a couple of creative activities initiated and directed by teachers.

Both the spontaneous and teacher-initiated physical activities were communicated as collective and joint activities, but participating in joint physical activity was also discussed in the framework of individual well-being. The teachers envisioned a school-yard in which individual children find interesting and enjoyable activities and where they have positive individual experiences of participation in collective activities:

> We want to turn every break-time into a pleasurable moment and to make sure that every child feels that he or she can participate.

As the excerpts have demonstrated, encouraging physical activity was a main topic in the plans, although the methods to obtain this varied. When relating this theme to previous research where children themselves are questioned, physical activity is also something that children–at least some children–seem to appreciate. As has been recognised in studies where children's views are highlighted, children often enjoy opportunities for physical movement. They also seem to be quite self-initiating when it comes to physical activity–at least they present themselves as active and self-initiating and not dependent on teachers to activate them (Rönnlund, 2015a).

Following the analysis, it is obvious that the teachers expected the children to be active in the school-yard and to enjoy physical activities. Furthermore, crucial for encouraging physical activity was the equipment in the school-yard.

Space for social interaction

The third theme in the teachers' representations was outdoor space as an arena for social interaction. By using words such as *meetings*, *communication*, *interactions*, and *togetherness*, they highlighted the school-yard as a space where social interactions and communication are processed. Following this idea, they wanted to support social relations and increase social interactions. They wanted school-yards that:

> [...] invite children to engage in social interactions.

By encouraging children to participate in collective activities in the school-yard, they wanted to support and strengthen a spirit of community among the children:

> All children should develop their awareness of how their choices affect themselves and others. Our goal is that all children should learn to play and interact with each other in order to feel connected.

From the texts, it is obvious that the teachers saw the physical milieu as supportive or hindering to social interaction. They emphasised *calm corners, peaceful oases, bowers,* and other tranquil places as particularly supportive to communication and interactions. The teachers intended to:

> [...] create places that invite children to meetings and talking, like bowers.

> [...] create small peaceful oases where they can find a quiet spot and reflect on things.

As was discussed above, children also appreciate calm and peaceful spaces in the school-yard. They desire and enjoy contact with other children and find that places for communication are an important element in the school-yard habitat (Norddahl and Einarsdottir, 2015). Similar to the teachers' arguments in the project plans in this study, children also seem to understand that the physical milieu can be either supportive or hindering to social interactions. In studies where children talk about their needs, they link certain activities and social relations to specific places and materiality (Rönnlund, 2015a). As discussed in a study of children's visions of the school environment, children want *suitable spaces* for a number of different activities such as physical activities, learning, stillness, socialising, and being alone (Kostenius, 2011).

Based on the analysis, the teachers saw the school-yard as space for social interaction between children, and the physical milieu–in particular its design–as supportive or hindering for this interaction.

Various spatial understandings

The three identified themes, which with some variations can be recognised from earlier research, were recurrent in the majority of the projects plans. But, regardless of whether individual project plans discussed all three themes, or only two of them, the themes mainly stood out as separated from each other in the texts. Learning was, for example, communicated separately from physical activities and social interaction and *vice versa*–the teachers did not explicitly talk about learning when they talked about physical activities and social integration. When communicating *learning*, the focus seemed to be on academic skills, even if in other parts of the plan they discussed social skills. Something that reinforced the impression that the teachers saw these activities as separated was the fact that they planned for pedagogical, physical, and social activities in more or less separate physical units. Following David Harvey's (2006) distinction between three different spatial understandings–space as absolute, relative and/or relational–this conveys a view of the school-yard, and places within the school-yard, as absolute space, i.e. discussing space in concrete physical terms and understanding space as a container. The teachers saw the school-yard, and places within the school-yard, as defined and designated space for different activities to take place. In line with this understanding they wanted to create specific places for specific activities, i.e. suitable spaces (cf. Kostenius, 2011).

Parallel with space as absolute were thoughts about space as relative. Following Harvey (2006), an understanding of space as relative originates from an interest in mapping and measuring space in order to analyse correlations. In this study, the tendency to create outdoor space using indoor space as a model can be seen as an example of understanding space as relative. The design of the educational indoor milieu, with special areas for gathering and teaching different classes, was the model when planning for teaching outdoors–the teachers wanted to create 'outdoor classrooms' and outdoor 'group rooms'. Relating the outdoor to the indoor is common in studies about nature as a context for learning. However, in many of these studies, the outdoor and the indoor are contrasted and discussed as opposites–nature is seen as a genuine and *authentic* context, and the classroom is seen as artificial and unnatural (e.g. Änggård, 2010). Opposing and contrasting the outdoor with the indoor was not done in the project plans in this study–it was rather a question of grounding the thinking about the outdoor environment on the indoor environment.

Some passages and formulations in the project plans, however, tied the three themes together and revealed a more integrated and less time-space bounded view on the relations between physical activities, social integration, and learning. This was seen, for example, in the idea to equip the school-yard with mobile play and sports material. The underlying idea in this plan was that attractive play equipment would entice children into non-fixed playing activities and that these activities in turn would encourage good social relations and hinder social exclusion and marginalisation. This was also the underlying idea behind providing the school-yard with teachers responsible for initiating games. By organising games and physical activities that attracted many and various children, the aim was to support social relations and a spirit of community among the children. These ideas reflect a relational understanding of school-yard space (Harvey, 2006). As argued by Harvey as well as by theorists such as Massey (1994: 2005) and Lefebvre (1991), many different relationships constitute and produce social space. Relationships between individuals and groups of individuals at the local and societal level, as well as intersecting relations that depend on aspects such as materiality, geographical distances, and individual and collective lived experiences traverse and construct space. Social space is thus constantly produced through various interconnected relations (Lefebvre 1991; see also Gordon et al., 2000).

The identified themes in which the school-yard was characterised as a space for teaching and learning, for physical activity, and for social interaction recurred repeatedly in the projects plans. The variation within individual plans, as well as the variation between them was linked to spatial understandings (space as absolute, relative, and/or relational) rather than to the content of the plans.

Active, creative, and agentic subjectivity

The project plans about how to improve the school-yard provided insight into how the teachers envisioned the ideal school-yard child. In the teachers' rhetoric, the ideal school-yard child stood out as an individual who is actively engaging in pedagogical, physical, and social activities. *Active* was a recurrent adjective, often referring to *physically* active and accompanied with *creative*, *engaged*, and *involved*:

> We want the children to be active during break-time.
> We want to see creative and engaged children in our school-yard.

Activeness also referred to social interaction–and the school-yard child was described as someone who *meets* and *communicates*, but also as someone who is active on an individual level, a *reflective* individual who also withdraws from socialising and interactions and who *can reflect and find a quiet moment*. In addition, activeness referred to learning, to being someone who takes an active and positive approach to education: *[children who are] open-minded and have a positive attitude to learning*. Overall, the analysis presented here gives a picture of the ideal school-yard child as an active, socially competent, and reflective subject–as an individual who plays and interacts with other children and reflects on herself and her environment. This is a picture that corresponds well with the kind of subjectivity that is highly valued in the neoliberal discourse on active citizenship (cf. Brunila and Siivonen, 2014). Actual education policy, in Sweden and in many other countries, nurtures the vision of a citizen who is presumed to be active, competent and well educated–a creative and enterprising subject who can handle and take growing individual responsibility in modern society.

However, what was striking in this part of the analysis was how the physically and socially active and reflective school-yard subject was contrasted against subject positions and behaviours that were communicated as problematic. Embedded in the teachers' rhetoric about the school-yard as a space for learning, physical activity, and social interaction were presumptions about some children not being physically active enough. When the teachers discussed activeness, they related active behaviour to 'inactive' behaviour, something that indicates that pupils in these school-yards performed subjectivity in various ways. In the project plans being *inactive* was seen as inappropriate behaviour, and in one of the plans it was literally and explicitly linked to gender and age–*inactivity* or *passivity* was something the teachers connected with *older girls*. In one of the plans it was stated:

> [...] there are many passive girls among the oldest ones.

In order to deal with the problem with *many passive girls among the oldest ones*, the teachers intended to contribute to increased activity among girls in grades 5 and 6. It was obvious from the text that these girls' behaviour was regarded as deviant in relation to the teachers' idea about ideal subjectivity in this local context and that their behaviour was troubling the school-yard culture.

So how can this idea of deviance be understood? Pupils perform subjectivity in multiple and various ways, but there were still some behaviours that were pointed out as deviant and in need of correction. This phenomenon has been discussed in research dealing with gender and embodiment issues, with the argument that the female body, regardless of age, is always deviant in some way and that the male remains the dominant norm in society (Young, 2005). Following this theory, girls' ways of physically occupying physical space and their use of school space is more controlled and limited than boys' (Gordon et al., 2000). As regards this study, it is not obvious what justified some girls' being described and considered as *passive* in the school-yard. It might just be that they were performing activeness in other ways than what was expected by the teachers. It might also be that their way of acting was interpreted by teachers as conscious counter actions against what they considered to be appropriate behaviour in the school-yard.

The talk about deviance also referred to social interaction, and embedded in the teachers' rhetoric about the school-yard were presumptions about some children not being socially active enough. Children who were not 'playing well' with other children were mentioned in several plans. The teachers described them as children *not being as good at taking initiatives as others*, children who *are socially inactive*, and children who *are not good at making contact with other children and therefore sometimes stand alone.*

> We want to support children who do not feel comfortable with their own play or with the team sports that usually take place in the school-yard.

However, in contrast to physical inactivity, inactivity in relation to social interaction was not gendered or aged in the plans.

Ideal school-yard subjectivity thus concerned being physically and socially active–being a competent child who plays actively and interacts socially. Social and physical *inactivity* was communicated as a problem–as troubling the school-yard culture. On the one hand, the teachers talked about children as a collective unit. However, when talking about shortcomings in terms of physical inactivity the children were gendered and aged.

Concluding remarks and discussion

There was a significant level of correspondence in how the school-yard was described among the project plans studied here. The most prominent themes included the school-yard as a space for teaching and learning, physical activity, and social interaction, and these themes recurred with only small variations in all project plans. The variation that was seen was linked to spatial understandings (space as absolute, relative, and/or relational) rather than to the content of the plans (the themes). Furthermore, common among the plans was the idea that an adequate physical environment will support teaching and learning, physical activity, and *good* social relations between the children as well as the idea that the teachers themselves are important agents in providing this.

From the representations, the ideal school-yard child turned out to be an active, competent, and participative subject–someone who is physically and socially active. The emphasis on active participation had both collective and individual dimensions, and the children were expected to participate in and adapt to collective activities as well as to perform agency in terms of taking individual initiatives.

Subjectivity in educational contexts refers to a great extent to socially becoming a pupil, which can be described as the very essence of schooling. From the teachers' perspective, schooling can be understood as the process of fostering individuals into desirable subjects, and from the pupil's perspective it can be seen as developing and performing situated knowledge of school life. The way ideal school-yard subjectivity and pupilness turned out in this study harmonises well with how ideal subjectivity in educational contexts has been portrayed in earlier research, and it fits well into the framework of neo-liberal societal ideals–schooling in the late modern period emphasises competences such as being active and competent as well as individual responsibility, autonomy, and self-regulation (e.g. Bjerrum Nielsen, 2009; Brunila and Siivonen, 2014; Irisdotter Aldenmyr et al., 2012).

From previous research, we know that processes of subjectivity are concerned with normality and deviance and with ideas about appropriate and inappropriate behaviour. This was also recognised in this study where social and physical inactivity were troubling the educational culture and were communicated as a problem. One contribution to previous research in this matter was the identified double nature of representing pupils in the data–the teachers expressed an ambition to cast every pupil in the same mould, as one big group, and the common pattern was to talk about pupils in *abstract* terms (cf. Gordon et al., 2000). However, when the school-yard culture was troubled by deviant behaviour such as physical inactivity, the rhetoric changed and became gendered and aged–and the teachers associated one group of pupils, i.e. *older girls*, with a particular school-yard behaviour. This raises questions about how we understand intersectional dynamics and patterns in relation to normality and deviance, and it points to the importance of taking a critical approach to both homogeneous and differentiated representations of school-yard behaviour.

With the theoretical framework outlined earlier in the chapter, one could argue that the teachers' representations of the school-yard–and the ideas of ideal subjectivity and adequate behaviour that are embedded in these representations–have a significant impact on 'the making of subjects' in school. Certain skills, competences, and behaviours are highly valued while others are regarded as troublesome, and this has an impact on the process of schooling. However, representations of space are just one spatial dimension influencing schooling (cf. Rönnlund, 2015b). With the understanding that subjectivity is situated and negotiated, and that individuals are active agents when it comes to creating social space (Massey, 2005), the analysis presented here gives just one glimpse of the subjectification that takes place in the school-yard. However, what stands out as obvious is that the educational space outside the classroom is also an arena where educative ambitions and schooling are played out–the school-yard is an important arena for processing subjectivity and socially becoming a pupil.

References

Alerby, E., (2003) 'During the break we have fun'. A study concerning pupils' experiences of school, *Educational research*, 45(1): 17-28.

Bjerrum Nielsen, H., (2009) *Skoletid: Jenter og gutter fra 1. til 10. klasse* [Schooltime: Girls and boys in first to tenth grade], Olso: Universitetsforlaget.

Bjerrum Nielsen H. and Rudberg, M., (1991) *Historien om pojkar och flickor*, Lund: Studentlitteratur.

Brunila, K. and Siivonen, P., (2014) Preoccupied with the self: towards self-responsible, enterprising, flexible and self-centred subjectivity in education, *Discourse: studies in the cultural politics of education*, 37(1): 56-69.

Carrier, S., (2009) Environmental education in the school-yard. Learning styles and gender, *The journal of environmental education*, 40(3): 2-12,

Connolly, P., (2003) Gendered and gendering spaces: Playgrounds in the early years, in Skelton, C. and Francis, B., (eds.) *Boys and girls in the primary school*, Berkshire: Open University Press.

Delamont, S., (1990) *Sex roles and the school,* London: Meuthen.

Epstein D., Kehily, M., Mac an Ghaill, M. and Redman, P., (2001) Boys and girls come out to play. Making masculinities and femininities in school playgrounds, *Men and masculinities,* 4(2): 158-172.

Evaldsson A-C., (2004) Shifting moral stances: Morality and gender in same-sex and cross-sex game interaction, *Research on language and social interaction*, 37(3): 331-363.

Evaldsson A-C., (2005) Staging insults and mobilizing categorizations in a multiethnic peer group, *Discourse and society,* 16(6): 763-786.

Fjørtoft, I., Kristoffersen, B. and Sageie, J., (2009) Children in school-yards: Tracking movement patterns and physical activity in school-yards using global positioning system and heart rate monitoring, *Landscape and urban planning*, 93: 210-217.

Frosh, S., Phoenix, A. and Pattman, R., (2002) *Young masculinities. Understanding boys in contemporary society*, New York: Palgrave.

Fägerstam, E., (2014) High school teachers' experience of the educational potential of outdoor teaching and learning, *Journal of adventure education and outdoor learning*, 14(1): 56-81.

Gordon, T., Holland, J. and Lahelma, E., (2000) *Making spaces. Citizenship and difference in schools*, New York: St. Martin's Press.

Gustafson, K., (2006) *Vi och dom I skola och stadsdel. Barns identitetsarbete och sociala geografier*, Thesis (PhD), Uppsala universitet.

Gustafson, K., (2009) Us and them - Children's identity work and social geography in a Swedish school yard, *Ethnography and education*, 4(1): 1-16.

Harvey, D., (2006) *Spaces of global capitalism*, London: Verso.

Holloway, S. and Valentine, G., (2000) *Children's geographies. Playing, living, learning*, London: Routledge.

Irisdotter Aldenmyr, S., Jepson Wigg, U. and Olson, M., (2012) Worries and possibilities in active citizenship: Three Swedish educational contexts, *Education, citizenship and social justice*, 7(3): 255-270.

Kofoed, J., (2008) Appropriate pupilness. Social categories intersecting in school, *Childhood*, 15 (3): 415-430.

Kostenius, C., (2011) Picture this - our dream school! Swedish schoolchildren sharing their visions of school, *Childhood*, 18(4): 509-525.

Larsson, A., Norlin, B. and Rönnlund, M., (2017) *Den svenska skolgårdens historia*. [The Cultural history of the Swedish School-yard], Lund: Nordic Academic Press.

Lefebvre, H., (1991) *The production of space*, Oxford: Blackwell Publishers.

Massey, D., (1994) *Space, place and gender*, Cambridge: Polity Press.

Massey, D., (2005) *For space*, London: SAGE.

Maynard, T. and Waters, J., (2007) Learning in the outdoor environment. A missed opportunity? *Early years*, 27(3): 255-265.

Norddahl, K. and Einarsdottir, J., (2015) Children's views and preferences regarding their outdoor environment, *Journal of adventure education and outdoor learning*, 15(2): 152-167.

Reay, D., (2001) 'Spice girls', 'Nice girls', 'Girlies', and 'Tomboys': gender discourses, girls' cultures and femininities in the primary classroom, *Gender and education*, 13(2): 153-166.

Renold, E., (2005) *Girls, boys and junior sexualities: exploring children's gender and sexual relations in the primary school*, London: RoutledgeFalmer.

Rosa, H., (2013) Leading a life. Five key elements in the hidden curriculum of our schools, *Nordic studies in education*, 33: 97-111.

Rysst, M., (2015) Friendship and gender identity among girls in a multicultural setting in Oslo, *Childhood*, 22(4): 490-505.

Rönnlund, M., (2015a) School-yard stories. Processes of gender identity at a 'childrens' place, *Childhood*, 22(1): 85-100.

Rönnlund, M., (2015b) Skolgården som socialt rum. [The school-yard as social space], *Nordic studies in education*, 3-4: 200-216.

Rönnlund, M. and Tollefsen, A., (2016) *Rum - Samhällsvetenskapliga perspektiv*, Stockholm: Liber.

Skelton, C., (2001) *Schooling the boys: masculinities and primary education,* Buckingham: Open University Press.

Thomson, S., (2007) Do's and don'ts. Children's experiences of the primary school playground, *Environmental education research,* 13(4): 487-500.

Thorne, B., (1993) *Gender play: Girls and boys in school,* Buckingham: Open University Press.

Titman, W., (1994) *Special places, special people: the hidden curriculum of school grounds,* Surrey: The World Wide Fund for Nature.

Tranter, P. J. and Malone, K., (2004) Geographies of environmental learning. An exploration of children's use of school grounds, *Children's geographies,* 2(1): 131-155.

Ulleberg, H-P., (2006) *Et vidløftig sted. En analyse og diskusjon av skolegården som et sted for pedagogisk virksomhet,* Thesis (PhD), Norges teknisk-naturvitenskapelige universitet.

Villanen, H. and Alerby, E., (2013) The sense of place - voices from a school-yard, *Education in the North,* 20(special issue): 26-38.

Wodac, R. and Meyer, M., (2001) *Methods of critical discourse analysis,* London: SAGE

Young, I. M., (2005) *On female body experience. 'Throwing like a girl' and other essays,* New York: Oxford University Press.

Änggård, E., (2010) Making use of the 'nature' in an outdoor preschool. Classroom, home and fairyland, *Children, youth and environments,* 20(1), 4-25.

Änggård, E., (2012) Att skapa platser i naturmiljöer. Om hur vardagliga praktiker I en Ur och Skur-förskola bidrar till att ge platser identitet, *Nordisk barnhageforskning,* 5(10): 1-16.

Öqvist, A., (2009) *Skolvardagens genusdramaturgi. En studie av hur feminiteter och maskuliniteter görs i år 5 med ett särskilt fokus på benämningar som hora och kärring,* Thesis (PhD), Luleås tekniska universitet.

Chapter 3

Getting along–social skills required to be *normal* in the Finnish school

Ina Juva and Touko Vaahtera

In this chapter, we analyse how teachers and other school personnel construct the *normal* student through the concept of social skills and how this echoes the needs of the state to produce citizens who can agree with a capitalist society. The chapter unpacks the idea of social skills. The examination of social skills became part of research themes in Finland in the 1970s, when the first programs to influence children's aggressive behaviour were implemented. Social skills have been researched in the field of social psychology and educational psychology since then, as part of social competence (Pulkkinen, 2002). The earlier research on social skills in schools addressed topics such as teaching and developing social skills in the school environment (Mäntynen, 2007; Pulkkinen, 2002; Hynninen, 1999), and supporting students' social skills and social competence (Neitola, 2011). However, we want to situate social skills and moreover the aims to mould students' personalities and worries about the wrong kind of personalities, in the context of schooling, in the mechanism that reproduces, naturalises and strengthens the idea of an individual driven by their self-interests.

In what follows, we investigate how the teachers and other school personnel define normal social behaviour. They equate normal behaviour with having good social skills. Indeed, in the nineteenth century the term *normal* was used to create a means to measure an ideal of how an average human should be (Davis, 1995). In the following sections, we explore how social skills cannot be separated from the wider cultural norms of a society. We will consider first how the concept of social skills in the context of schooling emphasises competition rather than co-operation and connects social skills with the needs of the labour market. Then we turn to the question of how the discourse of social skills underscores the capacity to be a part of a wider system without challenging it. In the final section, we consider how not all modes of sociality are recognised as a social behaviour.

On methodology

This chapter is part of a wider two-year ethnographic project that examines teachers' and students' perceptions of marginalisation in two lower secondary schools (the age range of pupils is thirteen to fifteen years-old) in the capital area of Finland. In particular, this chapter is based on an ethnography which was conducted in two schools that are located in multicultural areas in southern Finland. The students accordingly have different religious backgrounds, different migrant and non-migrant backgrounds, different social class backgrounds, different home languages and different gender identifications. Some of the students also have special needs. However, we do not distinguish between the two schools in this chapter since there were no demographic differences in the composition of their student bodies or in terms of how the schools went about their official business or the way the issues we were engaging with in the research were approached and studied.

Deriving from interviews with thirty-one teachers and other staff members in the two schools we examine how teachers and other staff members understand the notion of social skills.[1] To contextualise the teachers' constructions and to understand them as part of larger discursive field we studied their responses alongside the manuals and textbooks used in the field of educational psychology. We have been able to contrast the teachers' views with the definitions of social skills provide by the manuals and textbooks. There are similarities and differences between the teachers' constructions and the definitions of social skills in the manuals and textbooks. We will concentrate on what kind of meanings are given to social skills or more widely for social behaviour.

The interviewees were asked about their perceptions of whether and why certain students are excluded and others included in the school community. One theme that constantly came up in the interviews were students' social skills. To contextualise this, Ina researched earlier studies in the field of education in Finland, especially focusing on how these studies define and conceptualise social skills. Ina found out that there are manuals and textbooks, which focus on social skills, and which are constantly mentioned in master's theses in the field of educational psychology. These books and manuals belong to the type of

1 The material of this chapter consists of thirty-one semi-structured in-depth interviews. They were conducted with twenty-eight teachers, one teaching assistant and two school counselling staff. Ina conducted the interviews in one school and two other researchers did the same in another school. The interviews were conducted in the schools and lasted between one and one-and-a-half hours each.

literature that is mostly directed at teachers, educators and parents; and in a few cases at students. They share the use of semi scientific language and scientific sources, and mix it with personal opinions and points of view. Some of the books are written by scholars and some by professionals such as teachers and psychologists. Previously, Touko has investigated the uses of popular scientific texts and explored how the ideas introduced by scientists can be used in various ways (Vaahtera, 2016). When Touko became a co-author for this chapter, they noticed that the data gathered by Ina resonated with Touko's aims to investigate various texts as cultural texts; that is emphasising that it is not possible to state that only particular kinds of texts would be political and others would not (Jameson, 1993 [1981]).

The manuals and textbooks that we analyse in this chapter, consist of six books, of which four are manuals/handbooks, one is a textbook and one is a non-fiction popular science book. These manuals and textbooks are significant because they are a part of a literature that is used in professional training and teacher education and the books are referenced regularly in the masters' theses that examine social skills in the field of educational psychology in Finland.

The transcribed interviews and the manuals/textbooks were thematically analysed and contrasted by reading them with the themes partially emerging from the data and partially from theory and earlier research, and partially from then ongoing participant observation. We combine ethnography with the methodological approaches of cultural studies. Cultural studies foregrounds that the ways in which we write a research paper cannot be separated from our political aims (Slack, 1996; Grossberg, 2010). Moreover, this process seeks to re-articulate contexts, rather than describing a context in a seemingly unpolitical way (Slack, 1996).

The concept of social skills

The overarching concept for social skills is social competence and research exists on students' and children's problems with social competence (Kangas and Kolehmainen, 2007; Kaukiainen, 2002). The teachers and students assessments of social skills have also been researched (Ristimäki, 2011). In international literature a research connection was drawn between the deficit of the social skills of students and future mental health problems, social isolation, learning disabilities and marginalisation in general (Maag, 2006; Hansen et al., 1998; Parker and Asher, 1987). In the Finnish research there was a similar connection drawn between the deficit of social skills and social problems. The importance of social skills was seen essentially through preventing *problematic* behaviour such as aggressiveness and it was connected to the risk of marginalisation (Hiltunen and Perälä, 2011; Ristimäki, 2011; Mäntynen, 2007). This is also seen in the manuals/textbooks that are used to define the concept of social skills for educational professionals and university students referred to earlier (i.e. Keltikangas-Järvinen, 2010; Kauppila, 2005; Laine, 2005; Salmivalli, 2005; Pulkkinen, 2002; Kalliopuska, 1995 and Poikkeus, 1995).

The manuals focusing on social skills often emphasised the institutional context of social skills. The assumption appeared to be that social skills are needed in the future work place and for the functioning of the classroom (Keltikangas-Järvinen, 2010; Kauppila, 2005; Kalliopuska, 1995; Poikkeus, 1995). For example, the skills that are seen to contribute to studying, such as listening, obeying rules and pleasing teachers, were seen as more important than other interpersonal skills and cooperation with other students (Kauppila, 2005). Here the formal school, and other formal settings such as a work place, are assumed to be the main contexts of social skills.

Our aim in this chapter is to re-articulate social skills through situating them in the ideological struggle about how capitalism functions. Urciuoli (2008) describes how the skills (such as communication, leadership or in the case of this study, social skills) have been constructed through discourses as an aspect of workers performance, which means something that can be acquired, quantified, measured (or tested) and that can bring positive outcomes in labour markets in a way that can be measured in money (Urciuoli, 2008). This means for example that the social skills of students are something that can be measured and later converted to something that makes it easier for the person to create an image of themselves as a capable worker and to acquire a position in the labour market. At the same time social skills are clearly not delimited but ' … cover a range of disparate practices, knowledge, and ways of acting and being. In short, they are denotationally indeterminate' (Urciuoli, 2008: 212). Thus, it becomes a difficult task to be aware of what exactly one must know to have for example *good* social skills, as the content of the concept is all the time shifting. In order to pay attention to its *indeterminacy*, we explore how the notion of social skills is used, what kind of work it does and in particular, what is the function of social skills in the context of schooling?

The competitive individual and capitalist common sense

In the quote below Ursula describes the *normal* student through what kind of behaviour is expected:

> *Ursula*: … someone who can independently study, can do group work, can take care of school work and homework, when needed to can be in contact with classmates and to ask for homework. The not normal student does not send a message, or even worse the mother sends a message and asks for homework. The student needs to be able to take care of their own school work.

Here Ursula emphasises the ability to work independently and the ability to be active when defining an abstract normal student. The definition of normal by Ursula resonates with the definition of good social skills. Interviewees defined a student with good social skills as someone who does not disturb classroom activity and who participates responsible in school activities. Interaction with other students was recognised mainly as a social skill, when it did not disturb the functioning of the school system. Furthermore, also in the manuals, an idea of efficiency seemed quite important, for example *good* social skills were described as the variety of models of behaviour and capacity of choosing what is most suitable for the situation (Keltikangas-Järvinen, 2010).

This idea of a student, who knows how to behave in the school and as some interviewees indicated in the future work place too, was also present in the manuals/textbooks, where the good social skills were connected to ability to act *correctly* in the formal school and in the future work place. Already in 1977, Paul Willis noted how teachers maintain the idea that there would be a continuity between maintaining school norms and accessing respectable jobs (Willis, 1977). In earlier research in the context of special education, the student who knows how to act *correctly* has been referred as *a professional pupil* (Leino and Lahelma, 2002, Braun, Maguire, and Ball, 2010), which means 'a competent student [who] knows how to behave and does so willingly' (Leino and Lahelma, 2002: 80). The term *professional pupil* connotes working life and the capacity to be a *professional*. Indeed, students who were understood to possess good social skills were understood as beings who possess skills needed in their future working life.

In the manuals and textbooks, social skills were mainly described as behaviour models that help us to obtain our objectives in situations with social interaction, and all of them shared the notion that social skills are learned and not permanent personality traits. The idea of improving poor or even absent social skills was very present in the manuals/textbooks, as they offered ways to educate children and students–and in some cases adults–to have the right set of social skills (Keltikangas-Järvinen, 2010; Kauppila, 2005; Kalliopuska, 1995). Importantly, good social skills were seen as an essential part of employees' competence in the labour market (Kauppila, 2005).

Institutions such as schools understand their subjects as beings who are individuals but behave in a similar way and with a similar logic (Echeverría, 2007). This came up in the interviews and in the manuals/textbooks confirming the contradiction between the pressure to individualise and at the same time expecting that those individuals behave in very similar ways. The demand for autonomy resonates with a wider shift in the sphere of social politics in Finland where different institutions produce and reproduce the citizenship of social politics, where one of the aims is to create active and accountable/responsible subjects that are then measured in the labour markets (Julkunen, 2006; Miller and Rose, 2010).

Interestingly labour market expectations of skills such as collaboration, mutual aid and other forms of relating to others that are not based on competition between autonomous individuals were not part of the discourses of the interviewees on social skills. Collaboration was limited to working together in teaching situations and also to getting along with others. Salmivalli (2005), critically, points out that the measured skills seem to be in many cases more connected to obedience than to co-operation. Stuart Hall (1996: 33), a cultural theorist, remarks how capitalist common sense assumes an individual who is not 'driven by goodwill, or love of his neighbour or fellow feeling to succeed in the market game.' Rather, the market is assumed to function in its best when people are solely driven by their self-interests (ibid.). Moreover, Hall (1996: 38) emphasises how 'the market experience' frames everyday life and situations that ostensibly appear to be outside economics. In this respect, we suggest that the ways in which good social skills are understood in the context of school echoes 'the market experience.'

However individual competition as the only way to organise human societies and especially processes of work has been contested by authors such as Pyotr Kropotkin and Karl Marx. Kropotkin (1906) states that cooperation and mutual aid have been more of a norm than an exception in organising human communities and work; meanwhile Marx (2013: 232-233) highlighted the efficiency of cooperation of workers and saw its ambiguous potential both for benefiting capital as well as the workers own organisation against it.

When students with good social skills are understood as beings who do not disturb the functioning of the school system and when this ability is connected with the ability to enter to the labour market, we must ask how the capacity to not disturb dominant systems resonates with the aims to produce workers who do not challenge the dominant mode of production. While Marx (2013) connected co-operation with an efficient working method at the moment of industrial capitalism, he also suggested that labourers can co-operate to their own ends (see Jossa, 2005). Kropotkin saw that cooperation or mutual aid was not possible in the context of capitalist wage labour because work was not done for the community formed by labourers. Rather, the nature of capitalist forms of work is in contradiction to mutual aid and cooperation, as the fruits of this labour are not collective (Kropotkin, 1906). In this respect, it is important to note that co-operation can function in different ways and as such it does not guarantee anything. The ways in which social skills, too, emerge from our data should–methodologically–be understood as a formation 'without guarantees' as Hall (1996: 45) describes the methodological assumption of cultural studies.

Social skills functioned in the interviews and in the manuals in different ways. An interesting contradiction in the notion of social skills in the interviews and the manuals was that the teachers and school personnel presented them as individual characteristics, whereas in the manuals social skills appeared as something to be learned. Overall in the teachers responses, the construction of the right kind of social skills highlights the importance for individual students to be able to function with other students and teachers without causing problems.

There were only few mentions of solidarity or cooperation as part of social skills in the school personnel's interviews, even though they were mentioned in two of the manuals/textbooks (Keltikangas-Järvinen, 2010; Kauppila, 2005). Thus, manuals about social skills understood social skills in a wider and less individualistic way. Social skills were described in these materials as behaviour appreciated by others, and as positive or affirmative for others (Kalliopuska, 1995). They were also described as behaviour that brings positive social results (Kauppila, 2005; Poikkeus, 1995). There were lists of types of behaviour that is part of *good* social skills these varied between different authors but nearly all mentioned, the ability to communicate and act with others with empathy and regulation of emotions and without problems.[2]

2 The way that receiving and interpretation of some behaviour or action as positive or affirmative

Reetta Mietola and Sirpa Lappalainen (2006) have paid attention to how teachers and other education professionals, when they use the research texts to make sense of the everyday practices in schools, sometimes use them in a way that obscures the aims of the original texts. This is, of course, a general mechanism of cultural texts: those who write the texts cannot control to what ends other people use them (e.g. Vaahtera, 2016). Even though particular ideas and concepts can, in some situations, challenge dominant understandings, their capacity to engender visions which dispute the dominant common sense cannot be related to these concepts as such.

'The normal student is a very adaptable being'

As we have seen in the previous section it seems that one of the main points of social skills is that the student is able to blend in, and does not cause any trouble. Virpi describes a normal student as:'definitely [someone who does not] open their mouth in the case there is some dispute which somehow expresses that one thinks differently about something or to defend someone weaker. So it is very adapt ... normal (Ina: student) is a very adaptable being.' In this quote Virpi points out that a *normal* student would not voice different opinions or views than their peers have and they would not stand up to defend a student in a weaker position. She concludes that the *normal* student is *a very adaptable being*. The way in which Virpi emphasises adaptability echoes with the historical meaning of the term normal as it emphasises capacity to be a part of a wider system without challenging it.

According to Georges Canguilhem (2007), the term *normal* appeared in the French language in 1759, at the same time as the use of statistics was first introduced. The term *normal* was used in this context where the aim was to gather information about the population. In Great Britain, the term *normal* surged forth with the rise of eugenics where it combined an intention to define an average human being in the framework of how ideal human beings should be or what are the ideal traits of this abstract person. Thus, it allows a use of the language of natural sciences in order to manage a population (Davis, 1995). Michel Foucault (2010) remarked how the term *normal* emerged as a way to understand the intersection between the population as a whole and health, sickness and mortality.

In this sense, the term normal cannot be separated from the attempts to understand and control the bodies/minds of people. The context of schooling

---

can vary inside the school. was not discussed.

was also one of the first sites for the term *normal*. In the nineteenth century, the term *normal school* was introduced. In this context, normal was a prototype; it was a model school. As Michael Warner (1999) points out the term normal is here substantially connected with the aim to normalise; that is to make everyone identical with the specific model. Bolivar Echeverría (2007) describes the process of creating a *model* of an ideal subject or human being in modern time. He pays attention to how the historical process that enabled homogenising ways to maintain abstract identities of private proprietors coincided with the birth of universalism.

Modernity and a capitalist mode of production require an abstraction of the human being, an ideal average which can be the imagined worker or student, when planning factories, schools or other institutions. In the most recent mode of capitalism–neoliberalism–the ideal abstraction might seem to be more individual, but there still exists an ideal: flexibility and autonomy (on flexibility, see Martin, 1994), which become visible when we examine how *being normal* as a requirement operates in school (see also Beach and Dovemark, 2007). Moreover, Warner (1999) pays attention to how the term *normalisation* means a process which authorises someone as a member of society. Thus, let us return to the quote from Ursula where she defines a normal student.

> *Ursula*: But in another way, otherwise we have all kinds of (students), everyone has their own character, I would not define that kind of norm, normal, but that kind of student who can cope with the ordinary day to day life, can manage the day to day life.

Here we can notice how Ursula emphasises how students can be different from each other and assumes that they need to have their individual character. Thus, being normal does not mean that one is not specific somehow. However, Ursula still states that a normal student is someone who fits into the school world which assumes students to independently 'cope with the ordinary day to day life.' Similar to social skills *to be normal* is an indeterminate condition. Although Ursula challenges the concept of normal, at the same time she describes how one can become or be constructed as normal, and in this case it is through behaviour that can be recognised as normal. (We return to the theme of recognisability in the next section).

If we consider the way that a normal student should not voice out different opinions and should cope with the expectations of the school, we can start to notice that here the members of the school staff defend the notion of the normal in the sense of *adapted to the environment* (cf. Canguilhem, 2007: 200). As we consider normal as a capacity to be able to adapt or a requirement to be able to adapt, we should pay attention to what are the specific requirements for this; in other words how one should operate in a specific context in order to be someone who can adapt to it.

When Canguilhem investigated the ways in which the term normal has been used in the history of science, he enabled us to notice that the term normal could have been emerged in a different way. Canguilhem (2007: 184) claimed that while sickness and pathology, which are assumed to be the opposites of the normal, are often understood as states that are 'the normal mode of life minus something which has been destroyed,' they could also be understood as states that are substantially different from the states that appear to be normal. He paid attention to how, in the history of science, scientists have also maintained how pathological states could be understood as states that have their own order and how that what is understood as a recovery could also be understood as a new arrangement. For example, the use of electric shocks in neuro-psychiatric therapy showed, according to Canguilhem, how this treatment engendered new chemical arrangements rather than maintain the previous arrangements. This makes it possible for Canguilhem to suggest that we should not confuse health with normal, because healthy organisms do not just maintain their current state but are able to modify themselves. Further, he claimed that 'man feels in good health […] only when he feels more than normal–that is adapted to the environment and its demands–but normative, capable of following new norms of life' (Canguilhem, 2007: 200). Warner (1999: 58) remarks that Canguilhem's ideas highlight that 'variations of the norm' should not be rejected but embraced because they show us modes of being that 'can become new norms.'[3] Indeed, Canguilhem's ideas make it possible to remark that students who are not able to exemplify a capitalist common sense, could actually introduce new modes of social skills.

Knowing the rules–becoming recognisable

In this section, we analyse the norms of recognisability and normality in regards to social skills. Not all behaviour is recognised as a social skill. As mentioned in

3 Interestingly, Mikko Tuhkanen (2004: 311) suggests that Michael Warner (1999) who theorises the notion of normal calls for interpretations that would emphasise new conditions. Tuhkanen (2004) connects these ideas with Deleuzian philosophy..

the earlier section, one of the main themes that was connected to social skills in the interviews, was the capability of the pupils to adapt to the functioning of the formal school. There was a range of modes of behaviour that were described by the teachers and other personnel as problematic. In the quote below, Raakel describes how a student can be too open and come too close and how this disturbs a school.

> *Raakel*: … students might not see the difference that between being at home or (laughs) or somewhere else … But also it could be at some point like, like to understand a bit that it is a strange adult and one may not say straightforwardly like in home one says … it can be in that one is too open and somehow comes too close.

There seems to be an expectation that the students have to have a good and positive attitude towards teachers but at the same time maintain a certain distance. In the focus group interviews the students mentioned the pressure of when they have to tell very personal information to the staff. At the same time the teachers and other school personnel mentioned that they keep the professional and personal sides separated. Hence it is easier for the teachers to control the line between being *too open* and showing one's personal life in the context of the school or maintaining it strictly outside of the formal school. This should make us ponder on the ways the distinction *public/private* is unstable. [4] The ways in which the distinction *public/private* functions in school settings is complex and even contradictory. For example, students are supposed to describe personal information in a professional context but still they should not tell *too* much. The main issue in this negotiation and what *guarantees* correct social conduct, is ability to recognise the rules of social relations.

A mode of behaviour that is intelligible and recognisable echoes wider social relations. Robert McRuer (2006) has argued that the naturalisation of the *public/private*–distinction intertwines with the production of capitalist common sense and compulsory able-bodiedness. For McRuer (2006), compulsory able-bodiedness means assumptions and practices that produce an able-bodied identity as a monolithic *composition* (ibid., 156) which shapes the ways that bodies and minds can emerge in a particular time and place. McRuer (2006: 8) explains how the reinforcement of the binary *public/private* intertwined with the

4 For the ways in which the *public/private* distinction can be used to different ends in regards to disability and sexuality, see Kulick & Rydström, 2015.

ways in which labourers' bodies were controlled in the nineteenth century when industrial capitalism emerged. McRuer (2006: 8) paraphrases Marx and states that the labourer was then 'free to sell one's labour but not free to do anything else effectively' (ibid., 8). Thus, here the life of the labourer, who has a body that is able to work, is divided into two spheres. Marx (Economic and Philosophic manuscripts, cited in McRuer, 2006: 86) puts it as: 'He is at home when he is not working, and when he is working he is not at home.' Thus, the rules that students have to be able to recognise are contextual and historical; they frame the way that an ideal subject should be able to operate in a society. Only some forms of behaviour are acceptable and rewarded in the context of the formal school. Not all behaviour can be recognised as social skills. They require those 'a prior conditions of recognisability' (Davies, 2011: 279), which are related to the capitalist common sense mentioned earlier in this chapter.

When the school staff crosses the line between public and private, by obligating students to expose personal information, while at the same time maintaining limits by separating teachers' private life as something that can be kept separated from school, we can start to notice that the distinction *public/private* is far from a self-evident formation. Rather, we should ask to what ends the distinction is used. In this context, maintaining proper distance and handling personal information in a controlled way might be quite an essential part in constructing students as abstractions, so they can blend into the mass system.

In the interviews, *lack of* social skills was understood in complex ways. Interviewees connected it with both shyness, passiveness and being unpredictable, aggressive or noisy. In the textbooks, the importance of social skills are seen essentially through preventing *problematic* behaviour such as aggressiveness (Hiltunen and Perälä, 2011; Ristimäki, 2011; Mäntynen, 2007). As not all behaviour is recognised as social skills, students have to be able to recognise the limits and the rules of the behaviour that is considered normal or socially skillful. Thus, the essential point is the ability to perceive the rules.

Indeed, the notions of social skills and normal social relations are exclusive. We want to pay attention to how the category of normal excludes those students whose behaviour is not recognisable in the context of social skills. When behaviour is not recognisable in the context of social skills, students can *become* unrecognisable, and might face attempts at correction or exclusion.[5] Social skills or behaviour that differ from the norm are also constructed in medical

5 For the career paths of adults, whose modes of behaviour were named *antisocial*, *maladjusted* or *wild* when they were in school, see Kivirauma and Jahnukainen (2001).

terms. In the International Classification of Diseases (WHO–World Health Organisation, 2010) behavioural disorders are described to be'... characterised by a repetitive and persistent pattern of dissocial, aggressive, or defiant conduct. Such behaviour should amount to major violations of age-appropriate social expectations; it should therefore be more severe than ordinary childish mischief or adolescent rebelliousness and should imply an enduring pattern of behaviour (six months or longer).' (WHO, 2010, F91)

In the same manner that the body can be constructed as pathology, as unable to function in a *correct* way, behaviour too can be pathologised, and a person can be named as disabled for violating social expectations. As we have seen in this chapter, there are attempts to fix poor social skills in the context of schooling.

Such an idea of remedying the pathological individual by offering a correct set of social skills has been problematised by Fahlgren, Johansson and Mulinari (2011). They describe how different processes of marginalisation are explained as a fault or issue of the individual and not as a structural issue that would require a deeper scrutiny of structures. When the notion of social skills is connected with the labour market, as we have seen in this chapter, it is a category that not only expresses the characteristics of an individual, it also expresses how we think about labour. However, the ableist ideology wants us to assume that it only expresses an individual. This contradiction here is nothing else than ideological struggle (cf. Hall, 1996).

Conclusions

As earlier research in Finland shows, pupils can be defined as *normal* when they are open to norms, rules and moral codes and can cope with them (Rinne, 2012). In the school individuals learn their own position and place regarding the *official* constructions of normality in the school. Normality as a discursive construction favours some qualities such as autonomy/independence, adaptability, competitiveness. It justifies positioning in hierarchies of different subjects by neutralising the process, by saying that the position is based on individual capacities, although what is considered as *normal* represents the logic that is needed to function *appropriately* in the society and working life. Now the question is how can a student adapt to the existing system, not if the system should adapt to our needs as individuals and communities. When the aim is to tackle marginalisation and discrimination the question cannot be about how students adapt to the existing system but how the system should, and if it can, adapt to the needs of individuals and communities.

Part of the individualising emphasis on social skills underscores the ways in which poor social skills can be fixed. As a consequence the weight of resolving the situation moves from the institutions to individuals that have to fix their behaviour to be able to be recognised as *normal* subjects and to adapt to the formal school and to a society. This is not, of course, the ideology we want to put forward in this chapter. Rather, we want to change the ways in which the notion of social skills is understood. Stuart Hall (1996) remarks how Antonio Gramsci emphasised how a popular thinking, common sense, is substantially historical rather than natural, and in that sense contestable. Our aim in this chapter has been to interrogate a capitalist common sense in the context of schooling. We have used the formulation of *the capitalist common sense* (Watkins, 1999) in order to pay attention to everyday practices in school settings that reinforce and prioritise adaptability and competitiveness as norms.

It is important to note that not all activity of the students was recognised as having social skills. Only the forms of activity that illuminated the ability to adapt to the norms of the school; the activity which did not cause any problems in the formal settings was understood as a skillful activity. Intriguingly, while the school staff were seemingly able to challenge the definition of *normal* as behaviour which resonates with the social norms, they maintained the view that students should be able to adapt to the environment. That is, their understanding still maintained the idea of normal.

Christina Salmivalli (2005), who has studied social skills, states: 'We can ask, if it is socially skillful to be able to cooperate with peers or to adapt to expectations of the teachers?' Salmivalli's question challenges the ideal of being able to adapt to social norms. Still, the question does not interrogate social skillfulness. What about students who do not cooperate with others because their peers find them too difficult or unpredictable? What about students who would like to cooperate but cannot concentrate on working with others? Where does the emphasis on social skills leave these students?

References

Beach, D. and Dovemark, M., (2007) *Education and the commodity problem: Ethnographic investigations of creativity and performativity in Swedish schools*, London: the Tufnell Press.

Braun, A, Maguire, M. and Ball, S.J., (2010) Policy enactments in the UK secondary school: examining policy, practice and school positioning, *Journal of Education Policy*, 25(4), 547-560.

Canguilhem, G., (2007) *The Normal and the Pathological*, 5 ed., New York: Zone Books.

Davies, B., (2011) Bullies as guardians of the moral order: re-thinking the origins of bullying in schools, *Children and Society*, 25(4): 278-286.

Davis, L. J., (1995) *Enforcing normalcy: Disability, deafness, and the body*, London: Verso.

Echeverría, B.,(2007) Imágenes de la 'blanquitud', in Echeverría, B., Lizarazo Arias, D. and Lazo Briones, P., (2007) *Sociedades Icónicas: historia,ideología y cultura de la imagen*, México: Siglo XXI.

Fahlgren, S., Johansson, A. and Mulinari, D., (2011) Introduction: Challenging normalization processes in a neoliberal welfare state, in Fahlgren, S., Johansson, A. and Mulinari, D., (eds.) *Normalization and "outsiderhood". Feminist readings of a neoliberal welfare state*, Bentham Science Publishers, 1-166.

Foucault, M., (2010) *Turvallisuus, alue, väestö. Hallinnallisuuden historia. Collège de Francen luennot 1977-1978*, Helsinki: Tutkijaliitto.

Grossberg, L., (2010) *Cultural studies in the future tense*, Durham: Duke University Press.

Hall, S., (1996) The problem of ideology. Marxism without guarantees, in Morley, D. and Chen, K-H., (eds.) Stuart Hall: *Critical dialogues in cultural studies*, London: Routledge: 25-46.

Hansen, D. J., Nangle, D. W., and Meyer, K. A., (1998) Enhancing the effectiveness of social skills interventions with adolescents, *Education and treatment of children*, 21(4): 489-513.

Hiltunen, S. and Perälä, P., (2011) *Olen muutakin kuin koululainen -narratiivisen identiteetin ja sosiaalisten taitojen tukeminen perusopetuksessa*, Thesis (master), University of Tampere, Faculty of Education.

Hynninen, T., (1999) *Lasten sosiaalisten taitojen kehittäminen koulussa skidikantti-ohjelman avulla*, Thesis (licentiate), University of Jyväskylä.

Jameson, F., (1993 [1981]). *The political unconscious: Narrative as a socially symbolic act*, London: Routledge.

Jossa, B., (2005) Marx, Marxism and the cooperative movement, *Cambridge Journal of Economics,* 29(1): 3-18.

Julkunen, R., (2006) Vastuupuheen esiinmarssi. Avaukset, *Yhteiskuntapolitiikka*, 71(5): 533-540.

Kalliopuska, M., (1995) *Sosiaaliset taidot*, Helsinki: Painatuskeskus.

Kangas, I. and Kolehmainen, A., (2007) *Esikouluikäisen lapsen sosiaalinen kompetenssi*, Thesis (master), University of Joensuu.

Kaukiainen, A., (2002) Onko aggressio ja kiusaaminen aina sosiaalisen kompetenssin puutetta? *Psykologia,* 37(2): 115-123.

Kauppila, R., (2005) *Vuorovaikutus ja sosiaaliset taidot. Vuorovaikutusopas opettajille ja opiskelijoille*, Jyväskylä: PS-kustannus.

Keltikangas-Järvinen, L., (2010) *Sosiaalisuus ja sosiaaliset taidot*, Helsinki: WSOY.

Kivirauma, J. and Jahnukainen, M., (2001) Ten years after special education: Socially maladjusted boys on the labor market, *Behavioural Disorders*, 26(3): 243-255.

Kropotkin, P., (1906) *The conquest of bread*, New York: G. P. Putnam's Sons.

Kulick, D. and Rydström, J., (2015) *Loneliness and its opposite: Sex, disability, and the ethics of engagement*, Durham: Duke UP.

Laine, K., (2005) *Minä, me ja muut sosiaalisissa verkostoissa*, Helsinki: Otava.

Leino, M. and Lahelma, E., (2002) Constructing and educating 'problem children': the case of post-communist Estonia, *International journal of inclusive education*, 6(1): 79-90.

Maag, J, W., (2006) Social skills training for students with emotional and behavioral disorders: A review of reviews, *Behavioral disorders*, 32(1): 4-17.

Martin, E., (1994) *Flexible bodies. The role of immunity in American culture from the days of polio to the age of AIDS*, Boston: Beacon Press.

Marx, K., (2013 [1867]) *Capital: A critical analysis of capitalist production. Vol 1 and 2*, London: Wordsworth Classics of World Literature.

McRuer, R., (2006) *Crip theory. Cultural signs of queerness and disability*, New York: New York University Press.

Mietola, R. and Lappalainen S., (2006) Storylines of worry in educational arenas, *Nordisk pedagogik*, 26(3): 229-242.

Miller, P. and Rose, N., (2010) *Miten meitä hallitaan*, Tampere: Vastapaino.

Mäntynen, M., (2007) *Voiko sosiaalisia taitoja opettaa? Opettajien kokemuksia Askeleittain - ohjelman käyttämisestä koululuokassa*, Thesis (master), University of Jyväskylä.

Neitola, M., (2011) *Supporting the social competence of a child - parents' indirect and direct influences*, Thesis (Phd), University of Turku.

Parker, J. G. and Asher, S. R., (1987) Peer relations and later personal adjustment: Are low-accepted children at risk? *Psychological bulletin*, 102(3): 357-389.

Poikkeus, A.-M., (1995) Lasten toverisuhteet ja sosiaaliset taidot, in Lyytinen, P., Korkiakangas, M. and Lyytinen, H., (eds.) *Näkökulmia kehityspsykologiaan. Kehitys kontekstissaan*, Helsinki: WSOY: 122-138.

Pulkkinen, L., (2002) *Mukavaa yhdessä. Sosiaalinen alkupääoma ja lapsen sosiaalinen kehitys*, Jyväskylä: PS-kustannus.

Rinne, R., (2012) Koulutus normaaliuden ja poikkeavuuden historiallisena tuottajana, in Silvennoinen, H. and Pihlaja, P., (eds.) *Rajankäyntejä. Tutkimuksia normaaliuden, erilaisuuden ja poikkeavuuden tulkinnoista ja määrittelyistä*, Turku: Kasvatustieteiden laitos: 27-56.

Ristimäki, H., (2011) *Social skills evaluated by 6th grade pupils, class teacher and parents*, Thesis (master), University of Jyväskylä.

Salmivalli, C., (2005) *Kaverien kanssa. Vertaissuhteet ja sosiaalinen kehitys*, Jyväskylä: PS-kustannus.

Slack, J. D., (1996) The theory and method of articulation in cultural studies, in Morley, D. and Chen, K-H., (eds.) *Stuart Hall: Critical dialogues in cultural studies*, London: Routledge: 112-127.

Urciuoli, B., (2008) Skills and selves in the new workplace, *American ethnologist*, 35(2): 211-228.

Tuhkanen, M., (2004) Mustista venuksista pervoihin sekasikiöihin. Rodun ja seksuaalisuuden hydridisistä tieteistä, in Kekki, L. and Ilmonen, K., (eds.) *Pervot pidot: Homo-, lesbo - ja queer-näkökulmia kirjallisuudentutkimukseen*, Helsinki: LIKE: 289-311.

Vaahtera, T., (2016) "We swam before we breathed or walked": able-bodied belonging in popular stories of evolutionary biology, *Disability and society*, 31(5): 591-603.

Warner, M., (1999) *The trouble with normal: Sex, politics, and the ethics of queer life*, Cambridge: Harvard University Press.

Watkins, E., (1999) Gramscian politics and capitalist common sense, *Rethinking Marxism*, 11(3): 83-90.

WHO, (2010) *International Statistical Classification of Diseases and Related Health Problems 10th Revision*, F91, http://apps.who.int/classifications/icd10/browse/2010/en.

Willis, P. E., (1977) *Learning to labour: How working class kids get working class jobs*, Hampshire: Gower.

Chapter 4

Troubling an embodied pedagogy in science education

Kathrin Otrel-Cass and Liv Kondrup Kristensen

Nordic education is often valued for its ideals of naturalness, equality, freedom, autonomy, emancipation and solidarity. Also noted is the informal and uncomplicated way that students and teachers work together (Björk Eydal and Satka, 2006; Laursen, 2013; Wagner and Einarsdottir, 2008). At the same time Nordic education has been criticised for assuming to seek sameness in classrooms (Kryger, 2004). This presents an interesting challenge and this chapter intends to present and discuss this, in the context of recent developments in the Danish primary school setting.

In 2012 Denmark introduced an ideological policy, *Ny Nordisk Skole*–the New Nordic School to challenge every child to become the best they can be and reach their potential; disrupt the causal relationship between social background and learning outcomes; strengthen and build confidence between professional knowledge and practice (*Mål, Manifest og Dogmer for Ny Nordisk Skole,* 2017). One way to achieve this aim was through a reform that asked for the deliberate integration of physical activity, movement and exercise into everyday schooling (so not within physical education). The intention was that this should not only promote learning, but also lower the impact of a declining health in the general population and in particular in children (Herskind and Rønholt, 2007).

This new school reform was introduced in 2014, and mandates forty-five minutes of physical activity and movement every day across all grades at primary school. The initiative seeks to promote a culture and pedagogy of movement. Policy makers in Denmark promote physical activity for its apparent positive effect on learning outcomes. The idea is that by infusing everyday teaching practices with more exercise and bodily movement, the improved health in children and young people will support an increase in motivation to learn across all school subjects (Bailey, 2006; Bailey et al., 2009; Coe, Pivarnik, Womack, Reeves, and Malina, 2006; Keeley and Fox, 2009; Kulturministeriets Udvalg for Idrætsforskning, 2011; Rasberry et al., 2011).

In this chapter, we are concerned that this reform is based on simplistic ideas that integrating movement and physical activity will automatically lead to better learning. However, we see that classrooms represent *sensitive learning ecologies* in which very small changes in boundary conditions or interaction patterns can alter the intended direction of learning (Horn, 2008). We are also concerned that an embodied pedagogy has ramifications for teaching. To concretise this, we are examining the case of integrating movement into science lessons. We will expand on this concern in the following section.

Including movement in science education

The focus on integrating more physicality and movement into every day schooling may be interpreted in different ways; on the one hand, it signals the realisation that (young) people learn in more complex ways, and may need a degree of freedom in experiencing school. It may even indicate a heightened degree in respecting children's individual learning needs. On the other hand, it can be seen as a new way to manage and control learning, reducing it to a formulaic procedure that is claimed to result in improved educational performance. It can also be viewed as another form of governance, expecting that children and young people will accept bodily activity as a productive and enjoyable condition for their learning. This new rhetoric of learning experiences and reformed pedagogy is continuing with the search for new ways to accomplish old desires, namely to produce flexible and autonomous learners. The search for ways to improve educational outcomes seeks, in this case, to combine and promote two educational goals: academic success and physical wellbeing. Research that looks at increased physical activity leads to on-going renewed examination of its effectiveness and refinement of theory. As a result, teachers are confronted with policy implementation that requires them to seek new ways to enhance students' engagement in learning and create a learning environment that supports such wishes. Seen this way, the teacher's role is that of a facilitator; who shapes the setting and conditions for learning (Kryger, 2004). Concurrently, the teacher can implement the policy maker's wishes on how to integrate movement into the teaching of everyday subjects at school.

We are interested in what this integration means for a subject like science. The continued concern about the overall decline in student interest and engagement in science (Bybee and Mccrae, 2011; Fensham, 2006) may provide a plausible argument for initiatives such as the integration of movement. Nevertheless, policy makers have acted even though there has been little research attention on what an embodied pedagogy entails nor how to create one. This is acutely relevant when it is operating within a subject such as science that has a very strong culture of its own (McKinley, 2005). This is of interest because student participation and achievement in science education is a matter of equity and social justice, because of the role science plays in today's society. Many of the big societal challenges intersect with science and technology, and feeling knowledgeable in science supports active decision making and participation in science related activities, ranging from the mundane (choosing toothpaste with or without fluoride) to the complex (participating in decision-making that shape the world's climate). Being successful in formal science qualifications opens doors into high level education (Osborne and Dillon, 2008) and potentially careers. Internationally competitive tests, such as PISA have identified discrepancies between achievement and engagement (e.g. OECD, 2007) and it has been reported that the (lack of) identity formation in science can marginalise individuals (Roth and Tobin, 2007).

This chapter, explores a *pedagogy of embodiment in science* and draws on ethnographic fieldwork conducted at a school in the larger Copenhagen area. We used video recordings and observational notes as well as video prompted recall interviews that were conducted with young people and their primary school teacher. The idea was to identify the consequences of integrating movement in science lessons for young people. We examined students' participation when movement was part of their science activities, and their personal investment when they made their body public.

We will start by discussing what we understand as *embodied pedagogy* and how it may be possible to examine it.

A pedagogy of embodiment in science education

Our examination of methods and practices of science teaching with and through physical activity or movement starts with looking at those studies that analyse students' experiences. A number of those report an increase in student motivation when there is more movement and physical activity. One traditional way is that teachers create *breaks* to integrate physical activity or get students to move around while doing some learning tasks (Palmer, 2009; Svendler, Wehner, and Herskind, 2015; Vazou, Gavrilou, Mamalaki, Papanastasiou, and Sioumala, 2012). When specific learning outcomes are reinforced by movement abstract concepts can become embodied. Specific movement has been reported to support learning of some students under certain conditions (Herskind, Lysemose, and

Svendler, 2015; Svendler et al., 2015) for example in maths (Bautista, Roth, and Thom, 2011; Chen, Cone, and Cone, 2011) and language (Anderson and Chung, 2011; Cole and Boykin, 2008; Yang, Chen, and Jeng, 2010). Although these studies highlight that including activities such as relay runs, small games, technology-supported activities or dancing, is beneficial for students and their learning, this is only the first step. Embodied pedagogy is about recognising that body is not only of significance to the individual, but shapes interactions between people (Jordon, 2001). If teachers want to include movement in classroom activities they should select activities that are relevant to the learning goal, allow children to co-decide on activities, plan activities where children can interact with their peers, consider activities that may have an element of competition, or include possibilities for progression of activities over time (Herskind et al., 2015; Svendler et al., 2015). This suggests that a pedagogy of embodiment in science education needs fine-tuning of what it means to consider the whole body for the learning process.

For this reason we draw on the ideas of Maurice Merleau-Ponty (1962, 1968) who unified thinking about the body and the mind in what he termed *the lived body*. The lived body is the body that embeds our existence, and is not just a body that sustains, but also a body that makes it possible to experience reality. The lived body is therefore the 'subject of everything that we do and experience' (Bengtsson, 2013: 6), and if our body is moved, hurt, or otherwise changed, then experiences with the world change. From this we deduce that utilising movement activities in the science classroom involves teachers having to think about how their students inhabit the world with and through their bodies.

Building on Maurice Merleau-Ponty's ideas, our intention is to question what the currently popular educational trend of movement integration affords to students' experiences at school. Our specific interest is in science classrooms and what this means for an embodied pedagogy in science education. Examining what it means to include physical activity in science education is interesting because this subject has had a history of focusing on cognitive processes. The inclusion of movement into science education could support the conditions for science learning. However, science learning is also a construction of individuals, based on their prior understanding and socio-cultural conditions (Vygotsky, 1978). This implies that investigating a movement-enhanced pedagogy in science education is a complex endeavour. Not to foreground the body is according to Maurice Merleau-Ponty problematic because the lived body is more than just a shell, we are the body (Thøgersen, 2004). Merleau-Ponty describes embodiment by taking note of bodily intentionality and the challenges that this highlights. While he does not reject the presence of mental experiences, he emphasises that thinking and sensing are intertwined. Bringing Merleau-Ponty into the discussion concerned with learning means to consider the body as a constitutive part of experiencing the world through the body while being aware of one's own perceptions through one's mind.

To illustrate how we use Merleau-Ponty's ideas we are examining examples from classroom observations. The next section presents the data collection and choice of analysis.

Data collection and analysis

Data were collected by way of classroom observation using video, digital photographs, field notes, the collection of student and teacher work samples, and interviews with the teacher and students regarding their experiences. The analysis for the chapter proceeded through a process of inductive analysis (Patton, 2002) in which the researchers reviewed the data for themes and patterns.

Bearing in mind that we worked with a considerable amount of visual data we want to outline briefly here how we protected our participants' privacy. The data collection involved asking students, their parents, the teacher and the school leadership for informed consent, outlining the aims and details of the study, the nature of the intended data collection and use of data collected for research purposes, as well as the right for participants not to give consent or withdraw consent given at any stage of the investigation. To protect our participants we did not use any material without our participants' permission (Cerezo, Martinez, and Ranera, 1996). Where students had not given consent to be involved in the study, they were not filmed or if they appeared in the video their images were blurred and not considered during the analysis process. Visual data was used during prompted video recall interviews (Morgan, 2007) and students were asked again if they objected to the data selected to being discussed and shared. We gained informed consent from our participants but regarded it as provisional (Flewitt, 2005), reflecting our understanding that the researcher-participant relationship is one that needs to build on trust and requires degrees of flexibility to accommodate the needs of the participants (Cowie, Otrel-Cass, and Moreland, 2010). Therefore, when episodes of interest had been identified, one of the researchers returned to the students to show them the episodes to reflect on and ask again if we receive their permission to analyse and share those scenes. All selections detailed in this chapter received such permission. Despite signed consent forms we wondered how *informed* participants really are when they consent to representations and how others may interpret those (Pink, 2007). Since the nature of some of the actions that we captured visually may make our participants uncomfortable in the future, we decided to anonymise the data presented here despite signed consent forms.

During the observations one researcher followed a group of students with a video camera. We supplemented the resulting video-recorded episodes with field notes and student interviews. Interviewing involved casual conversation during the observations, structured group interviews post observations, as well as individual video prompted interviews (Morgan, 2007). We used prompted video recall interviews with the students that were video-recorded to capture not only verbal but also embodied responses when the students were watching their own embodied performances. The selected video-episodes were fully transcribed, noting both verbal and non-verbal communication (such as facial expressions, gestures, pitch, emotive interjections and stance) to expand on the analysis of the selected themes from the video. To gain insights into how activities were conceptualised, planned and evaluated, we conducted pre- and post-interviews with the teacher before and after each class. Video footage became a central information source in the meaning-making process at the micro-level.

Classroom data were collected in a school in the larger Copenhagen area that had just recently adopted policies to infuse all teaching with movement and physical activity, including science teaching. In this study, we were interested in the transformation of movement policies into science teaching activities. While we could have looked at any curriculum area or subject field we focused on science because we anticipated that the traditional notion of the *Cartesian split*, that implies that learning in science happens only in the mind (Alsop and Watts, 2003), may produce tensions for both teacher and students alike when pedagogical approaches deliberately integrate physical activities.

Observations were conducted in a Year 8 (fourteen to sixteen year-olds) physics class, during double lessons conducted over a four-week period. The observations were conducted in late spring, when students of this class had easy access to the adjacent school-yard. This meant that students would move outside to go for a walk or jump rope either as part of learning activities or just for fun. The episodes presented here concern students given tasks situated both inside and outside the physics classroom. The theme of the first three double lessons was *light and sound*, and the theme for the last and fourth double lesson was *ions*. During the light and sound unit the teacher asked the students to work in groups. The activities involved testing the properties and qualities of light and sound in various ways. Some of these activities involved lab work inside the classroom, such as the refraction of light through different liquids, while other activities such as experimenting with sound waves, took place outside the classroom, in the adjacent hallway.

We start with an activity that took place outside the classroom, namely in the hallway, where the task was to explore sound waves and the Doppler Effect. The Doppler Effect is the change in frequency of a wave for an observer who is moving relative to its source, such as may be experienced when a siren approaches, passes and recedes from an observer. What the observer should experience is a higher pitch during the approach, true at the moment that it passes by, and lower when it recedes (for more information see e.g. www.grc.nasa.gov/www/k-12/airplane/doppler.html). We were interested in this particular activity for a number of reasons. First, we wanted to examine teaching activities in science that used a body pedagogy to answer our question concerning what the infusion of exercise and bodily movement into everyday teaching practices could look like in a Danish primary school. Second, we were also interested in identifying episodes that were rich in explicit or embodied actions to find answers to our question what kind of embodiment would result from a body pedagogy in science.

The presentation of our findings is organised in the following way: We present our findings in the context of body consciousness in a science activity; next, we offer an account of students' experiences; we build an argument based on the data that refers back to students' conversation, body posture, and facial expressions; the final section of the chapter will draw these elements together, reflecting upon insights gained from the video-recorded ethnographic work and how we connect this with theories on embodiment and movement.

Body-consciousness in the hallway

Objectification theorists such as Fredrickson and Roberts (1997) posit that people, and in particular in their research girls, internalise an objectified observer's perspective of their own bodies. We suggest that the combination of media and actual or anticipated everyday social encounters shape how a person perceives their own physical appearance and performance. This argument builds also on work by Iris Marion Young *Throwing like a girl* (1980). To consider the role of the body and how it is perceived in the performance of science activity is shedding new light on these ideas. Performance in science and the research thereof, has often focused on cognitive work or the outcomes or processes connected to it. Here we want to examine the affordances of embodied learning and consider the mind and the body. Maurice Merleau-Ponty writes that our perceptions in and of the world are intertwined with how we experience the world through our bodies. These experiences are not fleeting but are retained as a kind of embodied memory of the things our bodies can or cannot do. Using the term body-consciousness helps to shed light on how we examine the body in performing certain tasks. Richard Shusterman (2008) explains that there are different levels of body consciousness and to examine body consciousness it is necessary to examine the living, feeling body rather than just the physical body.

Taking a point of departure in the living, feeling body also means considering students' embodied (inter)actions as acts of sense making. In doing so, it is important to remember that we experience others as subjects and have access to their life. Although, this access is never complete as we all have a different history of experience, which gives direction and meaning to our actions in the present moment. Bengtsson (2013a) notes that 'intersubjectivity lives in the tension between the otherness and sameness of individual human beings' (p. 50). Building on this understanding, social interaction is based on past (embodied) experiences, or information, that enables us to act in the present. This information concerns the context, situation and the individuals present in our immediate environment. Such information helps to define the situation, and according to Goffman, enables 'others to know in advance what he will expect of them and what they may expect of him' (1959: 13). This perspective proposes that observed actions are not always what they may appear at first and that individuals have the ability to manipulate their embodied expressivity in order to promote and maintain certain impressions of themselves (Crossley, 1995a).

During the observed learning episodes, we realised that body foregrounding activities made the students conscious of their bodies and how others may perceive their performances as a consequence. We observed one of these episodes where students were asked to conduct sound experiments to explore the Doppler Effect. The experiment took place in a hallway that was approximately 50 meters long and about 2.5 meters wide. The hallway had lines on the floor, marking every 5 meters. Hallways can be busy places in schools and this was the case here. Several classrooms opened into the hallway while the doors to the adjacent school-yard were open, making the hallway available to younger students who were having a break at the time the group was doing their investigation.

For their task, the students were asked that one student should run from one end to another with a mobile phone using a high pitch sound on full volume.

The remainder of the group had to position themselves halfway, listen to, record and evaluate how the sound changed when the runner was approaching, passing by, and running away from them. The recordings were done by making videos when the runner was passing by with a cell phone in the hand making a noise. The task for the students was that each one had to take a turn running, so each one had an opportunity to experience the sound with their whole body being either stationary as an observer or moving as a runner.

The group that was observed doing this experiment consisted of three boys Hai, Adi and Alfons, two girls Mira and Anna (pseudonyms used throughout). Although instructed that all should take turns to run, only two of the boys ran, Hai and Adi. These two are good friends. Hai enjoys physics, and explained during interviews that he regards himself as an able student. He likes physical education and doing sports, but does not participate in competitive sports. Hai is friends with Adi, their two families have lived next to each other for four years. Adi transferred to the school at the end of Year 5. He moved to Copenhagen from a marginalised residential area on the mainland. Adi described not caring too much about school during an interview. He told us that he is friends with everyone, and a keen sportsman. He does regular fitness, and plays competitive soccer four times a week.

Alfons and Mira both announced at the start of this activity that they did not want to run and sat down on the ground of the hallway with their backs firmly pressed against the wall. Anna did the same when she joined the group later on.

Hai: All right I'll run. (Puts down paper and starts walking down the hallway)

Adi: I'll run now. (Still looking down at his phone). I'll run Hai.

Alfons: No Hai'll run. Hai runs twice and you run twice.

Hai: (Walks down to the middle of the hallway) Is it from here? Is it just from here?

Alfons: No. It is from there–(Points to the end of the hallway)

Hai: It doesn't have to be from far away

Alfons: Yeah. We have to measure all the way from (Points from one end of the hallway to the other)

Hai: We'll just say from here. (Standing two-thirds down the hallway)

Adi: No Hai. All the way!

Alfons: He is lazy? (Looks up at Adi and smiles)

Adi: If you are lazy then let me run, you lazy dog

Shiota, Campos and Keltner (2003) refer to this as a drop-jaw Duchenne smile (this description refers back to Darwin's Expression of Emotion in Man and Animals). They explain that this physiological expression indicates amusement. In comparison, when Adi ran passed the students were also smiling. Alfons was observed with a jaw dropping laugh while the others showed a more contained smile, which is described as a display more typical for an expression of pride where the smiling lips move closer together (Shiota et al., 2003).

What we want to identify through this microanalysis of discreet positive emotions is that we detected slightly different bodily responses to the performances of the two runners.

Adi appeared as the 'performer' and comfortable about this role. We noticed him 'performing bodily' both for the video recording of the researcher but also to entertain his classmates (see images 7 and 8).

Image 7: Adi performing for the researcher's camera

Alfons and Mira were discussing things. Hai was observing Adi, while Adi turned his body towards the camera of the researcher and danced.

Image 8: Adi performing for the group

Later, Adi 'performed' for the group and received full attention from Mira and Alfons.[1]

1 It is speculative how much the presence of the researcher may have influenced how comfortable the young people were about being watched and recorded but when asked they explained that part of the task had been to record each other.

Using the ideas of Merleau-Ponty we interpret that bodily performance and embodied activities were evaluated from two perspectives. First, an inside perspective–how one feels and experiences their body. Merleau-Ponty (1962) explains that we use our conscious, explicit perception or sensing of the body when we are in contact with the world. Second, there is also an outside perception of the body. Shusterman (2008) writes that Merleau Ponty's stance of the awareness of feelings, movements or orientations includes also the assessment we make of our body when we are evaluating its performance as an observer.

Goffman (1959) describes that evaluating one's own performance as an observer is *impression management*. This concept draws our attention to howthe Doppler Effect experiment not only foregrounded the student's body consciousness, but also turned the hallway into a stage where the students were both actors and audience. As actors on a stage they expressed themselves including intentional poses, facial expressions, things they say, expressions they have less control over, and what can be identified as inconsistencies between speech and body language. This establishes social identity (Goffman, 1959). In our example, Adi was performing on the stage (the hallway), while Anna, Mira and Alfons were the audience who was observing Adi. The hallway defined the setting, where physical settings such as the length of and lines along the hallway were props for the actions that played out upon it. Adi's appearance was characterised by his strong physique, clothing that reveals his arms, in particular his biceps and a bodily restlessness. His manner supports the impressions given off by his appearance: eagerness and aggressiveness, which came across in the language he used and actions employed. Consciously or unconsciously, Adi managed his social identity by means of these signals. This way of managing identity is not a one-way communication. The hallway as a front was a *collective representation* (ibid.: 27) in that it established the setting, appearance and manner for the role assumed by Adi, and united Adi's personal front with interactive behaviour. Adi's role had, in other words, already been established for him, and it is this information that Alfons, Mira, Anna and Hai *read* in his performance.

To Adi there was a purpose of knowing about his embodied performance, both by experiencing himself but also by getting feedback from the others. He perceived his performance from the position of the observers as positive. He had the reassurance of being an acknowledged bodily performer because he is acknowledged as a talented soccer player. In his performance during the video-recorded episode, it becomes obvious that he likes to demonstrate his ability to himself and others. He explained also that he likes to push himself physically, and continuously seeks to improve e.g. his speed. Therefore, he used the task of running as part of the science experiment as a running opportunity on the *track* in the hallway. During the interview Adi explained that he had recently suffered a knee injury, which he was just recuperating from at the time of the observation. Being able to run was also an inside demonstration to test the body's weakness from the surgery. His outside perception of the body was made apparent when he explained to the interviewer that he takes pride in his body and demonstrated on a number of occasions during this observation when he posed in front of the camera or in front of other students. In doing so, he gave the impression of confidence, skill, and leadership that presented a favourable public image to which the others responded positively. Furthermore, Adi's history of competitive sports (the ability to run fast, and being tested and measured) in combination with his fit body provided him with physical capital (Shilling, 2004). The term physical capital stems from the works of French philosopher Pierre Bourdieu, who argued that individuals acquire certain bodily appearances, competencies and performances that gives them value within a social field and is most likely to reproduce their existing social status (Bourdieu, 1990; Shilling, 2005). In our case, we see that Adi placed value on having a competitive and *healthy* body, and was able to employ this form of capital in a legitimised way in the activity, as the rest of the group accepted and supported Adi's embodied actions by means of acknowledging Adi through i.e. eye-contact and smiles. In doing so the group and Adi co-shaped the boundaries of what is proper performance, and defined the boundaries for participation and contribution in the Doppler Effect activity to go beyond the problem solving process.

The task required the students to be conscious of their sensations and bodily perceptions. They were asked to listen to the sound of a runner passing by with a sound-producing device. They had to use their senses sight, hearing when watching a runner. Running was in this activity a necessary part to enable students as observers to experience sound waves moving relative to its source. However, the bodily performance of running was an activity that made the students conscious about their own body capital (Goffman, 1959) and the body performances of others. This pedagogy of embodiment resulted in that some students responded by taking the lead such as Adi, while Mira and Anna, responded by seemingly excluding themselves from taking part in some aspects of the activities because they perceived their body's performance would compromise how they perceive themselves as observers. When asked by the interviewer why this was the case Mira responded, 'It was because we had to record ourselves, and it's like ... I don't want to run and be recorded and for it to be shown ...' and when asked if she ran differently from the others since she did not want to have her performance video recorded, she said 'I don't know. I just don't think ... It is kind of uncomfortable'. While running may be characterised as a basic movement and one that all five students were capable of performing, they did not all decide to do so. For Merleau-Ponty (1968: 226) 'one imagines a being in itself, where it appears transposed according to a given ratio of sizes, so that the representations on different scales are different *visual pictures* of the same in itself.' He regards that these visual pictures shape the intentions or attitudes towards the world and this means that people experience and evaluate their transposed visual pictures. This evaluation leads to in making, or excluding decisions, on whether the exposure of the body may be threatening, uncomfortable or empowering. The students were body-conscious through what Merleau-Ponty regards as a mental representation at different scales of our body and what Shusterman (2008) explains is an explicit awareness and focused consciousness. This is what was observed when the students were asked to move their bodies in manners that made them take inside and outside notice of their bodies.

Connecting embodied experiences with learning science ideas and concepts

Learning in science can be separated from the outside world to be 'taught in special rooms at a particular time of the day' (Roth and Tobin, 2007: 157). Yet the intention was to utilise the physical space to learn with and through the body resulting in an assemblage of different experiences that formed the students' understanding (Stenner, 2008). These assemblages resulted in unique experiences for the individual and framed by the teacher, classroom, peers, school, family, interests but also educational policies. In our case in the hallway, the activity and the presence of recording devices positioned and situated the students, their relations to the rest of the group and other students passing by, and shaped their willingness and confidence as runners and public performers. In the examples provided above, we see that there is more at stake than learning and accomplishing a task. This created a conspicuous tension, between experiencing abstract concepts and communicating their embodied experience.

Interviewer: If I asked you to explain something about Doppler?
Hai: Ah, that Doppler thing... What was it that we used it for?
Interviewer: If you have to say anything at all about it. What could it be?

(Students are looking away from the interviewer then at each other and thinking. They whisper with each other then turn back to interviewer.)

Anna: The experiment with the sound.

Adi: Ah, the one with (makes a sound) shuuuuuuuuuuuu

Hai: Yeah!

Adi: Aaaaaah!

Alfons: The one … (He whistles softly)

Hai: The one with the sounds. Is that the Doppler Effect?

Adi: If it comes close like this (makes a sound of something approaching) schuuuuuw

Hai: The one about the tones getting higher or lighter. High notes and light notes.

Adi: Dark and light.

Hai: Plus and minus.

Alfons: Dark and light notes.

Hai: Yes, dark and light.

Alfons: Deep voice, light voice

Hai: (Changes pitch of his voice when uttering the first word). Light voice.

Interviewer: So was that what it was all about? Dark and light notes?

Hai: Yes, light and dark notes.

Interviewer: And how did you remember this?

Hai: I just remember it.

Interviewer: Okay.

Hai: Every time it (sound) came towards us it got … I cannot remember if it got higher or darker or lighter. But it was something along those lines, yes.

When the students were asked to explain what they know about the Doppler Effect, they seemed careful and aware of what may be expected from them. They referred in their explanations to their body memory of the experiment by relating to their experiences. They used an embodied language when Adi and Alfons made different sounds or when they distinguish between *light* and *dark* sounds, by changing the pitch of his voice when uttering the word *light*. The explanations were scientifically vague in that the students did not use the correct scientific terminology to describe the experiment, yet the effect seemed to be remembered in a bodily way, having to do with sound coming towards

Hai and his body. This is also, what Merleau-Ponty describes as body memory or a third dimension between imagined body movement and the execution of body movement. Yet in science it is also about the ability to put body memory into words and the students identified this as an important part that validates the acquisition of science knowledge in the next excerpt from the interview.

Interviewer:	When would you say that you have learnt something in physics? If you have physics and come home one day and say, 'oh, I have learnt something today'. When do you know that you have learnt something?
Hai:	When we have learnt something.
Alfons:	When we can remember it.
Interviewer:	How do you know this?
Hai:	When you can remember what you have learnt, or you have been taught in …
Mira:	When you can explain it.
Interviewer:	When you can put words on it?
Mira:	Yes!
Anna:	Well, when you can understand it.

Talking about their learning (in physics) meant for the young people that you need to able to explain and articulate ideas. This is not surprising, however, when a pedagogical approach is used that draws specifically on embodied experiences, the students still understood that valid evidence of their learning needed to be transformed, perhaps abstracted into language. Merleau-Ponty writes that the difficulty lies in, that 'one does not know how to speak' (1968: 252), and points to the difficulty to trust and transform embodied experiences into mental-verbal expressions that are recognised and validated by others. The science classroom environment for instance validates certain ways of expressing sensations. Finding representational explanations in science requires that learners sometimes have to re-interpret embodied experiences into explanations that are perceived to be acceptable in science. Merleau-Ponty writes that each of our senses describes a different world but that it is through the bringing together of these different *worlds* that we perceive and *be* in this world. Seeing, hearing and talking about sound, running with the sound source are those different worlds but not necessarily problematic as Merleau-Ponty explains: 'meaning is invisible, but the invisible is not the contradictory of the visible' (1968: 215). An embodied pedagogy in science education needs to find ways how to accommodate for body memory and validate the sensorial experiences, so that an expression like *schuuuuuw* (from the interview transcript above) has a legitimate place.

Conclusion

Merleau-Ponty explains that it is not possible to observe both the inner and the outer experiences but that we can revert between being the observed to being the observer. The young people were explaining that evidence of learning is indicated if the reflective mind can transform the lived experiences into words. Mira responded in the interview that you have to be able to explain things.

Taking an embodied pedagogy in science beyond the inclusion of disconnected physical activities means that young people will need to be regarded as lived beings that are moved through the embodied experiences they have. Building on the French philosopher Merleau-Ponty who details that 'hands do not suffice for touch–but to decide for this reason alone that our hands do not touch, and to relegate them to the world of objects, or of instruments, would be ... the bifurcation of subject and object...' (1968: 137) we think that a pedagogy of embodiment in science will need to consider the deliberate inclusion of how to experience the natural world through the whole body because our experience of the world happens through meaningful configurations of sensations that belong to the body (Crossley, 1995b). A pedagogy of embodiment validates the embodied experiences we all have. Yet these sensations have different meanings and consequences for each student, as history, culture and prior experiences rest in their bodies to form the basis for how they make sense of their sensations to also evaluate as an observer their own performance. Young people's experiences of embodied activities such as running resonate differently for the individuals who are body conscious about their performances. This means that the decision to perform in this case required that the young people had to evaluate how they wanted to be perceived and experienced by others. The example we shared is unique but also representative for the diversity of individuals that can be found in everyday classrooms in Denmark. With this we mean the diversity of young people's backgrounds and experiences including also how they perceive themselves. A pedagogy that assumes that embodiment is simply a task to be performed neglects that we observe our own bodies differently to how we observe external objects in this world. Adopting an embodied pedagogy in science will require considering *body-consciousness* and that the students' bodies are considered as the condition for learning. The troubling aspect is that a body sensitive pedagogy in science requires a subjective attitude to how learning is perceived and this is in contrast to the abstract representational thinking advocated for in science. As shown in our examples this is not so easy to achieve, also because the understanding of reality and how we perceive it has empirical implications when we want to investigate how students' perceptions and sense-making processes are shaped by this movement culture.

This (Danish) focus on embodiment in science requires a fine-grained conceptualising of the conditions for young people's learning activities. Embodiment also requires respecting that performativity will be perceived differently by individuals. If this is a new strategy to control learning and governance, it can be expected that the outcome will not necessarily have the desired result. Being interested in the perspectives by Maurice Merleau-Ponty, who sees people as embodied perceivers of the world, we find that the implications of the deliberate inclusion of more movement in science education is not without consequences such as being or feeling exposed by the nature of an activity. Our example showed that individuals can desire such experiences or not.

We conclude that a pedagogy that focuses on body-based performances in science to make use of experiences in a contextual frame shift and direct the attention for those who are involved from how science activities are usually completed. Considering that movement in science teaching is something that can be simply added ignores the fact that science inquiry and the production of knowledge and insight in science is traditionally based on rationality and objectivity. For example, the American Association for the Advancement of Science (AAAS) Atlas of scientific literacy states that 'scientific investigations usually involve the collection of relevant evidence, the use of logical reasoning, and the application of imagination in devising hypotheses and explanations to make sense of collected evidence' (2001: 14). If scientific observations are made with, through and about embodied activities it will be necessary to consider the implications of working with body capital to address whether an individual's projected self is exposed and perhaps endangered when being there (Goffman, 2008). On the other hand, if movement and embodiment is to be included in science we may need to find ways for accommodating body memory (Merleau-Ponty, 1968) to expand pedagogies in science to include utterances, gestures, movement, body and voice as legitimate ways of learning and sharing of knowledge in science.

Acknowledgement

The video analysis was conducted at the video research lab (VILA: www.vila.aau.dk) at Aalborg University, a DIGHUMLAB initiative. The authors are part of the JustEd–Justice through Education network.

References

Alsop, S., and Watts, M., (2003) Science education and affect. *International Journal of Science Education*, *25*(9): 1043-1047. https://doi.org/10.1080/0950069032000052180

American Association for the Advancement of Science. (2001). *Atlas of Science Literacy* (Volume 1). Washington, DC: Author.

Anderson, J., and Chung, Y.-C., (2011) Finding a voice: arts-based creativity in the community languages classroom, *International Journal of Bilingual Education and Bilingualism*, 14(5): 551-569. https://doi.org/10.1080/13670050.2010.537742

Bailey, R., (2006) Physical Education and Sport in Schools: A Review of Benefits and Outcomes, *Journal of School Health*, 76(8): 397-401. https://doi.org/10.1111/j.1746-1561.2006.00132.x

Bailey, R., Armour, K., Kirk, D., Jess, M., Pickup, I., Sandford, R., and Bera Physical Education And Sport Pedagogy Special Interest Group, R., (2009) The educational benefits claimed for physical education and school sport: an academic review, *Research Papers in Education*, 24(1): 1-27. https://doi.org/10.1080/02671520701809817

Bautista, A., Roth, W.-M., and Thom, J. S., (2011) Knowing, Insight Learning, and the Integrity of Kinetic Movement, *Interchange: A Quarterly Review of Education*, 42(4): 363-388. https://doi.org/10.1007/s10780-012-9164-9

Bengtsson, J., (2013a) Embodied Experience in Educational Practice and Research. *Studies in Philosophy and Education*, 32: 39-53. https://doi.org/10.1007/s11217-012-9328-1

Bengtsson, J., (2013b) With the Lifeworld as Ground. A Research Approach for Empirical Research in Education: The Gothenburg Tradition, *Indo-Pacific Journal of Phenomenology*, 13: 1-18. https://doi.org/10.2989/IPJP.2013.13.2.4.1178

Björk Eydal, G., and Satka, M., (2006) Social work and Nordic welfare policies for children—present challenges in the light of the past, *European Journal of Social Work*, 9(3): 305-322. https://doi.org/10.1080/13691450600828358

Bourdieu, P., (1990) *The logic of practice*, Cambridge: Polity.

Bybee, R., and Mccrae, B., (2011) Scientific Literacy and Student Attitudes: Perspectives from PISA 2006 science, *International Journal of Science Education*, 33(1): 7-26. https://doi.org/10.1080/09500693.2010.518644

Cerezo, M., Martinez, A., and Ranera, P., (1996) Tres antropólogos inocentes y an ojo si parpado. In M. Garcia Alonso, A. Martinez, P. Pitarch, P. Ranera, and J. Fores (Eds.), *Antropologia de los Sentidos: La Vista*, Madrid: Celeste Ediciones.

Chen, W., Cone, T. P., and Cone, S. L., (2011) Students' voices and learning experiences in an integrated unit, *Physical Education and Sport Pedagogy*, 16(1): 49-65. https://doi.org/10.1080/17408989.2010.491818

Coe, D. P., Pivarnik, J. M., Womack, C. J., Reeves, M. J., and Malina, R. M., (2006) Effect of physical education and activity levels on academic achievements in children, *Medicine and Science in Sports and Exercise*, 38(8): 1515-1519.

Cole, J. M., and Boykin, A. W., (2008) Examining Culturally Structured Learning Environments with Different Types of Music-Linked Movement Opportunity, *Journal of Black Psychology*, 34(3), 331-355. https://doi.org/10.1177/0095798408314137

Cowie, B., Otrel-Cass, K., and Moreland, J., (2010) Multimodal ways of eliciting students' voice, *Waikato Journal of Education*, 15(2): 81-94.

Crossley, N., (1995a) Body Techniques, Agency and Intercorporeality: On Goffman's Relations In Public. *Sociology*, 29(1): 133-149.

Crossley, N., (1995b) Merleau-Ponty, the Elusive Body and Carnal Sociology. *Body and Society*, 1(1): 43-63. https://doi.org/0803973233

Fensham, P. J., (2006) Humanistic science education: Moves from within and challenges from without. In *Paper presented to the Annual Conference of the Australasian Science Education Research Association (ASERA)*. Canberra.

Flewitt, R., (2005) Conducting Research with Young Children: Some Ethical Considerations, *Early Child Development and Care*, 175(6): 553-565.

Fredrickson, B. L., and Roberts, T. A., (1997) Objectification Theory, *Psychology of Women Quarterly*, 21(2), 173-206. https://doi.org/10.1111/j.1471-6402.1997.tb00108.x

Goffman, E., (1959) *The presentation of self in everyday life*, London: Penguin Books.

Goffman, E., (2008) *Interaction Ritual: Essays in face-to-face behavio*, New Brunswick, New Jersey: Transaction Publishers.

Herskind, M., Lysemose, C., and Svendler, C., (2015) Kvalitativ undersøgelse af skole i LCoMotion-projektet. In A. Bugge, J. von Seelen, M. Herskind, C. Svendler, A. K. Thorsen, J. Dam, K. Froberg (Eds.), *Rapport for "Forsøg med læring i bevægelse" 2* Odense: Institut for Idræt og Biomekanik, Syddansk Universitet, 99-111.

Herskind, M., and Rønholt, H., (2007) Idræt, krop og bevægelse mellem sundhed og dannelse, *Utbildning and Demokrati*, 16(2): 57-74.

Horn, J., (2008) Human Research and Complexity Theory. In M. Mason (Ed.), *Complexity theory and the philosophy of education*, Chichester: Wiley-Blackwell, 124-136.

Jordon, S., (2001) Embodied Pedagogy: The Body and Teaching Theology. *Teaching Theology and Religion*, 4(2): 98-101. https://doi.org/10.1111/1467-9647.00100

Keeley, T. H., and Fox, K., (2009) The impact of physical activity and fitness on academic achievement and cognitive performance in children, *International Review of Sport and Exercise Psychology*, 2(2): 198-214. https://doi.org/10.1080/17509840903233822

Kryger, N., (2004) Childhood and "New Learning" in a Nordic Context. In H. Brembeck, B. Johansson, and J. Kampmann (Eds.), *Beyond the competent child : exploring contemporary childhoods in the nordic welfare societies*, Frederiksberg: Roskilde University Press, 153-176.

Kulturministeriets Udvalg for Idrætsforskning. (2011) *Fysisk aktivitet og læring – en konsensuskonference*. København. Retrieved from http://idrætifolkeskolen.dk/uf/30000_39999/38790/3791ca2d0671e588e16ae1a29ea216cc.pdf

Laursen, P., (2013) Hvad er Ny Nordisk Skole. In T. Balle, H. Haue, and M. Schelde (Eds.), *Nordisk pædagogisk tradition?: mellem Grundtvig og Ny Nordisk Skole*, Odense: Institut for Kulturvidenskaber Syddansk Universitet, 115-123.

McKinley, E., (2005) Locating the Global: Culture, Language and Science Education for Indigenous Students, *International Journal of Science Education*, 27(2): 227-241.

Merleau-Ponty, M., (1962) *Phenomenology of Perception*, London: Routledge.

Merleau-Ponty, M., (1968) *The visible and the invisible: followed by working notes*, Evanston: Northwestern University Press.

Morgan, A., (2007) Using video-stimulated recall to understand young children's perceptions of learning in classroom settings. *European Early Childhood Education Research Journal*, 15(2): 213-226. https://doi.org/10.1080/13502930701320933

Mål, Manifest og Dogmer for Ny Nordisk Skole, (2017). Retrieved June 1, 2017, from http://www.emu.dk/modul/mål-manifest-og-dogmer-ny-nordisk-skole

OECD., (2007) *PISA 2006 science competencies for tomorrow's world.* Paris: OECD.

Osborne, J., and Dillon, J., (2008) Science Education in Europe: Critical Reflections. London: The Nuffield Foundation. Retrieved from http://efepereth.wdfiles.com/local--files/science-education/Sci_Ed_in_Europe_Report_Final.pdf

Palmer, D. H., (2009) Student Interest Generated During an Inquiry Skills Lesson. *Journal of Research in Science Teaching*, 46(2): 147-165. https://doi.org/10.1002/tea.20263

Patton, M. Q., (2002) *Qualitative research and evaluation methods* (3rd ed.), Thousand Oaks, Calif.: Sage.

Pink, S., (2007) Walking with video, *Visual Studies*, 22(3): 240-252. https://doi.org/10.1080/14725860701657142

Rasberry, C. N., Lee, S. M., Robin, L., Laris, B. A., Russell, L. A., Coyle, K. K., and Nihiser, A. J., (2011) The association between school-based physical activity, including physical education, and academic performance: A systematic review of the literature, *Preventive Medicine*, 52: 10-20.

Roth, M. W., and Tobin, K., (2007) *Science, learning, identity: Sociocultural and cultural-historical perspectives*, Sense Publishers.

Shilling, C., (2004) Physical Capital and Situated Action: A New Direction for Corporeal Sociology, *British Journal of Sociology of Education*, 25(4): 473-487.

Shilling, C., (2005) *The Body in Culture, Technology and Society*. London: Sage Publications Ltd.

Shiota, M. N., Campos, B., and Keltner, D., (2003) The Faces of Positive Emotion, *Annals of the New York Academy of Sciences*, 1000(1): 296-299. https://doi.org/10.1196/annals.1280.029

Shusterman, R., (2008) *Body Consciousness : A Philosophy of Mindfulness and Somaesthetics*, New York, N.Y: Cambridge University Press.

Stenner, P., (2008) A.N. Whitehead and Subjectivity, *Subjectivity*, 22(1): 90-109. https://doi.org/10.1057/sub.2008.4

Svendler, C., Wehner, S. K., and Herskind, M., (2015) Kvalitativ undersøgelse af Dansematematik-projektet: læring i bevægelse med fokus på kreativitet. In A. Bugge, J. von Seelen, M. Herskind, C. Svendler, A. K. Thorsen, J. Dam, K. Froberg (Eds.), *Rapport for "Forsøg med læring i bevægelse"*, Odense: Institut for Idræt og Biomekanik, Syddansk Universitet, 112-126).

Thøgersen, U., (2004) *Krop og fænomenologi : en introduktion til Maurice Merleau-Pontys filosofi*, Aarhus: Systime.

Vazou, S., Gavrilou, P., Mamalaki, E., Papanastasiou, A., and Sioumala, N., (2012) Does integrating physical activity in the elementary school classroom influence academic motivation? *International Journal of Sport and Exercise Psychology*, 10(4): 251-263. https://doi.org/10.1080/1612197X.2012.682368

Vygotsky, L. S., (1978) *Mind in society: the development of higher psychological processes*, Cambridge, Mass.: Harvard University Press.

Wagner, J. T., and Einarsdottir, J., (2008) The good childhood: Nordic ideals and educational practice, *International Journal of Educational Research*. https://doi.org/10.1016/j.ijer.2008.12.005

Yang, J. C., Chen, C. H., and Jeng, M. C., (2010) Integrating Video-Capture Virtual Reality Technology into a Physically Interactive Learning Environment for English Learning. *Computers and Education*, 55(3): 1346-1356. https://doi.org/10.1016/j.compedu.2010.06.005

Young, I. M., (1980) Throwing like a girl: A phenomenology of feminine body comportment motility and spatiality, *Human Studies*, 3(1): 137-156. https://doi.org/10.1007/BF02331805

Chapter 5

Disconcerting processes of marginalisation and boys' opportunities for performing identity work in a Swedish special education need unit

Yvonne Karlsson

The Swedish National Education Act aims to achieve a longstanding historical goal of *a school for all*. This objective aims to educational inclusion for all children within regular education irrespective of social background, geographical location, disability, or other difficulties in school. Despite this strong political commitment to equal educational opportunities, there have always been groups of children who do not have the same access to education as the rest of society. Differentiation and segregation of children into varying categories and groups remain evidently central in the public school system. This chapter supports the notion that schools may play a significant role in defining children who are regarded as having school problems (e.g. Conrad, 2006; Hester, 1998) and who thus cannot be accommodated by Sweden's regular primary education system. It also elucidates how the education of these pupils is organised. The processes by which the pupils are defined present disconcerting and inferential problems for the children to whom the definitions are directly applied.

In this chapter I aim to explore the strategies and opportunities of pupils in a special needs education unit (SENU) in Sweden for negotiating their school's negative and disconcerting definitions of them. I analyse the boys' strategies for communicative agency when performing category work as they participated in and responded to the social processes used by their school to define them and organise their activities. I focus on how these strategies could be observed and described in a talk-in-interaction context during two remedial special education activities: pedagogic circle time and regulative talk. Two specified research questions are asked: (i) how the boys participated in pedagogic circle times and regulative talk; and (ii) how the boys responded to their teachers' initiatives during these pedagogical activities.

These two remedial activities offer a particularly interesting perspective on how boys in the SENU perform category work by rejecting or negotiating the teachers' descriptions and categorisations. Teachers' descriptions and categorisations were focused on the boys' deficiencies with the intention of remedying their emotions and behaviour.

The data in this chapter derives from an ethnographic study conducted in a Swedish SENU attended by a group of five boys, aged between seven and twelve years-old. All of them were regarded as having school difficulties and needing full-time special support. Swedish schools use the following criteria to identify children with school difficulties: children who have *social and emotional deficiencies*, who *act out behavioural difficulties*, who have *conduct disorder*, and who have ADHD or Aspergers syndrome. The boys in this study were described as having *difficulty concentrating, finding it difficult to remain attentive*, and having *anxiety* or *depression*. These definitions and the ways in which they are used to organise students within schools present a troubling marginalisation process with which students must cope, since it occurs daily at the SENU.

The Swedish education system and special needs units–a school for all children?

The Swedish state school system comprises compulsory school and upper secondary school. Compulsory school includes nine years of compulsory basic school, school for the Saami people of Northern Sweden, special school, and compulsory school for intellectual disabilities. The Swedish National Education Act stresses the schools' responsibility to give all children the guidance and encouragement they need during their learning and personal development, based on individual circumstances. According to The Act, the schools mission is to compensate for students' different social backgrounds and to promote learning by stimulating the individual while developing knowledge and democratic values (e.g. SFS, 1985:1100; SFS, 2010: 800). Moreover, legislators (e.g. Unesco, 1994) focused on children's rights in terms of the inclusion of all students in ordinary classrooms, and aimed to reduce segregated education.

The latest Education Act (SFS, 2010: 800) incorporated key principles from the United Nations Convention on the Rights of the Child (UN, 1989), specifically, that children have the right to be involved and heard in matters affecting them. The Act establishes that education must consider the child's perspective, give them voice, listen to them, and take them seriously. It also reinforces ideas of inclusion of all children, irrespective of disability or difficulties in school (SFS, 2010:800). However, separating children with SEN from other children has been considered best for providing extra support to those with

SEN while facilitating successful teaching for those with ordinary or superior learning capabilities (Börjesson and Palmblad, 2003; Persson, 2003).

Furthermore, despite the inclusive intentions of the Education Acts (e.g. SFS, 1985:1100; SFS, 2010: 800), a move towards a category-based system of special support is exacerbated by the common use of medical diagnoses such as ADHD and Aspergers syndrome, and of labels such as *social emotional and behavioural difficulties* in school practice (Giota and Emanuelsson, 2011). These school practices demonstrate that medical diagnoses are commonly required before children are entitled to specialist teaching at a given school. The children are then described as having school problems, and teaching practices and organisation of study groups offered for those pupils are seldom questioned.

An estimated 17-20 per cent of all students in the ordinary comprehensive school system in Sweden are defined as having special educational needs (SEN), and thus need special support (Giota and Emanuelsson, 2011). The reasons for being defined as having SEN vary, but students at risk of not achieving the expected educational targets in one or more subjects, and those who have behavioural difficulties, are most likely to be given additional support. The number of students described as having SEN has increased, possibly because teachers have found it so difficult to meet the needs of individual students (Andreasson, 2007).

The Education Act stipulates that the school principal be informed of students who do not *reach the minimum knowledge requirements*, or *present other difficulties in their school situation* due to social, emotional and behavioural difficulties (SFS, 1985:1100; SFS, 2010:800). The Act also stipulates that an assessment of such students should be conducted, usually involving the student health team. In Sweden, teachers often use various kinds of standardised tests to identify students' having difficulties with reading, writing, and mathematics. Conversely, students with social, emotional and behavioural difficulties are often assessed by teachers' subjective definitions of *normal* behaviour and ability (Andreasson, 2007; Karlsson, 2007: 2012). Consequently, the identification and definition of students whose behaviours deviate from school norms and expectations are highly subjective processes.

One form of SEN support in Sweden is student placement into special needs units (SENUs; SFS, 1985: 1100; SFS, 2010:800; SNAE, 2014). According to self-reported data, Swedish municipalities have about four SENUs where students marked as having SEN spend more than fifty per cent of their time. However, and as previously mentioned, separating SEN students from other students is deemed best for providing educational support to SEN children. Thus it seems likely that the existence and use of these SENUs are underreported (Göransson, Nilholm and Karlsson, 2011). The prevalence of SENUs is remarkable considering the stipulations of the Education Act (SFS, 1985:1100; SFS, 2010:800) that organisational solutions in the form of SENUs should be avoided whenever possible within the comprehensive school system.

Learning and behavioural problems, categorisation and social processes of institutions

This chapter concerns the assumption that schools and teachers play a significant role in defining and labelling children considered to have school difficulties. In recent decades, numerous researchers have raised critical perspectives on the labelling and medicalisation of children's problems with learning and behaviour in school. Conrad (2006) was an early contributor of a sociological perspective, criticising the treatment of student deviance from school norms as a medical problem. He emphasised that medicalisation of deviant behaviour is part of a larger phenomenon that is prevalent in our society, the individualisation of social problems. Individualisation involves the tendency to look to the individual for causes and solutions to complex social problems, rather than to the social system. More than thirty years after Conrad's critique of 1975, Harwood (2006) argued that the frequency with which children are diagnosed with behavioural disorders and referred to as disorderly is still increasing and common in western countries. She further states that current conceptualisations of disorderly children are far reaching.

A majority of the children who are defined as having behavioural problems and ADHD are boys from socially disadvantaged backgrounds (Emanuelsson and Persson, 2002; Hey, Leonard, Daniels and Smith, 1998; Visser and Jehan, 2009). More boys than girls are excluded from mainstream classes, and a majority of these boys are designated as having *social and emotional difficulties* and *acting out problems* (Reed, 1999; Persson, 2004). These boys also generally obtain lower grades and are more likely to experience failure in school and difficulties adapting to adult life (Frank, Sitlington and Carson, 1995; Koyangi and Gaines, 1993). Moreover, boys who are considered to have *social, emotional, behavioural difficulties* and ADHD in school tend to remain in marginalised positions throughout school and later in life (Landrum, Tankersley and Kauffman, 2003). Although, results show that a majority of the children excluded from school are boys, research demonstrates that the gender disparity is seldom expressed as an issue and is not acknowledged during the remedial practices in the SENU (see Evaldsson and Karlsson, 2012; West and Zimmerman, 2009).

Even though psychologists and educators strongly tend to link problems and difficulties at school with certain psychological and physiological syndromes, no standard definitions of children with *social and emotional difficulties* or *showing behavioural problems* currently exist. Various behaviour-screening questionnaires typically use criteria such as: 'behaviour that goes to an extreme, behaviours or emotions that are outside societal norms; behaviours or emotions that negatively affect a child's educational functioning' (Soles, et al., 2008: 276). From the ethnomethodological perspective of this chapter, a fundamental problem remains with how these questionnaires predetermine the descriptive categories of children's problem behaviours in terms of underlying problems with psychological and physiological states. In this way, children's problem behaviours are abstracted from the institutions' daily practices and the interactions during which the teachers and the boys themselves attempt to interpret these descriptive categories (see Hester and Francis, 2000).

Previous research on schools' local social processes for describing and defining children's social, emotional and behaviour problems and ADHD showed that teachers invoke and define limits for deviant and desirable behaviours among boys in everyday practice. This results in the confirmation of identities such as having *social and emotional difficulties* and *acting out behaviour*, and ADHD, which in turn leads to children with such identities being defined as *students with deficiencies* and *failing students*. These definitions are then solidified in local social processes embedded within school activities (Evaldsson and Karlsson, 2012; Hester, 1992; Hjörne, 2004; Mehan, 1993). Social categorisations during interaction simultaneously define and construct a person's identity as a member of a specific social group, and are thus resources for organisational activities (Baker, 2000). Descriptions of people and things are building-blocks for categorisations and identities. When members describe others or themselves in different ways, they simultaneously build social categorisations and identities which, in turn, refer to specific social worlds or institutions (e.g. social and emotional deficiencies, behavioural problems, and ADHD; see Douglas, 1974; Antaki and Widdicombe, 1998).

Hester (1998) points to the powerful role of institutions in controlling *children's deviance*. In this study, I observed that the boys were marked out, identified and described as deviating from the local norms of school conduct and order (cf. Hester and Francis, 2000). Further, in the local social processes, individual boys are ascribed a set of emotional and social deficiencies and behavioural difficulties that become a daily topic of inquiry during teacher-student talks comprising SENU remedial practice (Evaldsson and Karlsson, 2012). The descriptions of a person, thing or event do not consist entirely of true statements. Statements expressed by a person who has a specific position (i.e. teacher) in an activity with a specific aim must be interpreted within that specific context (see Antaki and Widdicombe, 1998). In other words, any knowledge about a given category may be considered relevant to the person to whom the label is being applied. The problem behaviours that teachers refer to, for example *controlling anger, not listening, exaggerating,* and similar terms, are linked to the psychological categories of *the student assigned to SEN, boys with social, emotional and behavioural deficiencies* and the medical category *boys with ADHD.* This link is based on knowledge of conventional use of the categorisations in the psychological literature and, particularly, in the education setting (see Antaki and Widdicombe, 1998; Evaldsson and Karlsson, 2012).

Categorisation and attribution processes occur when a teacher directly refers to a student with an obvious group label such as *having social and emotional difficulties.* Alternatively, a teacher may succeed in categorising a student into a certain social group more subtly by indirect description of the student (see Day, 1998). Indirect description may serve to set up what Day (1998) terms 'a case of special relevance'. This description is then considered relevant to the remaining participants in the group. Evaldsson (2014) found that direct naming of a medical diagnosis is seldom used in teacher-student talk in Swedish school practice. Evaldsson investigated boys diagnosed with ADHD participating in a SEN classroom and showed that their conduct in school was minimally associated with the criteria for ADHD and related pathological syndromes. Overall, Evaldsson highlighted that in everyday classroom practice, teachers mostly expected boys to be normal, ordinary students. They seldom used a medical perspective to understand the boys' behaviours and interactions in the classroom. Instead the boys were held accountable for their conduct.

Children's actions as their communicative agency

In contrast to an individualistic perspective (Rutherford, Quinn and Mathur, 2004), I use childhood sociology to analyse children's competence as communicative agency during SENU practices. This approach emphasises that children's social relations and interactions are inherently worth studying, apart from adults' definitions of them (Danby, 2002; Danby and Farrell, 2004;

James, Jenks and Prout, 1998), and that children are considered as active meaning-making participants who understand experiences, and reflect and interpret their social world during interaction (Corsaro, 2005). Thus children use, construct, and reproduce knowledge and information they glean during experiences with adult relations and culture. In this chapter, I analyse how the boys' expressions, social actions and interactions acted as instruments through which they demonstrated social competence during interactions with teachers in daily SENU practices (see Hutchby and Moran-Ellis, 1998). Children's active meaning-making participation was evident in my study when the boys registered their experiences and commented on the teachers' negative definitions of them with a one-sided focus on deficiencies.

Corsaro (2005) stressed that children use their space for agency when they participate in a given situation. As such, they are constantly striving for and contributing to current changes in routines, rules and normalities of everyday practises. Linell (2015: 1-2) defines agency as something communicative and practical during interactions. I used an ethnomethodological approach and Linell's definition of agency to analyse children's communicative agency in this study. Communicative and practical agency are closely related to the participants' actions. Furthermore, agency is related to one's potential to take the initiative, during SENU practices and interaction, to choose opportunities for active interventions. This includes the ability to reject, comment on, modify and negotiate, within limits, reactions that are situationally expected, or forced onto the participant. Agency was demonstrated in this analysis when the children in the SENU attempted to take control during pedagogic circle time and regulative talk, where they were defined by the teacher as having behavioural deficiencies and school difficulties.

Category work and rejection of social identities

I use Sacks (1995) Membership Categorisation Analysis (MCA) to understand how identities are accomplished in institutional interactions. I analyse how the boys performed category work by rejecting or negotiating membership in a specific social identity group (e.g. social and emotional deficiencies and behavioural problems) that may have been attributed to them during talk-in-interaction. I also looked at the children's strategies for performing category work as they participated in and responded to the social processes that their school used to define them as having school deficiencies. MCA demonstrates how *identity work* is negotiated in morally accountable ways (cf. Antaki and Widdicombe, 1998; Jayyusi, 1984; Sacks, 1972). In analysing the boys' understandings of the social categories attributed to them during the daily talk-in-interaction event, I have used ethnographic and ethnomethodological perspectives (cf. Antaki and Widdicombe, 1998; Hester and Eglin, 1997; Hester and Francis, 2000).

The perspective on identity in this chapter is grounded in ethnomethodology and explores how people orient to, describe, and assess themselves and others as particular kinds of people in everyday social life and as members (or non-members) of identity-relevant categories. Identities are put to local work turn-by-turn during interactions, a phenomenon viewed as identity work. In ethnomethodology, identity work is performed by the participants. Identity work focuses on the organisation of social life during, and through, talk and social interaction, and who each person is to another is a concern of the members of a given identity-relevant category. Identity work is what the boys and teachers were doing together during talks, demonstrating the details on how identities are displayed, negotiated and co-produced. Identity work implicates a thoroughly social view of self, embedded within social action and interaction (see Widdicombe, 1998).

Schools' and teachers' processes for categorising students as having school difficulties may also present unfavourable inferences for boys to whom the category membership is directly or indirectly applied (e.g. Drew, 1987). Day (1998) emphasises that individuals can function as active agents by indirectly and subtly resisting undesirable categorisation during talk-in-interaction. Individuals who perceive themselves as being categorised by others in a negative manner perform category work during such interactions by resisting these descriptions. This category work can be expressed ardently, or softly and indirectly.

According to Antaki and Widdicombe (1998), a person's identity is his or her display of, ascription to, or rejection of membership in some feature-rich category. Any individual can be regarded under a multitude of categories. In my analysis, I identified a variety of ways through which students in the SENU accomplished comments on, objections to, and rejection of the appropriateness of the teachers' descriptions of them as having difficulties with school such as *social and emotional difficulties* and *behaviour problems*.

Methodological considerations and the data

As presented above, this study aims to explore and identify children's communicative agency and identity work during pedagogic practices in a special needs education unit (SENU) in Sweden. I explore local social processes occurring in a group of five boys as they responded to, and attempted to negotiate, their school's disconcerting, negative definitions and categorisations during two pedagogical activities: pedagogic circle time and regulative talk. Pedagogical circle time is the first activity of the school day for students, and regulative talk occurs at the end of the school day. During interactions with the boys in the SENU, teachers did not explicitly express descriptions of the boys as having social and emotional difficulties, behavioural problems, and ADHD. Instead they used descriptions (e.g. being angry, using dirty words, exaggerating) as resources for organising social activities (e.g. praise, blame, accountability) that referred to the construction of the students' identity as having social and emotional deficiencies, behavioural problems, and ADHD.

My study focuses on interactions and their social functions, both of which are related to the school being an institution in society. Thus, teachers and students talking and interacting (e.g. explaining, correcting, blaming, and praising) in the SENU simultaneously refers to school norms and rules (e.g. how students should behave, feel, and perform; see Cicourel, 1981; Sarangi and Roberts, 1999). In addition, the aim is to elucidate students' activities in the SENU and to establish their meaning-making, agency and competence in an institutional context (Hutchby and Moran-Ellis, 1998). In my study, ethnographic analysis of the educational setting, including spatial arrangements, was central to understand how the categorisations attributed to the boys in the SENU were contextually embedded within institutional practice, and how the boys responded by doing category work (Mehan, Hertweck and Meihls, 1986).

As research data, I have used video recordings to identify and explore children's communicative agency and identity work in detail during pedagogic practices. Thus I could study local social processes occurring amongst the five boys as they responded to their school's negative and disconcerting definitions in the two daily remedial practices. Video recordings of everyday activities were required to identify and understand the meaning the boys ascribed to social categories, identities, values, norms, and relations (Corsaro, 2005; Danby, 2002). The video recordings allowed me to observe non-verbal communicative resource like gestures, gazes, and body positions, e.g. someone turning away, or bending the head as a *quiet* response. In corroboration of Duranti's (1997) work, I noticed that the participants were engaged in their everyday social activities and used the same communicative resources despite the presence of the researcher and video camera (see Cromdal, 2000; Evaldsson, 2003; Tholander, 2002).

The data was produced in the special educational needs unit (SENU) in one comprehensive school with six hundred students from mixed socioeconomic circumstances in a medium-sized town in Sweden. Five boys aged seven to twelve years-old attended the unit. The boys had been removed from their ordinary classes and from regular school activities with other students. They participated full time in separate educational and social activities conducted in a building located on the periphery of the school property. Each boy had spent between eight months and three years in the unit. A lack of official mention of the SENU in the school's publicly accessible informational materials (i.e. its webpages, catalogues, schedules, etc.) demonstrated the marginal and subordinate positions of these boys in everyday school life.

Four female teachers with different professional backgrounds (special needs education teacher, leisure-time pedagogue, youth recreation leader, and child minder) were responsible for the boys' education. Children were assigned to the unit because they were classified as having emotional and social deficiencies and behavioural problems, and these classifications identified the children as different, and as *needing remedial help*. As Hester (1998: 142) explains, the category *remedial* implies various predictors, including a need for help, falling behind in a subject, and similar descriptions that ascribe incompetence to the categorised individuals. The school's categorisation of each individual boy as needing remedial help was acknowledged and interpreted in daily school activities over a long period of time (see also Hester and Francis, 2000; Mehan, 1991).

Organising pedagogical circle time

Pedagogical circle time is a group activity that occurs at the start of every school day in the SENU during which teachers and students discuss topics and evaluate student behaviour.

Pedagogical circle time is a regularly-occurring group activity in the SENU. Its main purpose is to improve children's self-esteem, social and emotional behaviour, group identity, and learning. (e.g. Lang, 1998; Lang and Mosley, 1993; Margerison, 1996). During pedagogical circle time, teachers and children sit in a circle on the same level to discuss a topic or theme. Simultaneously, children's behaviour, and social and personal development are the central foci of this circle time. Pedagogical circle time usually follows a set of key rules such as only one person speaking at a time, all children/students listening to each other without interruption (e.g. Lown, 2002; Mosley, 2009; Taylor, 2003).

Each school day in the SENU begins with a pedagogical circle time. Teachers and students call this event 'breakfast' and it lasts for forty minutes. It is conducted in a room for gatherings, where all of the teachers and students sit around a table and eat breakfast. Different teachers lead the group and instruct the students on different days of the week. According to the teachers, the aim of the breakfast is to encourage the students to 'calm down', 'drink something warm' and 'eat something' before the school day starts. The breakfast also includes both pedagogic and social activities, as well as a brief discussion of the day's planned activities and advice on: being a good friend, taking turns, table manners, eating habits, social and emotional behaviour, discussion of students' past weekend activities, the date and day of the week, the school schedule, and instruction on the alphabet, numbers, seasons and suchlike.

Repeated category work during pedagogic circle time

During the pedagogic circle time, the teachers in the SENU categorised the students as having poor table manners and eating habits, both at school and at home. One teacher said that the students 'don't eat breakfast at home.' The students often responded to teachers' categorisations by performing category work and by refuting the teachers' statements: 'I eat breakfast at home ... but I eat bread and butter here anyway.' This example indicates that students complied with the rules of the SENU and ate breakfast even if they had already eaten at home. In the passage quoted below, the teachers told the students why they had to eat in a separate dining room in school and not with the other students. This discussion comes from a pedagogic circle time involving three teachers and five students. Lena is the teacher, and Jesper and Oskar are students in the SENU.

Example 1 The following discussion occurred during a 'breakfast' pedagogic circle time that was recorded on video:

1	*Lena:*	it's much easier to talk to one another when we sit in there (referring to the separate dining room for
2		the students in the SENU)
3		
4	*Jesper:*	yes... you don't hear anything
5	*Lena:*	no... and it is important for you to know how to eat nicely... when you're invited to someone's
6		house... or something like that... it is quite nice to know... how to eat with a knife and fork... and

7		[that one uses]
8		
9	*Oskar:*	[at home we have]
10	*Lena:*	[and that you say thank you]
11	*Oskar:*	at home we have four forks
12	*Lena:*	yes... we practice every day
13	*Oskar:*	at home we have four forks
14	*Lena:*	four forks?
15	*Oskar:*	yes... two knives and two forks... for dessert
16	*Lena:*	yes... that's right (2s) we don't have dessert that often... so we can't practice that... some of you
17		might already know (8s) but it's good to practice every day
18		
19	*Oskar:*	sometimes when we have dinner parties... we have six pieces of cutlery... starting with spoons for
20		the soup

In this discussion, the teacher explained how the boys were benefiting from being separated from the other students (lines 1-3), and highlighted the reasons for having lunch in a separate dining room and the need for the boys to develop their table manners (lines 5, 7-8, and 10).

The teacher indirectly categorised and addressed all the boys in the SENU as though they had poor table manners at home (lines 5-8, and 10). Oskar rejected this assertion and repeatedly performed category work as someone who has good table manners at home, interjecting at lines 9, 11, 13, 15, 19 and 20. Oskar performed this category work in a soft and subtle way (Day, 1998), repeatedly positioned himself as an active agent, and commented on the teacher's categorisation of him as someone with problematic table manners at home. Moreover, Oskar described his own experiences at home and implied his desire to portray himself as a good person. According to Widdicombe (1998), the scenario depicted in the dialogue above may be interpreted as follows: the descriptions of the boys' concerning poor table manners at home were linked to the social category of *boy having behaviour problems*. In response to these descriptions, Oskar performed category work by describing himself in a more favourable way, i.e. as someone who has good table manners at home. In doing so, it can be interpreted that Oskar refers to his social background with experiences of taking part of dinner parties at home. Further, that the teacher had different expectations about what Oskar is doing at home and what kind of family life he has.

Arranging regulative talk *smile* and *daily rose*

Regulative talk occurs at the end of every school day and involves the teachers evaluating how the boys behaved during the school day. The regulating talk activity occurred at the end of every school day and consisted of two parts: *smile* and *daily rose*. *Smile* is further described in examples 2 and 3, and the *daily rose* in example 4 below. During these activities the students answered teachers' questions about how they had behaved throughout the school day. The *smile* activity focused on students' problematic behaviour and the *daily rose* activity focused on students' desirable behaviour. Both activities were performed in a specific physical space in the classroom that is used only for these two activities. During regulating talk, the students sit on chairs arranged in a semi-circle in front of a wall. Each student had a map placed on the left section of the wall on which they pasted their smiley stickers. The teacher used a collective map on the right section of the wall to document instances of desirable behaviour during the *daily rose* activity. During the activity, the teachers stood behind or beside the students.

Figure 1 Seating arrangements during the regulative talk *smile* and *daily rose*

The seating arrangement (in which the students sat facing the wall) positioned the boys as subordinate to the teacher while the teacher, who stood behind the children and monitored their activities, took on a position of power. The teachers routinely evaluated the boys' problem behaviour through talk-in-interaction (see Hester, 1998). Only students who managed to remedy their emotional, behavioural and social deficiencies were rewarded with a smiley sticker. The stickers each student had obtained were displayed on a map that was hung on the wall in front of the boys. In this way, the deficiencies attributed to each individual boy became manifested and a public matter for the whole group.

During the *smile' activity, teachers asked questions about the students* behaviour during the day. *Smile* lasted for twenty-five minutes and focused on aspects of the students' behaviour that were considered problematic. During the *smile* activity, the students were told about four or five problematic situations/occasions that the teachers had identified during a conference held at the start of the school semester. Predefined problem behaviours were documented in a written record at this conference, and the record was used to structure the activity.

Example 2

To get a 'Smiley' sticker you have to:
Anton * Control your anger. * Don't say no. * No exaggerating. * Don't make mistakes even if your friends are doing wrong things.
Jesper * Did you do your homework? * Finish your school tasks. * Listen to adults and obey. * Don't make bad faces.
Marcus * Talk nicely. * No dirty words. * No complaining. * Confess when you make mistakes. * Do not tease.
Oskar * Don't correct others. * Don't say dirty words. * Do not exaggerate. * Tell and explain what you want. * Leave the room when told to do that.
Tom * Leave the room when you get disturbed. * Don't say what. * No unpleasant tone. * Undress before you enter the room and be attentive to the social situation. * Eat up the food you have put on your plate.

In the written record, the teachers categorised what they identified as students' problematic behaviours and characteristics from students' behaviour, interactions, and relations with adults and peers in school. A majority of the behaviours relate to social/school norms for interaction and emotions e.g. what the students did, what they said and their responses during interactions. Jesper is an exception in that he should be expected to do his schoolwork. The problematic behaviours were associated with a specific student and name, demonstrating individualisation of school problems.

Reinforcing a description as a *good and desirable* student–*smile*

The discussion below came from a *smile* activity during which Anton was asked to discuss his behaviour problems. In this activity, the teachers started by addressing the students by name. In this way, school problems are individualised and made a matter of concern for the individual child (see Hester, 1998). Anton uses a strategy to avoid being described as having problematic behaviour and, instead, describes himself as a good student.

Example 3. Discussion during a *smile* activity that was recorded on video

Karin:	Anton
Anton:	(looks at Karin) (2s)
Karin:	have you managed to control your anger? (reads the written record and looks at Anton) (4s)
Anton:	I have not had any anger (looks at Karin)
Karin:	(nods yes) (6s)
Karin:	and not said no? (reads in the written record and looks at Anton)
Anton:	I have not said that
Karin:	(nods yes)
Karin:	not made any mistakes... even if your friends do wrong things? (looks at Anton)
Anton:	I have not done that (looks at Karin)
Karin:	(nods yes)
Karin:	not exaggerated? (looks at Anton)
Anton:	not done (with low voice, looks at Karin)
Karin:	(nods yes, cuts out a smiley sticker) (4s)
Oskar:	then it's my turn... after Anton
Lena:	you got a sticker (with low voice, looks at Anton)

20	*Karin:*	[great… Anton]
21 22	*Karin:*	[he deserved that] … give it to him (hands over the smiley sticker to Lena)

Anton was clearly adapting to what the teacher was saying, and trying to answer the questions in the manner expected of him as a student. Teachers asked questions and students were expected to answer (Initiate-Response-Evaluate (I-R-E) sequences; Mehan, 1979; Hester and Francis, 2000). However, Anton's involvement was minimal, and he answered the questions as briefly as possible (lines 5, 9, 13 and 16). Moreover, he used the same phrasing and vocal tone as the teacher. This observation of Anton may be interpreted as his conformation to the teacher's talk. He was performing category work by adapting his responses to match the teacher's phrasing to avoid being defined as problematic. In other words, he was attempting to minimise the risk that the conversation would move in a direction the teacher would consider problematic (Goodwin and Goodwin, 1997).

Example 3 may be interpreted as Anton establishing agency and a form of category work aimed at getting himself out of a difficult situation and avoiding categorisation as a problematic student. At the end of the discussion, Anton was described positively (lines 20-22), which invoked a desirable student identity. This identity was further reinforced when Anton received the smiley sticker. Anton reinforced his position as a 'good and desirable student' using the strategy of adapting his responses.

Intensifying redefinitions of categorisations and distancing to problem talk in *daily rose*

As mentioned previously, the *daily rose* activity immediately follows *smile* during regulative talk, and is the last scheduled activity of the school day. The *daily rose* activity is shorter than *smile*, lasting ten minutes, and is intended to highlight instances of students' desirable behaviour during school. In contrast to the *smile* activity, *daily rose* does not rely on predefined written records or stickers as rewards. Instead, the teachers established a written desirable behaviour record during the ongoing activity. Desirable social and emotional behaviours during class activities (e.g. 'you did very well in handicraft'), break times (e.g. 'you had so much fun on the sledge'), or relative to peers (e.g. 'you played very well with Tom during this breakfast break') were highlighted and praised.

The *daily rose* activity was also controlled by the teachers' questions. The teachers led the activity by asking questions, and used traditional turn-taking to facilitate initiate-response-evaluation (I-R-E) sequences (Mehan, 1979; Hester and Francis, 2000). In the discussion quoted below, a student (Tom) performed category work by distancing himself from the activity and redefining problematic school categories.

Example 4. Discussion during a *daily rose* activity that was recorded on video:

Karin:	but you are worth the daily rose
Lena:	absolutely
Tom:	I don't want it (8s) it's unpleasant to say bad words
Lena:	no you... to not have a nice tone means 'I know... I know!'... are you screaming at us?
Tom:	why do you have the special needs unit?
Lena:	what do we have?
Tom:	why do you have the daily rose and not anyone else?
Lena:	because we work with who one is as a human being... very much
Tom:	I AM A HUMAN BEING! (with loud voice)
Lena:	yes... you are (2s) and we want you to be a nice little guy
Anna:	you are that most of the time
Lena:	so that you can be together with others... without that they will be angry at you (2s) because you don't know how to behave... that's not funny
Anna:	or if adults sometimes get angry... just because you answer... phu... PDU... HU... like that
Lena:	that is something you have to work on (2s) or else people around you will get very irritated (2s) but we help each other with that
Tom:	they are not angry at me
Lena:	they will be if you answer like that
Anna:	that's a bit like I told you in the English lesson... in the classes

29	*Tom:*	°hm° (with low voice)
30	*Anna:*	then you can't be like that
31	*Tom:*	°I don't want to be here° (with low voice, getting up from the chair)

The teachers asked an indirect question about the definition of a desirable behaviour (line 1). Tom did not answer in the expected manner, i.e. with a desirable behaviour. Instead, he identified and confessed to having problematic behaviour by saying, 'it's unpleasant to say bad words' (lines 3 and 4). Unpleasantness and saying bad words are included in the membership category *school difficulties*. Tom's response may also be interpreted as his implementation of a good student identity during the regulative discussion. During the *smile* activity, the descriptions *being unpleasant* and *saying bad words* are used by teachers to define the boys.

During this dialogue, Tom appropriated and reproduced the teachers' descriptions (Corsaro, 2005) from the *smile* activity, but the teacher interpreted Tom's response as resistance to their request (lines 7 and 9-10). The teacher demonstrated this interpretation by initiating intensified and detailed negative descriptions of Tom (lines 14-24 and 26-28) (Evaldsson and Karlsson, 2012). Tom performed category work by distancing himself from the regulative talk (lines 29, 31 and 32) and redefining negative categories (lines 13 and 25). Throughout the activity, Tom seemed to experience the teachers describing and categorising him negatively (Day, 1998).

Tom also redefined the participation framework by asking the teachers critical questions such as 'why do you have a special needs unit?' (line 7), 'why do you have the daily rose and not anyone else?' (lines 9-10). Widdicombe and Wooffitt (1995: 55) argued that by producing these questions and comments, the participant is able to re-characterise the conversation. Instead of question-answer sequences during which the teachers ascribed descriptions and categories, the subsequent utterances focused on other concerns. In this way, Tom avoided being associated with problematic school identities in local social processes in the SENU. Further, he attempted to redefine his problematic categorisation by saying, 'I AM A HUMAN BEING' (line 13) and 'they are not angry at me' (line 25). Tom also distanced himself from the activity (line 29, and 31), which may be interpreted as an attempt to voice his own experiences with the teachers' authoritarian and negative categorisations.

Conclusion: Boys' responses and identity work regarding negative categorisation processes in a SENU

I have examined the local social processes occurring amongst a group of five boys as they responded to their school's negative and disconcerting definitions during two pedagogic activities: pedagogic circle time and regulative talk. The results show that the students have to manage the school's social organisation and teachers' definitions and categorisations of them, while attempting to control their circumstances. Moreover, boys' agency and social competence is related to the school context and social structure, which includes the boys themselves.

Boys' agency must be viewed within the institutional structures to which they react. The way in which teachers from the SENU describe and categorise boys' behavioural problems could be interpreted as an attempt to guide the boys' development so that they will change and improve. Conversely, from the boys' perspective, daily activities in the SENU could be a minefield where it is necessary to adopt several different strategies to control and strengthen their identity. The fact that the boys in the SENU are indirectly resisting and subordinating themselves during the pedagogic activities suggests they believed it risky to oppose negative, disconcerting definitions of them. My results also indicate that boys must cope with discouraging organisation and categorisation processes as they participate in, relate to, and register experiences during daily pedagogic practices in the SENU. The boys were isolated from other children in a separate school building in a corner of the school property, and ate in a separate dining room. Moreover, they were primarily described in negative terms, with a one-sided focus on their deficiencies. Their teachers dictated how they were to behave, talk, account for themselves, act and feel. The boys attempted to position themselves as active agents by indirectly resisting or subordinating themselves to the school's definition of them as having behavioural problems and school difficulties. The students also positioned themselves as being *good students*.

The school focused unilaterally on boys in the SENU as having deficiencies, problems, and difficulties, which is a disconcerting practice, especially because the purpose of the SENU is to give these boys special needs support and to help them with school difficulties. I argue that educational approaches in which the boys were mainly regarded as problematic and having deficiencies tended to obscure boys' own perspectives of their experiences, and their own reflections and actions during social interaction in daily SENU practises. These observations highlight the importance of detailed analyses, and of appropriate interpretation of the social purpose of the boys' communicative activities during interactions with teachers and peers. For example, instances in which the boys did not answer questions, made no comments, objected, or raised their voice in response to teachers' statements during a specific situation in the SENU were all important aspects for objective observations, assessments, and evaluations of the boys' behaviour. Contrary to the individualised perspective that focused on the deficiencies of each boy, I found that the more accurate perspective consisted of boys constantly interacting with teachers and peers in different contexts. I have interpreted the boys' behaviours in the context of interactions and identity work during talk-in-interactions with teachers and peers instead of viewing their behaviours from an individualistic perspective.

Although school staff emphasised that students should improve their social behaviour and academic skills, this paradoxically appeared to be reducing the boys' agency and sense of responsibility for themselves and their behaviour, feelings, and academic skills. Boys in the SENU are marginalised on different levels in the educational environment, even though Sweden has a strong democratic agenda that values egalitarianism and the concept of *a school for all children*. The rights of children with special needs to equal educational opportunities and academic skills, participation with other children, confirmation, and self-expression according to their experiences and emotions are eliminated.

Studies of children during peer interaction stress that when children break school rules, or playtime rules, observations of them playing games and talking with peers provide important knowledge about how they experience and apply norms in the adult world (see Corsaro, 2005; Evaldsson, 2002). Such experiences allowed the boys to contribute to (re)construction or transformation of rules and norms during pedagogic activities. The boys' negotiations of rules and norms in school demonstrated that they were active agents, but their agency depended on whether the teachers paid attention to the boys' unique experiences and reflections, and highlight their communicative contributions during pedagogic activities. Instead, I found that teachers in SENU reduced the boys' opportunities to be heard and seen during pedagogic activities. The boys were categorised as troublesome and problematic, and as a result, were declined opportunities to comment on disconcerting, negative descriptions of themselves, to perform identity work, and to negotiate school rules and norms. In this study, the boys showed that that they had their own unique opinions about the school's cultural and institutional assumptions.

I found that the school and teachers applied descriptions of negative behaviours to the boys, which in turn, were associated with different social identities (e.g. *boys with behaviour problems, boys with social and emotional difficulties* and *boys with difficulties concentrating*). Furthermore, my analysis shows that boys in the SENU had few opportunities to describe themselves and influence the negative descriptions and deficiencies assigned to them during pedagogic circle time and regulative talk. Such descriptions, by teachers, as having a deviant identity pose serious threats to the personal identity of boys with special needs.

The categorisation of boys as deviant, with disconcerting descriptions and deficiencies, affects the construction of their identity (Antaki and Widdicombe, 1998; Goffman, 1959; Karlsson, 2007). This work explored the opportunities children have for negotiating and responding to such negative categorisations, and for being assigned such identities, as revealed during the daily practises conducted within a SENU in Sweden. My analysis has shown that boys expressed their agency during the pedagogical circle time and regulative talk activities by attempting to: gain control, remove themselves from the environment, or evade being assigned problematic definitions and deficiencies. By taking these actions, they responded to societal norms of social position and consolidated their identity position as *good students*.

References

Andreasson, I., (2007) *Elevplanen som text - om identitet, genus, makt och styrning i skolans elevdokumentation* [The individual education plan as text. About identity, gender, power and governing in pupils' documentation at school], Thesis (PhD), University of Gothenburg.

Antaki, C. and Widdicombe, S., (1998) Identity as an achievement and as a tool, in Antaki, C. and Widdicombe, S., (eds.) *Identities in talk*, London: SAGE Publications, 1-14.

Baker, C., (2000) Locating culture in action: membership categorization in texts and talk, in Lee, A. and Poynton, C., (eds.) *Culture and text. Discourse and methodology in social research and cultural studies*, Lanham Maryland: Rowman and Littlefield publishers, 99-113.

Börjesson, M. and Palmblad, E., (2003) *I problembarnens tid. Förnuftets moraliska ordning.* [The problem child. Sense of moral order], Stockholm: Carlsson.

Cicourel, A., (1981) Notes on the integration of micro - and macro - levels of analysis, in Knorr-Cetina, K. and Cicourel, A., (eds.) *Advances in social theory and methodology. Toward an integration of micro - and macro - sociologies*, London: Routledge and Kegan Paul, 51-80.

Conrad, P., (2006) *Identifying hyperactive children. The Medicalization of Deviant Behavior,* expanded ed., Lexington Massachusetts: Lexington books.

Corsaro, W., (2005) *The sociology of childhood,* London: Pine Forge Press.

Cromdal, J., (2000) *Code-switching for all practical purpose. Bilingual organization of children's play,* Thesis (PhD), Linköping University.

Danby, S., (2002) The communicative competence of young children, *Australian journal of early childhood,* 27(3): 25-30.

Danby, S. and Farrell, A., (2004) Accounting for young children's competence in educational research: new perspectives on research ethics, *The Australian educational researcher*, 31(3): 35-49.

Day, D., (1998) Being ascribed, and resisting, membership of an ethnic group, in Antaki, C. and Widdicombe, S. (eds.) *Identities in talk,* London: Sage Publications, 151-170.

Douglas, J. D., (1974) Understanding everyday life, in Douglas, J. D., (ed.) *Understanding everyday life,* London: Routledge and Kegan Paul, 3-44.

Drew, P., (1987) Po-faced receipts of teases, *Linguistics*, 25: 219-253.

Duranti, A., (1997) *Linguistic anthropology,* Cambridge: Cambridge University Press.

Emanuelsson, I. and Persson, B., (2002) Differentiering, specialpedagogik och likvärdighet. En longitudinell studie av skolkarriärer bland elever i svårigheter, *Pedagogisk forskning i Sverige,* 7(3): 183-199.

Evaldsson, A-C., (2002) Boys gossip telling: Staging identities and indexing (unacceptable) masculine behaviour, *Text,* 22(2): 199-225.

Evaldsson, A-C., (2003) Throwing like a girl? Situating gender differences in physically across game contexts, *Childhood*, 10(4): 475-497.

Evaldsson, A-C., (2014) Doing being boys with ADHD. Category membership and differences in SEN classroom practice, *Emotional and behavioural difficulties*, 19(3): 266-283.

Evaldsson, A-C. and Karlsson, Y., (2012) Shaping marginalised identities and indexing deviant behaviours in a special educational needs unit, in Hjörne, E., van der Aalsvoort, G. and de Abreu, G., (eds.) *Learning, social interaction and diversity - exploring school practices,* Rotterdam: Sense, 119-138.

Frank, A., Sitlington, P. and Carson, R., (1995) Young adults with behavioral disorders: A comparison with peers with mild disabilities, *Journal of emotional and behavioral disorders,* 3: 156-164.

Giota, J. and Emanuelsson, I., (2011) Policies in special education support issues in Swedish compulsory school: a nationally representative study of head teachers' judgements, *London review of education*, 9(1): 95-108.

Goffman, E., (1959) *The presentation of self,* Hammondsworth: Penguing Books.

Goodwin, C. and Goodwin, M., (1997) Assessments and the construction of context, in Duranti, A. and Goodwin, C., (eds.) *Rethinking context. Language as an interactive phenomenon*, Cambridge: Cambridge University press: 147-189.

Göransson, K., Nilholm, C. and Karlsson, K., (2011) Inclusive education in Sweden? A critical analysis, *International journal of inclusive education,* 15(5): 541-555.

Harwood, V., (2006) *Diagnosing 'disorderly' children. A critique of behaviour disorder discourse,* New York: Routledge.

Hester, S., (1992) Recognising references to deviance in referral talk, in Watson, G. and Seiler, R., (eds.) *Text in context. Contributions to ethnomethodology*, London: SAGE Publications, 156-174.

Hester, S., (1998) Describing deviance in school. Recognizable educational psychological problems, in Antaki, C. and Widdicombe, S., (eds.) *Identities in talk,* London: Sage Publication.

Hester, S. and Eglin, P., (1997) The reflexive constitution of category, predicate and context in two settings, in Hester, S. and Eglin, P., (eds.) *Culture in action. Studies in membership categorization analysis,* Lanham, Maryland: University Press of America, 25-48.

Hester, S. and Francis, D., (2000) Ethnomethodology and local educational order, in Hester, S. and Francis, D., (eds.) *Local educational order. Ethnomethodological studies of knowledge in action,* Philadelphia: John Benjamins, 197-222.

Hey, V., Leonard, D. Daniels, H. and Smith, M., (1998) Boys' underachievement, special needs practices and questions of equity, in Epstein, D., Elwood, J., Hey, V. and Maw, J., (eds.) *Failing boys? Issues in gender and achievement,* Buckingham: Open University Press, 128-144.

Hjörne, E., (2004) *Excluding for inclusion? Negotiating school careers and identities in pupil welfare settings in the Swedish school,* Thesis (PhD), Göteborgs Universitet.

Hutchby, I. and Moran-Ellis, J., (1998) Situating children's social competence, in Hutchby, I. and Moran-Ellis, J., (eds.) *Children and social competence: Arenas of action,* London: The Falmer Press, 7-26.

James, A., Jenks, C. and Prout, A., (1998) *Theorising childhood,* New York: Teachers College Press.

Jayyusi, L., (1984) *Categories and the moral order,* London: Routledge.

Karlsson, Y., (2007) *Att inte vilja vara ett problem. Social organisering och utvärdering av elever i en särskild undervisningsgrupp.* [Resisting problem talk. Social organization and evaluation practices in a special teaching group], Thesis (PhD), Linköping University.

Karlsson, Y., (2012) Barns aktörskap och identitetsarbete i en särskild undervisningsgrupp. [Children's agency and identity work in a special teaching group], *Utbildning och demokrati*, 21(3): 35-52.

Koyangi, C. and Gaines, S., (1993) *All systems failure: An examination of the results of neglecting the needs of children with serious emotional disturbance,* Washington, D.C.: National Institute for Mental Health and the Federation of Families for Children's Mental Health.

Landrum, T., Tankersley, M. and Kauffman, J., (2003) What is special about special education for students with emotional or behavioural disorders? *The journal of special education,* 37(3): 148-156.

Lang, P., (1998) Getting round to clarity. What do we mean by circle time? *Pastoral care in education*, 16(3): 3-10.

Lang, P. and Mosley, J., (1993) Promoting pupil self-esteem and positive school polices through the use of circle-time, *Primary teaching studies*, 7(2): 11-15.

Linell, P., (2015) On agency in situated languaging. Participatory agency and competing approaches, *New ideas of psychology*, 42: 39-45.

Lown, J., (2002) Circle time. The perception of teachers and pupils, *Educational psychology in practice*, 18(2): 93-102.

Margerison, A., (1996) Self-esteem: its effects in the development and learning of children with EBD, *Support for learning*, 11(4): 176-180.

Mehan, H., (1979) *Learning lessons. Social organization in the classroom,* Cambridge: Harvard University Press.

Mehan, H., (1991) The school's work of sorting students, in Boden, D. and Zimmerman, D., (eds.) *Talk and social structure. Studies in ethnomethodology and conversation analysis*, Cambridge: Polity press.

Mehan, H., (1993) Beneath the skin and between the ears: A case study in the politics of representation, in Chaiklin, S. and Lave, J., (eds.) *Understanding practice. Perspectives on activity and context,* Cambridge, Massachusetts: Cambridge University Press, 241-268.

Mehan, H., Hertweck, A. and Meihls, J. L., (1986) *Handicapping the handicapped. Decision making in students educational careers,* Stanford, California: Stanford University Press.

Mosley, J., (2009) Circle time and socio-emotional competence in children and young people, in Cefai, C. and Cooper, P., (eds.) *Promoting emotional education. Engaging children and young people with social, emotional and behavioural difficulties,* London: Jessica Kingsley.

Persson, B., (2003) Exclusive and inclusive discourses in special education research and policy in Sweden, *International journal of inclusive education,* 7(3): 271-280.

Persson, B., (2004) Specialpedagogik och dokumentation i en skola för alla. En fråga om likvärdighet, rättvisa eller rättigheter? *Utbildning och demokrati,* 13(2): 97-113.

Reed, R., (1999) Troubling boys and disturbing discourses on masculinity and schooling: a feminist exploration of current debates and interventions concerning boys' in school, *Gender and education.* 11(1): 93-110.

Rutherford, R., Quinn, M. and Mathur, S., (2004) *Handbook of research in emotional and behavioral disorders,* New York: Guilford Press.

Sacks, H., (1972) On the analyzability of stories by children, in Gumperz, J. and Hymes, D., (eds.) *Directions in sociolinguistics: The ethnography of communication,* New York: Rinehart and Winston, 325-345.

Sacks, H., (1995) *Lectures on conversation. Volume I and II,* Oxford: Blackwell Publisher.

Sarangi, S. and Roberts, C., (1999) The dynamics of interactional and institutional orders in work-related settings, in Sarangi, S. and Roberts, C. (eds.) *Talk, work and institutional order. Discourse in medical, mediation and management setting,* Berlin: Walter de Gruyter, 1-57.

SFS 1985: 1100, *Swedish Education act.* Stockholm: Allmänna Förlaget.

SFS 2010: 800, *Swedish Education Act.* Stockholm: Fritzes.

SNAE (The Swedish National Agency for Education). (2014). *Arbeta med extra anspassningar, särskilt stöd och åtgärdsprogram. Allmänna råd med kommentarer.* [Work with additional adjustments, special educational needs support and individual education plans. General guidelines with comments], Stockholm: Fritzes.

Soles, T., Bloom, E., Heath, N. and Karagiannakis, A., (2008) An exploration of teachers' current perceptions of children with emotional and behavioural difficulties, *Emotional and behavioural difficulties,* 13(4): 275-290.

Taylor, M., (2003) *Going round in circles: Implementing and learning from Circle Time,* Slough, United Kingdom: National Foundation for Educational Research.

Tholander, M., (2002) *Doing morality in school. Teasing, gossip and subteaching as collaborative action,* Thesis (PhD), Linköping University.

Unesco, (1994) The Salamanca statement and framework for action on special educational needs, Paris: Unesco. http://www.unesco.org/education/pdf/SALAMA_E.PDF [Accessed June 6 2015].

United Nations, (1989) Convention on the rights of the child, New York: United Nations.

Visser, J. and Jehan, Z., (2009) ADHD: A scientific fact or a factual opinion? A critique of the veracity of Attention Deficit Hyperactive Disorder, *Emotional and behavioural difficulties,* 14(2): 127-140.

West, C. and Zimmerman, D., (2009) Accounting for doing gender, *Gender and society,* 23(1): 112-122.

Widdicombe, S., (1998) But you don't class yourself. The interactional management of category membership and non-membership, in Antaki, C. and Widdicombe, S., (eds.) *Identities in talk,* London: Sage, 52-70.

Widdicombe, S. and Wooffitt, R., (1995) *The Language of youth subcultures. Social identity in action,* Hemel Hempsted, United Kingdom: Harvester Wheatsheaf.

Chapter 6

Troubling normativities? Constructing sexual and gender diversity in the educational work of Finnish LGBTI human rights association Seta

Jukka Lehtonen

Introduction

Many lesbian, gay, bisexual, trans and intersex (or intergender) (LGBTI) associations undertake educational outreach work in the Nordic countries to advance knowledge on sexual and gender diversity, to help students, teachers, and other professionals, to acknowledge them and take them into account. This is necessary because educational institutions and professionals often lack the information and the tools to engage with such diversity, both in Finland and in other Nordic countries.[1] Although Nordic countries are often seen as front-runners in the fields of equality and justice, there is still much to be done in challenging heteronormative education practices. LGBTI human rights associations are criticising, and perhaps troubling, the heteronormative education system with their educational outreach work. It might also be asked whether they are challenging the structures of the system or just filling in the obvious gaps within a narrow area and adding to the knowledge of sexual and gender diversity by engaging in educational outreach work.

I focus on how gender and sexuality are constructed within the educational outreach work of Seta, a Finnish national LGBTI human rights association for twenty-four member associations. Seta does various kinds of human rights advocacy work, and educational outreach work is part of that. I understood Seta challenges the current heteronormative education system by offering knowledge on sexual and gender diversity to school students, but in this chapter I reveal how also Seta's own educational outreach work needs challenging.

I base my theoretical framework on a constructionist, feminist and queer theoretical thinking of sexuality and gender (Butler, 1990: 2004; Duggan, 2002; Foucault, 1984; Rubin, 1984; Sedgwick, 1991; Spivak, 1990; Vance,

1 Research in Finland (Alanko, 2013; Huotari et al., 2011; Karvinen, 2008; Lehtonen, 2003, 2010, 2014a; Suhonen, 2014; Taavetti, 2015) and in other Nordic countries (Bromseth & Wildow, 2007; Kjaran, 2014; Martinsson & Reimers, 2008; Rothing, 2008; Takacs, 2006).

1989; Warner, 1999; Weeks, 1986; Wittig, 1989). Developing from the 1970s onwards these feminist and social scientific works question binary gender thinking, heterosexist worldviews, and the focus on stable and categorical sexual and gender identities They also question essentialist or biologically based understandings of sexualities and gender, while also emphasising the need for intersectional analysis and the challenging of existing normativities around sex and the family.

I use the concepts of heteronormativity and homonormativity to analyse the educational outreach work. Heteronormativity refers to a way of thinking or reacting that refuses to see diversity in sexual orientation and gender, and that considers a certain way of expressing or experiencing gender and sexuality to be better than another. This includes normative heterosexuality and gender normativity, according to which only women and men are considered to exist in the world. Men are supposed to be masculine in the *right* way and women feminine in the *right* way. According to heteronormative thinking, gender groups are internally homogeneous, are each other's opposites, and are hierarchical, in that men and maleness are considered more valuable than women and femaleness. The heterosexual maleness of men and the heterosexual femaleness of women are emphasised and are understood to have biological origins. The existence of other sexualities or genders is denied, devalued or othered (see also Rossi, 2006; Martinsson and Reimers, 2008; Butler, 1990; Lehtonen, 2003; Wittig, 1989).

Lisa Duggan defines homonormativity as a 'politics that does not contest dominant heteronormative assumptions and institutions but upholds and sustains them while promising the possibility of a demobilised gay constituency and a privatised, depoliticised gay culture anchored in domesticity and consumption' (Duggan, 2002: 179). Homonormativity is used here as to analyse how Seta's educational outreach work supports and challenges the dominant understanding of sexuality and gender, in which heterosexuality and gender normative cis-genderism[2] are taken for granted as natural and normal starting points. Homonormativity includes in this analysis that kind of politics and understanding of sexuality and gender diversity in which heterosexuality and cisgenderism is accepted as normality and in which the aim is seen as opening

2 The term cis-gender is used to describe persons who are not trans. The term emerged in trans activist discourses that criticised the typical ways of using *man* and *woman* as natural starting points when talking on gender. *Cisgender* (or cis woman/ cis man) can be used in discussion on gender diversity without reproducing underlying norms associated with cisness (see Stryker, 2008).

or enlarging this cisgender heterosexual based normality to include LGBTI people. Within this kind homonormative thinking and strategy heteronormative structures are only partially criticised. The aim of trying to fit LGBTI people into normality, which is based on cisgender heterosexuality, can also include strategies that prevent visibility of sides of sexual and gender diversity which can be seen as problematic in aiming to fit LGBTI people into this normality.

I will first describe and analyse how the educational outreach work is organised in Seta and what kind of significance is given to it. Then I will analyse five key tensions from the point of view of constructing sexuality and gender. There are several issues which are controversial in the educational outreach work of Seta, and which also create discussion inside and outside the association. Here I will discuss aspects which could be named and analysed as tensions between universalistic identity-centred policy on the one hand and context-focused norm-challenging policy on the other. The more traditional Finnish LGBTI movement includes aspects which are common to universalistic identity-centred policy. Context-focused norm-challenging policy includes aspects which have become more popular especially in recent years, but which have been discussed from the 1970s onwards in feminist and social constructionist theorisation of sexuality and gender, and in queer studies from the 1990s onwards.[3] I argue that both universalistic identity-centred and context-focused norm-challenging policies exist side-by-side within the educational outreach work of Seta (see Sedgwick, 1991). In both of these policies heteronormative thinking, including binary gender thinking, is criticised. That is a fruitful starting point, and I want to emphasise that I have an over-all positive attitude towards the educational outreach work of Seta. I was developing this outreach work in early 1990s as the first Educational Secretary of the organisation. I will argue though that universalistic identity-centred policy includes homonormative tendencies which makes it difficult to fully resist heteronormativity in practice. My aim here is to support the current development of educational outreach work and I hope that it will adopt in the near future more aspects of the context-focused norm-challenging policy and resist the temptations of the universalistic identity-centred policy.

3 There are certain aspects of context-focused norm-challenging policy which are familiar from queer research and pedagogy, but context-focused norm-challenging policy is understood here to be distinct from queer pedagogy (see more on queer pedagogy: Bromseth & Wildow, 2007; Juvonen, 2014; Lehtonen, 2003; Martinsson & Reimers, 2008).

The discussion around universalistic identity-centred and context-focused norm-challenging policies is a larger package of various kinds of elements which people either emphasise or minimise. They are all meaningful to the construction of sexuality and gender in educational outreach work, but most of them are not pondered upon critically enough when educational activists are trained. The tensions of this discussion are the following: 1.) nature versus nurture; 2.) essentialism versus constructionism; 3.) abstract and pure LGBTI categories versus blurred identifications and intersecting differences; 4.) social versus sexual; and 5) focus on couples and families versus focus on diverse life situations. In a universalistic identity-focused policy, LGBTI identities are seen as based on biological factors and/or otherwise essentialistically constructed, and they are seen as universal, stable, and coherent identities free from other differences and not dependant on various life-situations and interests. A context-based norm-challenging policy, on the other hand, questions this kind of thinking, emphasising sexual and gender diversity, and intersecting differences, as well as normativities around them, while the various contexts in which people live their sexual and gendered lives are taken into account. I have constructed these policies based on my observation and analysis, and they are overlapping.

Ethnographic data on educational outreach work

I focused in my research project on LGBTI human rights association in Seta's youth work. I was interested in how sexuality, gender and other differences are constructed within youth work; what issues are discussed and what topics silenced; how youth, young people's agency and power are understood; and how the youth work of Seta is seen as part of the larger society and global interaction. Areas which I studied with Seta's youth work include national political advocacy around youth issues, educational outreach work, youth peer-group work, as well as youth related projects.

I did a multi-sited non-governmental organisation ethnography (see Honkasalo, 2011) on Seta's youth work, observing several occasions and events related to youth work and educational outreach work for over a year in 2013 and in 2014.[4] I kept a research diary, gathered documents, data on the internet and photos, and carried out fourteen ethnographic interviews. I interviewed employees of both Seta and its cooperation partners as well as young people in peer-support groups. I recorded not only the interviews but also many discussions in various educational seminars and meetings. In my

4 See more detailed discussion on my methodological choices Lehtonen & Taavetti, forthcoming.

research project I also used interviews of young people and material they have produced themselves as well as survey data (see more on this data Alanko, 2013; Taavetti, 2015).

I did my research as part of a large Finnish-South African research collaboration project, which was focused on young people, sexualities and gender. I visited Cape Town, South Africa, for six months, producing research data in the local LGBTI organisations (Triangle and GenderDynamiX). I interviewed five activists or researchers and observed several situations and seminars. I also gathered written material. The data produced there as well as the experiences I wrote about in my research diary helped me to look at Seta's youth work from a different angle. It made me think, for example, more about how the funding of the organisations affects the work and strategies. By looking from a distance, from another cultural viewpoint, I also had a chance to see the situation in Finland differently (see also Ratele, 2015). I focused more than before on various aspects such as racism, ethnic and socioeconomic differences in my analysis.

As I formerly had been an employee and an activist of Seta and had studied non-heterosexual and trans youth for a long time, I assumed that most of Seta's activities would be familiar to me. In the early phase of my ethnography, however, I understood that many aspects in Seta's youth work were new to me and that I would have difficulties in finding my way around the field (see Lehtonen, 2014b). It took time to get to know the new people, things, concepts and situations. It took more time and energy to find out how to gain contact with the youth peer-groups than it had in mid-1990s when I had done interviews with young non-heterosexual people for my dissertation research project, soon after I had finished my work as Seta's Educational Secretary (Lehtonen, 2003; see also Gordon et al., 2006). At that time, I felt that the association was familiar to me, but after twenty years many things were changed or new. My own position both as researcher and as Seta's Educational Secretary in the early 1990s made me think about how to challenge my own presumptions in relation to educational outreach work and Seta's youth related work in general.

I have analysed my position (see Lehtonen, 2014b; Taavetti and Lehtonen, forthcoming) and tried to take distance on my presumptions of Seta. I have pondered upon my experiences and their influence on this ethnographic project with the help of autoethnographic writing (see Ellis and Bochner, 2000; Chang, 2008; Crawley, 2012; Hearn, 2013; Ng, 2013). By analysing my own experiences, memories and the past I aimed at understanding my own premises for research. In addition, I aimed at constructing a temporal perspective for my work to help me to locate my research topic: Seta's youth work including the current educational outreach work. In going through my own experiences and doing the active memory work–which was partly done in the international research project–which was inspired by the thoughts of Frigga Haug (2014; see also Jansson et al., 2008; Widerberg, 2011). The memory work and autoethnographical approach stimulated me to look at Seta's youth work from historical and temporal perspectives. The current work could not be seen as self-evident or automatic but as a part of a longer development process and constant change (Lehtonen, 2014b). I also used this temporal aspect in my research interviews, asking the interviewees of their conceptions of the 1980s situation in the youth work of Seta. This helped me to understand how the interviewees saw the current situation compared to the past.

The chapter is based on some part of my ethnography on LGBTI youth work and non-heterosexual and trans young people's agency and transitions (see Lehtonen, 2014a, 2014b).[5] I have produced data within Seta during 2013-2014.[6] The data I selected from my overall data to use here relates to educational outreach work, which I understood in my research project as part of youth work.

The data I use here consists of twelve ethnographic interviews conducted with employees of Seta and its co-operation partners (from other associations or projects with which Seta was involved), observation data, and other material, such as leaflets, posters, and internet sites, related to outreach work. Ethnographic observation was done in several educational settings, including a three-hour session at an upper secondary school in which Seta activists and employees provided outreach training as part of the school's theme day on

5 By non-heterosexual, I mean a qualitative term used to describe a person who has sexual feelings towards or practices with their own gender, or self-definitions that refer to these feelings or practices (such as lesbian, gay, or bisexual). Trans refers to a person, who challenges the gendered norms and expectations in a way that their gender designed at birth contradicts the gender they identify with or express.

6 The interviewed co-operation partners of Seta were typically employees of projects of which Seta was part, and employees in other non-governmental associations that were in close co-operation with Seta. This research project is part of the research collaboration projects *Engaging South African and Finnish youth towards new traditions of non-violence, equality and social wellbeing* (2013-2016, grant number 271546) and *Social and Economic Sustainability of Future Working Life: Policies, Equalities and Intersectionalities in Finland* (2015-2017, grant number 292883), which are funded by the Academy of Finland. I am a member of the Nordic Centre of Excellence *Justice Through Education in the Nordic countries*. I would like to thank Seta and all the interviewees and people who helped me to produce data, and for the comments on this article by Jon Invar Kjaran, Riikka Taavetti, Deborah Youdell and the editors of this book.

well-being, as well as a training seminar for youth workers on LGBTI issues organised by Seta. Also offered were, a presentation on trans youth and children for teachers in a large annual event for teachers organised by the Teacher's Trade Union, and a two-day training seminar for Seta's voluntary educational activists. I was an observer at these educational sessions, gathering material used in the sessions, recording some sessions, writing field notes and afterwards entering my reflections in my research diary. The citations of data I use in the chapter are from the interviews, recorded educational sessions and published material. I have used this data to analyse the dynamics of negotiation within sexual and gendered language, and examine how the language used in educational work can be linked to a broader understanding of sexuality and gender (see Blackburn, 2012).

Filling the gaps—Seta's educational outreach work and its significance

In this section I describe, based on my ethnographic interviews and observations, how Seta's educational outreach work is organised, and what kind of significance the interviewees give to it. Seta trained voluntary educational activists from its local twenty-two member associations (at the time of the data production), which were mainly responsible for organising the outreach work at educational institutions in their area. Also Seta's employees, such as the Educational Secretary, the Youth Coordinator and the Social Secretary of the Transgender support centre, did some educational work, especially if the local association did not have enough resources. Based on the information I received from the employees in the interviews, I would estimate that there were around 200 educational activists, and they made 200-300 visits to educational sites annually. This means that every year thousands of people had the opportunity to hear an activist or an employee from Seta talking about LGBTI issues. I estimate that, annually, Seta provided training on LGBTI issues to around five to ten per cent out of each age group of 60,000 young people in Finland. There were higher numbers in the larger towns where Seta has active member associations, and lower ones in the countryside and small towns. Seta had and still has a significant role in constructing the idea of sexual and gender diversity in the Finnish education system.[7]

7 Seta and its member associations also participate in large conferences and festivals, such as the annual professional conferences of school health professionals, teachers, and social workers, as well as human rights and cultural festivals, in which Seta has its own table, with information and activists talking to participants. These situations can be meaningful in spreading the

Most educational outreach visits were to lower or upper secondary educational institutions, or to youth centres and camps, so the recipients of the training were mostly young people. Professional training was also organised mostly for other young people, such as students in tertiary education. According to Seta's Educational Secretary voluntary educational activists–also mainly young people–made about ninety per cent of the school visits, which is the most common form of educational work in Seta. Seta's Social Secretary of member association saw educational activism as part of youth work, and young people's participation as beneficial to their self-esteem. Most of the voluntary activists were non-heterosexual, with various identifications, and there were also some trans people, as well as a few cisgendered heterosexuals taking part in educational outreach work. The majority of the voluntary educators were women.[8] Most of the voluntary educational activists had been trained by Seta. The basic training enabled participants to make a school visit and talk about sexual and gender diversities in general, as well as speaking about their own experiences in relation to LGBTI issues. The special training gave them more knowledge on specific topics, such as intersexuality and teaching methods. There was also training for persons who focus on telling their personal life-story or experiences around aspects of their sexual orientation or gender identity as a so-called experience educator.

The Educational Secretary saw the aim of outreach work as not just filling the gaps in young people's and teacher's knowledge, but rather mobilising them to transform the entire education system. Often though, the free educational outreach visits were repeated year after year at the same schools, and teachers hardly ever took responsibility for changing the curricula or questioning its heteronormativity. There were not enough resources to transform the entire system and Seta was typically just responding to the superficial needs of schools, which consist of information that *fills the gaps*, instead of using the knowledge to criticise the heteronormative practises of the school or helping teachers to develop their own abilities so they can include sexual and gender diversity in

---

information to professionals, who might then become more aware of LGBTI issues in their work, and in turn reach young people, for example in schools. In 2013 Seta delivered 600 LGBTI youth specific training DVDs to teachers at a teachers' fair called *Educa*.

8 The majority of the people trained are women, but in schools and youth groups there are almost an even number of men and women, though there are more visits to general upper secondary institution, in which the majority of students are women, compared to vocational upper secondary institutions. Participants in the professional training are mainly women, while women dominate in the educational programs, such as nursing, social work and teaching.

their curricula and pedagogical interactions. The Educational Secretary describes Seta's educational outreach work as 'more like a first aid at a societal level', and she saw that the responsibility lies with the public sector. When asked whether there would still be a need for educational outreach work if the public sector accepted their responsibility to transform the education system, the Educational Secretary answered that there would still be a need for the experience-based knowledge gained from outreach work.

Seta received and still gets its funding for educational work from the National Slot Machine Association and from Ministries.[9] This was not seen to directly influence the content of the education, but it was mentioned that it might make Seta's approach slightly less courageous than it would otherwise have been. Schools were also seen to hesitate to ask for visits from Seta if they thought that the training would aggressively question the basic structures of the school. This point was also made in the interview with the Educational Secretary: 'We are now gently telling people that there are genders other than man and woman, and that could make people very upset, if we do it in a feisty way'. Seta is in active partnership with some ministries, but in the interview Seta's Secretary General made it clear that 'there is still a long way to go' before the situation is satisfactory. She stated that even if Seta visits schools, and even if some schools ask for these visits regularly, the underlying structural problem still lie at the foundations of the education system:

> The requirements of our curriculum documents are not demanding enough, nor are the requirements for teacher training, and so on, they are missing at the structural level. Though many people are pleased that someone is dealing with issues of sexual and gender minority youth in society, and in the lives of all young people, there are many who think that it is the business of Seta alone. That makes it unequal in a way, while with that kind of thinking majority youth would get support, service, information and teaching from the public services. There is some kind of ghetto thinking, and we don't want to have that kind of role, or aim at having. Our projects are filling the gaps. While there was no scientific information produced, we produced a research project, and when there was no norm critical study material available, we had a project, where it

9 Many non-governmental organisations get funding from the National Slot Machine Association for their work especially in the area of health and social work.

was developed.[10] We hope that, in the future, this would change so that the actors who are responsible would do this work themselves.[11]

The above extract from the General Secretary's interview expressed a tension between *filling the gaps* and the more transformational approach expressed in all the interviews with Seta employees. Seta is a publicly funded non-governmental association which educates thousands of mainly young people annually, but it has not been able to change the structures and curricula of the heteronormative education system. The demand for more progress in this direction has been expressed in many interviews, yet currently Seta continues mainly to *fill in* some of the gaps in the unjust and unequal heteronormative education system. Government funding posits Seta as responsible for taking care of sexual and gender minority youth. This might influence the public education system so that it sees the responsibility of sexual and gender diversity issues as Seta's field of activity, instead of their own. Even though Seta sees the situation as problematic, not much has been done to change it, and one can question how public funding or the heteronormative culture of the schools has influenced the content of Seta's educational outreach work.

Tensions and norms around identities and differences

Traces of both universalistic identity-centred policy and context-based norm-critical policy can be found in almost each interview and observed educational setting, and often even in a single sentence of an interviewee. In this section, I will analyse the tensions between nature versus nurture, essentialism versus constructionism, and abstract and pure LGBTI categories versus blurred identifications and intersecting differences.

I was fairly surprised that in the educational sessions I followed it was mentioned that homosexuality or gender diversity is part of natural development or has biological origins. When I worked as Seta's Educational Secretary in the early 1990s discussion of the biological origin of homosexuality was common in the media, and in Seta's educational outreach work critical stances were taken on these biological explanations. During my observation the discussion of biological origins came up in high school training, in a youth work seminar,

10 See Alanko, 2013; *Älä oleta – Normit nurin,* [*Do not assume–the norms!*] 2013.

11 The citations from the data have been edited and shortened partly to make them clearer, and partly to make them more anonymous. I sometimes mention the professional status of the interviewee, sometimes not.

and at the teachers' fair training. During Seta's educational visit to a general upper secondary institution Seta's Chairperson mentioned that homosexuality is something you are born with. In the training for youth workers a researcher, who was a co-operation partner of Seta, explained that biological causes had been found for sexual orientation. The leading social worker at Seta's Transgender support centre said in her speech at the teachers' fair that gender diversity is part of nature's diversity:

> In every one of us there are both masculine and feminine sides, and this is also a genetic issue, which determines how much we have of these kinds of characteristics genetically, which is then in our culture understood as girlyness or boyishness. [...] Gender diversity is part of humanity, and it is also known in nature, for example if you think of the animal world, there are frogs in Kilpisjärvi [in Northern Finland] which can change sex, and also certain species of fish are known which can transform themselves into a different sex. This is part of natural diversity, but at the same time it belongs to humanity.

During the last thirty years a considerable amount of scientific and popular literature on the biological causes of homosexuality have been published, and there have been criticism of this literature. Scientists have been seen to take animal physiology and behaviour to be the natural foundations for understanding the sexual expressions of humans, or more likely the cultural norms were first projected to into the animal world and then *the culture* was interpreted through *the nature* (Terry, 2000). Often biological reasoning has been used as a strategy to normalise non-normative sexualities and genders and seek acceptance for them (Lancaster, 2003; Sedgwick, 1991). This strategy includes a rather homonormative message, that 'we, as gays or trans, are as natural as cisgendered heterosexuals, and that is why you should accept us'. This leaves the normativities unquestioned.

The cultural and historical aspects of sexuality and gender were also raised in many observed educational settings, so the biological model was not the only one to attract attention. But there was no discussion of the causes of sexual orientation or gender identity in the training of activists for educational outreach; and they were not asked to talk about biological reasoning (nature) nor to explain sexuality and gender identity as cultural, historical and social constructions which were adopted from the surrounding culture as part of our upbringing (nurture). While this issue was not dealt during the training of activists, the decision on whether to emphasise the influence of nature or nurture was left to the individual outreach activists.

This nature/nurture tension can also be read as part of a discussion of essentialism versus constructionism. These discussions were familiar from the 1980s onwards in research, the media and in the LGBTI movements internationally (Vance, 1989; Weeks, 1986) as well as in the Finnish discussion (Lehtonen, 1995; Löfström, 1993; Pulkkinen, 1993). They were also topics in the early 1990s training, which I organised as Educational Secretary, for Seta's educational activists. The essentialist discourse expects an inherent and usually stable cause for people's sexual orientation. This can be, among others, an a/typical gene, dis/function during pregnancy, under/developed or ab/normal psyche, or a socially structured deviant or normal coherent and stable identity. Often in earlier essentialist thinking, homosexuality was seen as a problem in development and identity structure, but essentialism does not demand a negative approach towards homosexuality. It can be seen within essentialist thinking also as a healthy, well developed and normal alternative compared to heterosexuality, which typically is homonormatively seen as such from the start. The constructionist view questions the notion of inherent and stable identity, and it may find the whole understanding of sexual orientation and gender identity to be a cultural, a historical and a social discourse. Sexual and gender identities are seen as something that is possible to shape. It also questions heterosexuality and cisgenderism as a starting-point of normalcy, and analyses them as cultural and often linguistic products, which have an influence on social structures and everyday practices. Even if neither essentialism nor constructionism were used as terms in Seta's educational outreach work, I would argue, that elements of both kinds of thinking were present in it, as one can see from in the interview citation above and in the citation below.

The focus on identities was clear in the educational outreach work (see also Löfström, 1993). In Seta a person's identity was often linked to one sexual or gender category. A common strategy to start the outreach training was the listing of LGBTI letters and asking what they meant. This list of letters was typical of the educational material used in the training of educational activists. This categorisation and its visualisation as a list of terms (LGBTI) in educational outreach work makes people think of sexual and gender diversities through an abstract categorisation of people into pure and single category-based identities. The Educational Secretary spoke about this dilemma and realised the problem in trying to fit diversity into a system of categorisation, but still emphasised the power of presenting clear categories in educational work (see Spivak on strategic essentialism, 1990):

> These are culturally specific concepts, and changing, humanity cannot be put into these categories, but in a way it helps if you know what it is all about, especially in the case of identity process it would be good that the young boy in a high school will know what a transvestite is. Then he realises, that I am normal that I am not the only freak in the world, and that it is acceptable.

The listing of different terms, and at same time categories of identities, produces an understanding as to which various sexual and gender categories are seen as homogeneous inside and having clear boundaries outside. However, many people have various kinds of other meaningful parallel identities, and they do not fit or do not want to fit into a single and stable sexual or gender category (one from LGBTI), or they live in various life situations in which LGBTI-categorisation does not make sense. Judith Butler notes in the preface of the second edition of her book *Gender Trouble* that 'mobilisation of identity categories for politicisation always remains threatened by the prospect of identity becoming an instrument of the power one opposes' (Butler, 1990: 26). I understand her supporting identity politics as a way of getting recognised in discriminatory culture, but at the same time criticising it for creating problems for those who do not fit into the identity categories emphasised. One co-operation partner of Seta argued in an interview that many young people are left out of sight if identity politics is emphasised (see also Lehtonen, 1998).

> I think that it is not very clear, these experiences about gender and sexuality are not clear in the same way that in the association, in which you formulate that here is the identity, and then one is discriminated against based on that identity.

One way of questioning the pure LGBTI-categorisation-based identity approach is to analyse and discuss the other meaningful social and cultural differences which are intertwined in people's lives and experiences. These differences can relate to gender, age, health, ability, ethnicity, religious or cultural background and language, or to social class and urban/rural differences. Though an in-depth discussion of possible parallel identities and intersecting differences did not belong in the basic training of educational activists in Seta. Some of the issues are dealt with, to some extent, in educational outreach work, but not systematically and automatically. In Seta's project with student associations the intersecting differences were actively discussed and material on the themes produced, but the viewpoints of this project were not adopted actively in the Seta's outreach work (*Älä oleta–Normit nurin!* [*Do not assume–down with the norms!*], 2013). The issue is understood to be important at some level, but the actual ways of finding the connections between intersecting differences are still negotiable and constructed.

There is, on the other hand, concentration on LGBTI-specific issues, which are seen as clean and clear of other differences, and then there is the linkage to other minorities, that face discrimination in society (see Ciszek, 2014). Anti-discrimination legislation brings certain groups or differences together and the interaction between Seta and other human rights activists influences educational outreach work. It was briefly mentioned in the activist training that LGBTI people have different backgrounds in relation to ethnicity and to some other differences. The Educational Secretary mentioned that this issue is taken into account more often nowadays, and the topic comes up in the practical exercises during educational visits. For example, the cards used in the training sometimes have characters such as a seventeen-year-old gay who has an immigrant background, or a similar character with a disability and non-normative sexual orientation or gender identity. On the other hand, she mentioned that educational activists do not usually have enough knowledge and training in issues such as religion or HIV, and therefore these aspects should not be dealt with during outreach visits.

There has been an effort to include diversity issues in Seta's educational outreach work, but it has not always been very successful. A good example of this is a photo, poster and slide series produced by Seta for educational and informational purposes. The production of this material was a major effort for Seta, and that is why this is important data for the analysis of how sexuality and gender is constructed in Seta. This material was criticised for the way ethnicity and religion was handled and was seen to be incorrect (see Jungar and Peltonen, 2015). In this photo series *Love is love* [in Finnish *Rakkaus on rakkautta*] four pictures were shown of couples: one man-woman couple, one transwoman/transvestite-woman couple, one man-man couple, and one woman-woman couple. In the heterosexual and trans themed couple photos the people were white, in the man-man couple one was black and the other one white, and in the woman-woman couple one had a scarf over her head, representing a Moslem, and the other one was white. The aim seemed to be to represent different kinds of couples and to emphasise the equality between different kinds of love, with intersecting ethnicity or religion and sexual orientation. The reaction towards the poster series was not entirely positive, and the woman-woman poster raised most questions. The poster series was distributed to Helsinki City youth centres and the woman-woman poster was removed in at least one centre, especially as Moslem youths had reacted against it. The reasons were, if I understood correctly based on the interviews, that they were the only couple who kissed, and public kissing by a Moslem woman, whether with a man or a woman, was seen as problematic, as was the way the Moslem woman was represented in the photo. She was not a real Moslem, but someone who portrayed a Moslem, and the scarf had not been tied in the proper Moslem way. After the episode in the youth centre Seta still had all four posters on their office wall, and used them as part of a slide series for educational outreach work. In an interview with a co-operation partner of Seta it was suggested that there might have been a question of lack of resources for producing more sensitive educational materials. Including diverse intersecting aspects in a correct way for the educational outreach work can be time-consuming and difficult, but this work is needed to overcome the narrow image of LGBTI people.

In Seta's educational outreach work intersecting differences are seen to matter to a certain extent but there is still much to be learned. Compared to the early 1990s when I worked in Seta and produced educational material the topics of intersecting differences were clearly more invisible. Finnish society has changed into being more diverse and this is pressuring Seta to take these differences into account. When intersecting differences are not actively discussed during educational outreach work, LGBTI people are easily constructed as white, able-bodied, healthy, and middle-class, and normativities around various differences and problematic practices like racism are left unquestioned. White, able-bodied, healthy, and middle-class LGBTI people might fit more easily to the normalcy based on the Finnish heterosexual and cisgendered norms, but the policy focusing only or mainly on these people does not take into account others who might be even more in need of equal practices in education and in the society at large.

Tensions and norms around sex and family

Sex and family, and normative thinking on them, raised discussions in relation to Seta's educational outreach work. The topics were whether Seta should emphasise sexual practices and desires or refuse to deal with those in the educational outreach work, and whether it should focus on rainbow families and stable same-sex partnerships instead of emphasising the various ways of forming intimate relationships. The current school curricula on sex education are analysed to emphasise medical and normalising discourses of sexuality and gender, and are seen to focus on married couples and nuclear family constellations (see Honkasalo, 2014; Lehtonen, 2016). In that sense Seta's policy on sex and family in educational outreach work is understandable, but many–also in my interview data–criticised it for being too conservative.

Sex is not a topic focused on in Seta educational outreach work, and instead of sexuality it was at various times stated that LGBTI identities should be seen as social identities. This also became clear in Seta's training of educational activists, when the Educational Secretary stated that:

> The first thing is that sex is not a number one topic of Seta, [though this was said in a funny way]. Educating people about sex and sexuality is not part of Seta's objectives. [...] You will not get the ability to talk about these things during this weekend, as we don't talk about them. [...] Our area of speciality is sexual orientation and gender diversity, and the focus is on human rights.

In an interview the Educational Secretary expressed the same idea and said that it was a pity there was still the linkage between sex and gays, and that the focus should be, instead of sex or sexuality,'sexual orientation and gender diversity, preferably a little bit about rainbow families, and our viewpoint is human rights, the social aspect point'. There has been a change in this policy concerning sex from the early 1990s to today. In the past, partly based on the AIDS/HIV crises of the 1980s and the early1990s there was a huge need to educate people on safer sex and that was also undertaken within Seta's educational outreach work. There is still no proper non-normative safer sex education in schools, but there are many HIV transmissions between men having sex with men (Heikkinen, 2011; Lehtonen, 2016). This is not acknowledged in the current outreach work. This current no-sex strategy is partly justified by the over-sexualisation of people with non-normative sexualities and genders. The emphasis and demand to talk about *the sexual orientation diversity*, instead of sexual diversity and sexuality in general, is a strategy to avoid talking about groups other than gays, lesbians and bisexuals, such as asexuals, sado-maschocists, and pansexuals. There have been discussions in Seta's member associations and in general on the position of talking about sex in educational outreach work, and also in general when thinking about Seta's policy and image.[12] This unwillingness to talk about sex has raised discussion and was even named *sex-negativity* in the interviews, especially among the co-operation partners of Seta. The distinction between sexual and social aspects was questioned, particularly in regarding the life of young people. Seta's decision to distance itself from sex and diverse sexualities was seen as strategic, but problematic.

> School sex education or anything else, for example the media, does not reach the youth when it comes to gay sex, or at least in a way which would be identifiable or positive, but the topic or questions around it is one that is on the minds of many young people. My experience of the sexphobia of Seta, sex related questions are avoided, and even the word sexual is cleaned away. [...] And there is this side to it, that at the same time you will kick out some groups of people for whom being part of a minority is sexual. It feels funny sometimes, when these words with *sexual*-endings will be avoided, and it is quite an irritating thing. This is far from the view that sex is positive, and you rather get the idea of it as something to be covered and be ashamed of, which is not the aim. And it is also a bit contrary to the over-sexualisation of media and society, and the hiding of sex in Seta feels a bit funny. It sounds like gay sex would be especially dangerous, when you cannot talk about it.

Sex-negativity can be seen as problematic in the sense that it tries to erase the unwanted sexual image of sexual and gender minorities, and replace this sexual image with an image of morally acceptable citizens with rights (see Rubin, 1984; Warner, 1999). I see this as a sign of homonormativity.

A key issue of Seta during the last twenty years has been the equal-marriage legislation and the rights of rainbow families.[13] These topics started to become

12 Seta has changed its official name, which used to be Seksuaalinen Tasavertaisuus [Sexual Equality], into the shorter version of Seta.

13 In Finland it has been possible to register relationship between same-sex couples since 2002,

important in the early 1990s but they were not framing the educational outreach work as much as today. In the training of educational activists, the issue of rainbow families was mentioned as a topic you should talk about during educational visits. There were practices in which the right vocabulary should be practiced around the issue[14] Couples were also portrayed in Seta's new poster series called *Love is love*. There were no singles portrayed in this series or relationships of more than two persons. This kind of family and couple-centred discussion leaves out any discussion on polyamory, multiple relationships, open and closed relationships of men having sex with men, singles, asexuals, and aromantics. LGBTI movements have internationally, and also in Finland, been much criticised for the trend of focusing on marriage rights, and this has been seen as a construction of couple normativity (Butler, 2004; Lehtonen, 2009; Rubin, 1984; Rydström, 2011; Warner, 1999). Clearly, the focus on families and marriage and the discourses around these issues have included homonormative aspects, such as the arguments that same-sex couples are as good at taking care of their children as heterosexual couples. However, heteronormative love, marriage and family constellations have been used as ideal models and starting points for normalcy. This strategy has left little space to deal with the problems in same-sex relationships and rainbow families (Moring, 2013).

I would argue that the approaches which emphasise biological, essentialist and LGBTI-categorisation-based social identity focused views, as well as sex-negative, couple and family normative views, can include homonormative messages. Homonormativity in this case can mean begging for acceptance and normalisation for LGBTI-identified people, and leave heterosexuality and heteronormative structures and practises unquestioned. They do not take into account people's diversity and needs, and the diverse life situations in which LGBTI and other non-normative people live in.

---

and in 2014 Parliament approved the legislation for an equal marriage law, which came into force in 2017.

14 The terms *gay marriage*, *gay family*, *gender-neutral marriage*, *lesbian couple* were categorised as problematic or *no-no's*. The correct terms recommended were *equal marriage* law and *woman couple* [*naispari*]. In a way, a woman couple is more inclusive than a lesbian couple, while [sexual orientation or] identity of the partners can be lesbian, bisexual or something else. Maybe in the same sense *gay family* [*homoperhe*] was a more limited expression than *rainbow family* [*sateenkaariperhe*]. Also in the list of correct terms for the media the following terms were explained: registered partnership, rainbow family [*sateenkaariperhe*], inside adoption [*sisäinen adoptio*], outside adoption [*ulkoinen adoptio*].

Conclusions

The position of Seta in responding to the lack of a heteronormative education system is a difficult one. With a changing group of voluntary educational activists and over-burdened employees the non-governmental association should be able to transform the system and challenge the norms and structures which are reproduced by the public sector, teachers and politicians. Governmental funding of educational outreach work aims to add knowledge of sexual and gender diversity in education, but the dependence on such funding might also make it difficult for Seta to actively disturb the bases of current educational culture and its heteronormative starting-points. Or at least that seems to be the thinking of the people responsible for educational outreach work, to assess how radical one can be and still reach the public and the funding bodies. Seta has the important task of giving people more opportunities for recognising sexual and gender diversity, and it influences young people's lives with its educational work. If the education system were to start challenging its own heteronormativity more actively, and diversify its constructions of sexuality and gender, Seta could focus on the criticism of heteronormative culture, instead of having to eliminate gaps in the public's knowledge.

There are many tensions and discussions around the way Seta constructs sexuality and gender in its educational outreach work. Its more traditional universalistic identity-centred policy still plays a pivotal role in its educational outreach work. One can find many homonormative aspects within this family-focused sex-negative policy. Instead of focusing on criticising heteronormative models presented in the education system, it aims to achieve acceptance and normalcy for chosen groups of discriminated people side-by-side with already accepted and normalised heterosexual cisgendered people. To some extent it seems to be a strategy enabling Seta to work within the current heteronormative system, but mainly it seems to be an unproblematised strategy influenced by the heteronormative culture in which we all live. Universalistic identity-centred policy easily ignores people's diverse situations and backgrounds, whether it is a question of intersecting differences, often blurred and non-categorical sexualities or genders, or various kinds of sexual desires, relationships, families and life situations. It creates inequality between those who fit in to the identity categories presented in educational work and those who do not fit.

Context-focused norm-challenging policy, with its practical manifestations, is one opportunity to challenge universalistic identity-centred policy, and question the ways in which sexuality and gender are constructed in educational outreach work. It is important for Seta to ponder carefully upon what kind of constructions of sexuality and gender it should adopt in educational outreach work, and base the work in constructions, strategies and approaches whereby the heteronormative education system can most efficiently be challenged. More importantly, Finnish society and its educational institutions should fully engage with their responsibility to change the system into one which recognises diversity and questions normativity–perhaps with a little help from Seta.

References

Alanko, K., (2013) *Hur mår HBTIQ-unga i Finland?* [How well are LGBTQI young people doing in Finland?], Helsingfors: Ungdomsforskiningsnätverket and Seta.

Blackburn, M., (2012) *Interrupting hate: Homophobia in schools and what literacy can do about it*, New York: Teachers Collage Press.

Bromseth, J. and Wildow, H., (2007) *'Man kan ju inte läse om bögar in nån historiebok'. Skolors förändringsarbeten med focus på jämställdhet, genus och sexualitet* ['One cannot read about gays in the history books'. Schools' transformational work on equality, gender and sexuality], Stockholm: Friends.

Butler, J., (1990) *Gender trouble*, New York: Routledge.

Butler, J., (2004) *Undoing gender*, New York: Routledge.

Chang, H., (2008) *Autoethnography as method*, Walnut Creek: Left Coast.

Ciszek, E., (2014) *Identity, culture, and articulation: A critical-cultural analysis of strategic LGBT advocacy outreach*, Eugene: University of Oregon.

Crawley, S., (2012) Autoethnography as feminist self-interview, in Holstein, J. A., Gubrium, J. F., McKinney, K., and Marvasti, A., (eds.) *The SAGE handbook of interview research: The complexity of the craft*, Los Angeles: Sage, 143-160.

Duggan, L., (2002) The new homonormativity: The sexual politics of neoliberalism, in Castromore, R. and Nelson, D., (eds.) *Materialising democracy*, Durham: Duke University Press.

Ellis, C. and Bochner, A. P., (2000) Autoethnography, personal narrative, reflexivity: Researcher as subject, in Denzin, K.N. and Lincoln, Y., (eds.) *The handbook of qualitative research*, Thousand Oaks: Sage publications, 733-768.

Foucault, M., (1984) *The history of sexuality*, London: Penguin Books.

Gordon, T., Hynninen, P., Lahelma, E., Metso, T., Palmu, T. and Tolonen, T., (2006) Collective ethnography, joint experiences and individual pathways, *Nordisk Pedagogik*, 26(1): 3-15.

Haug, F., (2014) *Memory-work as method of social science research: A detailed rendering of memory-work method*, http://www.friggahaug.inkrit.de or http://www.friggahaug.inkrit.de/documents/memorywork-researchguidei7.pdf [Accessed 31 July 2014].

Hearn, J., (2013) On men, organizations and intersectionality. Personal, working, political and theoretical relations (or how organisation studies met profeminism), *Equality, diversity and inclusion*, 33(5): 414-428.

Heikkinen, T., (2011) *Peruskoulun terveystiedon seksuaalisuus seksuaalisen moninaisuuden näkökulmasta* [Sex education in basic education from the perspective of sexual diversity], Thesis, Helsinki: Metropolia.

Honkasalo, V., (2011) *Tyttöjen kesken: monikulttuurisuus ja sukupuolten tasa-arvo nuorisotyössä,* [Among girls: youth work, multiculturalism, and gender equality], Helsinki: Finnish youth research network.

Honkasalo, V., (2014) Exceptionalism and sexularism in Finnish sex education, *Global studies of childhood*, 4(4): 286-297.

Huotari, K., Törmä, S. and Tuokkola, K., (2011) *Syrjintä koulutuksessa ja vapaa-ajalla: Erityistarkastelussa seksuaali - ja sukupuolivähemmistöihin kuuluvien nuorten syrjintäkokemukset toisen asteen oppilaitoksissa* [Discrimination in education and leisure time: with special focus on discrimination experienced by young people belonging to sexual and gender minorities who study in the upper secondary education], Helsinki: Ministry of Interior Affairs.

Jansson, M., Wendt, M. and Åse, C., (2008) Memory work reconsidered, *Nordic journal of feminist and gender research,* 16(4): 228-240.

Jungar, K. and Peltonen S., (2015) 'Saving Muslim queer women from Muslim hetero-patriarchy' in LGBTI youth work in Finland, *Norma: International journal for masculinity studies*, 10(2): 136-149.

Juvonen, T., (2014) Kriittinen ja korjaava pervopedagogiikka luento-opetuksessa [Critical and reparative queer pedagogy in university lecturing], in Saarinen, J., Ojala, H. and Palmu, T., (eds.) *Eroja ja vaarallisia suhteita: keskustelua feministisestä pedagogiikasta* [Differences and dangerous relations: discussions on feminist pedagogy], Helsinki: FERA, 115-139.

Karvinen, M., (2008) Koulu [School], in Jämsä, J., (ed.) *Sateenkaariperheet ja hyvinvointi* [Rainbow families and well-being], Helsinki: PS-kustannus, 222-241.

Kjaran, J. I., (2014) *Queering the Icelandic upper secondary schools: Heteronormative discourse and the experiences of queer students in Icelandic upper secondary schools,* Thesis (PhD), University of Iceland.

Lancaster, R., (2003) *The trouble with nature. Sex in science and popular culture*, Berkeley: University of California Press.

Lehtonen, J., (1995) *Seksuaalivähemmistöt koulussa* [Sexual minorities in schools], Helsinki: Seta.

Lehtonen, J., (1998) Young people's definitions of their non-heterosexuality, in Helve, H., (ed.) *Unification and marginalisation of young people*, Helsinki: Finnish Youth Research Society, 185-192.

Lehtonen, J., (2003) *Seksuaalisuus ja sukupuoli koulussa* [Sexuality and gender at school], Helsinki: University Press.

Lehtonen, J., (2009) The diverse intimate relationships of non-heterosexual Finnish men, *Norma: International journal for masculinity studies,* 4(1): 66-82.

Lehtonen, J., (2010) Gendered post-compulsory educational choices of non-heterosexual youth, *European educational research journal,* 9(2): 177-191.

Lehtonen, J., (2014a) Sukupuolittuneita valintoja? Ei-heteroseksuaaliset ja transnuoret koulutuksessa [Gendered choices? Non-heterosexual and trans youth in education], *The Finnish journal of gender studies*, 27(4): 67-71.

Lehtonen, J., (2014b) Muistot ja ajallisuus - Setan nuorten toiminta muutoksessa [Memories and temporality - Seta's youth work in transition], *SQS: The journal of queer studies in Finland*, 8(1-2): 22-35.

Lehtonen, J., (2016) Sukupuolen ja seksuaalisuuden moninaisuus osana laaja-alaista seksuaalikasvatusta ja heteronormatiivisuuden purkamista [Gender and sexual diversity as part of Sex Education and questioning of heteronormativity], In

Bildjuschkin, K., (ed.) *Seksuaalikasvatuksen tueksi* [For the support of Sex Education], Helsinki: THL, 104-115.

Lehtonen, J. and Taavetti, R., (forthcoming) Ambivalent positions and challenging contexts in researching 'rainbow youth' in Finland, in Boonzaier, F., Hearn, J., Ratele, K. and Shefer, T., (eds.) *Gender, sex and race in research and pedagogical practices with young people: Transnational reflections on the politics of knowledge/praxis.*

Löfström, J., (1993) Identiteettipolitiikan loppu. Homo - ja lesbopolitiikka 2000-luvun kynnyksellä [The end of identity politics. Gay and lesbian politics in the threshold of the 21st century], *Tiede and Edistys*, 18(4): 284-297.

Martinsson, L. and Reimers, E., (eds.) (2008) *Skola i normer* [School in norms], Malmö: Gleerups.

Moring, A., (2013) *Oudot perheet - Normeja ja ihanteita 2000-luvun Suomessa* [Strange families - Norms and ideals in twenty-first century Finland], Thesis (PhD), University of Helsinki.

Ng, E., (2013) Relative deprivation, self-interest and social justice: why I do research on in-equality, *Equality, diversity and inclusion,* 33(5): 429-441.

Pulkkinen, T., (1993) Keinotekoista seksiä? Luonto, luonnottomuus ja radikaali sukupuolipolitiikka [Artificial sex? The natural, the perverse and the radical gender politics], *Tiede and edistys*, 18(4): 298-313.

Ratele, K., (2015) Location, location, location: reckoning with margins and centres of masculinities research and theory in an inter/trans-national South Africa - Finland project on youth, *NORMA: The international journal for masculinity studies*, 10(2): 105-116.

Rossi, L-M., (2006) Heteronormatiivisuus. Käsitteen elämää ja kummastelua [Heteronormativity: queering the concept and its brief history], *Kulttuurintutkimus,* 23(3): 19-28.

Rothing, Å., (2008) Homotolerance and heteronormativity in Norwegian classrooms, *Gender and education*, 20(3): 253-266.

Rubin, G., (1984) Thinking sex: Notes for a radical theory of the politics of sex, in Vance, C., (ed.) *Pleasure and danger: Exploring female sexuality*, London: Pandora, 267-319.

Rydström, J., (2011) *Odd couples: A history of gay marriage in Scandinavia,* Amsterdam: Aksant.

Sedgwick, E., (1991) How to bring your kids up gay, *Social text*, 29: 18-27.

Seta ry, (2013) *Älä oleta–Normit nurin! Normikriittinen käsikirja yhdenvertaisuudesta, syrjinnän vastustamisesta ja vapaudesta olla oma itsensä* [Don't presume–Down with norms! Norm critical handbook on equality, prevention of discrimination and the freedom of being oneself], Helsinki: Seta.

Spivak, G., (1990) *Post-colonial critic: Interviews, strategies, dialogues*, London: Routledge.

Stryker, S., (2008) *Transgender History*, Berkeley: Seal.

Suhonen, S., (2014) Sukupuolen määrittelyn käytännöt ja itsenään elämisen mahdollisuudet [Practices of defining one's gender and the possibilities of living one's life], in Gissler, M. et al., (eds.) *Nuoruus toisin sanoen* [Youth in other words], Helsinki: Finnish Youth Research Society and THL, 178-186.

Taavetti, R., (2015) *'Olis siistiä, jos ei tarttis määritellä...' Kuriton ja tavallinen sateenkaarinuoruus* ['It would be cool not to have to define yourself'. Undisciplined and ordinary rainbow youth], Helsinki: Finnish Youth Research Society and Seta ry.

Takacs, J., (2006) *Social exclusion of young lesbian, gay, bisexual and transgender people in Europe*, Brussels: ILGA-Europe and IGLYO.

Terry, J., (2000) 'Unnatural Acts' in nature: The scientific fascination with queer animals, *GLQ: A journal of lesbian and gay studies*, 6(2): 151-193.

Vance, C., (1989) Social construction theory: Problems of the history of sexuality, in Altman, D., Vance, C., Vicinus, M., Weeks, J. et al., (eds.) *Homosexuality, Which homosexuality?* Amsterdam: Schorer, 13-34.

Warner, M., (1999) *The trouble with normal: Sex, politics, and the ethics of queer life*, New York: The Free Press.

Weeks, J., (1986) *Sexuality*, London: Routledge.

Widerberg, K., (2011) Memory work: Exploring family life and expanding the scope of family research, *Journal of comparative family studies,* 42(3): 329-337.

Wittig, M., (1989) On the social contract, in Altman, D., Vance, C., Vicinus, M., Weeks, J. et al., (eds.) *Homosexuality, Which homosexuality?* Amsterdam: Schorer, 239-249.

Chapter 7

Teaching about the Pink Holocaust in an Icelandic upper secondary school classroom: Queer counterpublics?

Jón Ingvar Kjaran and Ingólfur Ásgeir Jóhannesson

Studies in the West, particularly in USA and UK, have shown that the dominant discourse within schools tends to be heteronormative and that LGBTIQ students often experience themselves as marginalised and excluded from their school environment (see, e.g. Allen, 2009; Epstein, 1994; Lipkin, 2004; Mayo, 2013). Furthermore, textbooks and curricula rarely address LGBTIQ issues (see Blackburn, 2012; Ferfolja, 2007). In Iceland, a new National Curriculum Guide for pre-, compulsory and upper secondary schools was released in 2011. It is an indication of positive changes since it provides a legitimate option to offer queer theory (in Icelandic: *hinseginfræði*) as a possible subject as well as a resource for teaching about queer topics (see Ministry of Education, Science, and Culture, 2012). Thus in our view, this clause in the National Curriculum Guide provides a space for teachers and students to trouble the curriculum and teaching in general.

This chapter is based on a study of a course taught in an Icelandic upper secondary school on the Holocaust. This course is an elective course that is very popular among the students; approximately forty-five per cent of each graduate class of student for the past three years (2014, 2015 and 2016), or 450 students altogether, attended the course. The study is focused on a three-week session of the course that dealt with the so-called *Pink Holocaust*, the persecution of sexual minorities, mostly gay men, during the Nazi period in Germany from 1933-1945. We call this part of the course the Pink Holocaust module. We explored the perceptions of the students, who participated in the Pink Holocaust module, in particular if the content of the module changed their understanding towards queer issues, and how gay students experienced the course.

In our analysis we draw on the concept of queer counterpublics. Nancy Fraser explains counterpublics as 'parallel discursive arenas where members of subordinated social groups invent and circulate counter-discourses to formulate oppositional interpretations of their identities, interests and needs'

(Fraser, 1990, p. 67). Michael Warner also emphasises the discursive character of publics as 'a space of discourse organised by nothing other than discourse itself' (Warner, 2002: 67). Moreover, the public is 'a kind of social totality' (p. 65), whereas its limits and discursive circulation is never fully known. It is also an imagined space (Warner, 2002). Counterpublics are in principle the same kind of space as publics but are characterised by their tension to the larger public. According to Warner: 'Discussion within such a public is understood to contravene the rules obtaining in the world at large, being structured by alternative dispositions or protocols, making different assumptions about what can be said or what goes without saying' (Warner, 2002: 56). This notion of counterpublics resembles Fraser's description of 'parallel discursive arenas'. However, in difference with Fraser, Warner puts more emphasis on the discursive character of counterpublics without necessarily connecting them with particular subordinated groups. In that sense, the concept of a counterpublic has a wider resonance and can be used in order to form new identities and worldviews within school settings.

Counterpublics can therefore be understood as transformative discursive spaces where counterknowledges can be cultivated through critical engagement with the dominant norms and contexts of the cultural environment (Warner, 2002). It is in that sense that we use the concept of counterpublics in this paper within educational settings. This approach has been advocated by queer pedagogy, which emphasises the critical and hence the troubling nature of education (see, e.g. Britzman, 1998; Kumashiro, 2002). However, by focusing on the concept of queer counterpublics, we want to emphasise the spatial and contextual notion of knowledge construction, and how new discursive spaces are produced within the classroom with the potential of troubling education. In that sense, queer counterpublics have the potential of troubling or queering education cultures and taken for granted knowledges.

The chapter sets out to answer the following questions: i) How did the module function as a queer counterpublic and how did it trouble education cultures? ii) How did the students and the researchers (teacher-researcher and co-researcher) experience the course? iii) How did self-identified gay students experience the module?

Berlin in the 1920 and the 1930s and the Holocaust

In Germany, the notorious Paragraph 175 criminalised homosexuality from 1871, although not always enforced to its full (Stümke, 1989). Importantly, during the liberal atmosphere of the Weimar Republic in the 1920s, there was a lively gay and lesbian scene in Berlin, with many venues and nightclubs, where same sex desires could be shown openly. Moreover, Magnus Hirschfeld, a physician, sexologist, and an advocate for sexual minorities, ran his *Institut für Sexualwissenschaft*, Institute of Sexual Research, in Berlin. It housed immense archives and library on sexuality and provided educational services and medical consultations for sexual minorities. It also housed a museum of sex, which offered educational resources for the public (Dose, 2014). Thus, Berlin in the 1920s and early 1930s could be understood as a counterpublic for manifold gender and sexual non-conformity. The homosexual subject was thus visible, at least in large cities, such as Berlin. After the Nazis came to power in 1933, they gradually closed all queer venues and nightclubs, along with Hirschfeld's institute. They also broadened Paragraph 175[1] and initiated persecutions of homosexuals, of which many were imprisoned in concentration camps, becoming victims of the brutal camp regimes, which Heinz Heger described so bluntly in his autobiography (Heger, 2013).

In this chapter, we have decided to use the term Pink Holocaust instead of words such as the Hidden Holocaust (see, e.g. Grau and Shoppmann, 1995), Homocaust, or the Gay Holocaust. By using pink instead of gay we refer to the *pink triangle* which gay men were required to wear in the concentration camps. Thus the focus here is on gay males because during the times of the Third Reich lesbians were not persecuted to the same extent as gay men. In fact the Nazis did not acknowledge lesbian sexual activities. Moreover, if lesbians or women who had sex with women were imprisoned, they had to wear a black triangle, a symbol of asocial behaviour. In that sense, women's same sex sexual acts were associated with asocial behaviour during the Third Reich (Elman, 1996; Plant, 1986, for the idea of a/social see also Juva and Vaahtera in this book).

The Icelandic upper secondary school and the National Curriculum Guide

The Icelandic upper secondary school is a three to four year long program for sixteen to twenty year-old students. It is comprised of a variety of schools, including academic, comprehensive, and vocational schools of various sizes and locations. A new legislation has been in implementation from 2008 (The Upper Secondary School Act, no 92/2008). This legislation only stipulates Icelandic, English and mathematics as mandatory subjects with competences defined in

1 Paragraph 175 was not abolished until 1994.

a national curriculum. The schools themselves define which courses they teach and study programs they offer, but the Ministry of Education, Science, and Culture must approve of the study programs (see, e.g. Kjaran and Jóhannesson, 2013; Ragnarsdóttir and Jóhannesson, 2014).

In accordance with the 2008 legislation, a new national curriculum guide was released in 2011. It consists of three books, each for one of the school levels, i.e., pre-school, compulsory school, and upper secondary school. Each book contains about a ten-page section explaining the so-called fundamental pillars of education (see, e.g. Ministry of Education, Science, and Culture, 2012). These cross-curricular pillars are literacy, sustainability, democracy and human rights, equality, health and welfare, and creativity. The text about each of the pillars is about one-page long, for instance, the equality pillar is explained in 560 words.

The inclusion of gender and queer studies in the fundamental pillar of equality

The equality pillar is defined broadly as *an umbrella concept* to include any possible dimension of inequality. It mentions thirteen such dimensions in an alphabetical order: 'age, class, culture, descent, gender, disability, language, nationality, outlook on life, race, religion, residence, sexual orientation' (Ministry of Education, Science, and Culture, 2012: 20). It further argues that a goal of equality education is to be a 'critical examination of the established ideas in society and its institutions in order to teach children and youth to analyse the circumstances that lead to discrimination of some and privileges for others' (ibid.). This notion of equality education seems to be more radical than included in the previous national curricula (Jóhannesson, 2015).

Gender is given some priority in the pillar text, by, for instance, that a relatively lengthy section of it refers to the Act on Equal Status and Equal Rights of Women and Men, no 10/2008. In accordance with this legislation, which is based on earlier legislation dated from 1976, the fundamental pillar text emphasises that 'boys and girls having as extensive and as equal opportunities as possible. Nowhere in school activities, content, or in working methods, should there be any obstacles for either gender' (Ministry of Education, Science, and Culture, 2012: 20). In the second last paragraph of the fundamental pillar text, 'studies of gender and sexual orientation' (ibid.) appear first in a discussion where some of the other dimensions are listed later. And in a list of new disciplines for schools to learn from, gender studies and queer theory are listed before 'multicultural studies and disability studies' (ibid.), without the alphabet inviting that order.

Finally, the text in Icelandic refers to *margþætt mismunun* which is translated as 'various kinds of discrimination when more than one of these factors come together, for example, gender and disability, sexual orientation and nationality, age and residence' (ibid.).

Importantly for the present study, this text in the National Curriculum Guide includes not only issues of *sexual orientation*, which it mentions, but acknowledges queer studies both as a resource and a possible course subject. Further by introducing a notion of intersectionality, it paves the way for integrating many kinds of studies of inequality, discrimination, and privilege.

The text about the fundamental pillars therefore puts the Pink Holocaust module in a certain context, as it offers a rationale to teach about queer reality and lives. The module is meant to do exactly what the curriculum calls for, i.e., to nurture a critical awareness and thinking among students in order to help them to 'analyse the circumstances that lead to discrimination of some and privileges for others' (Ministry of Education, Science, and Culture, 2012: 20).

Methodology

The data is drawn from an ethnographic study at one upper secondary school in Reykjavik, given the pseudonym Hilly, which is a traditional academic upper secondary school with a relatively long history. At the time of the study, it had around 1300 students. They shared similar backgrounds, in most cases from well-off homes in terms of economic, social, and cultural capital. The average grades of the students admitted into the school were also well above the average mean in Iceland. At Hilly, Jón taught a three-week long module about the persecution of sexual minorities during the Nazi period in Germany from 1933-1945, called the Pink Holocaust, as a part of an elective course about the Holocaust, the historical conditions under which it took place, its events, and its aftermath. The course, and thus the Pink Holocaust module was first offered to five different groups of students from January to April 2014 and again in 2015 and 2016 to five groups each year, also from January to April. A total of 450 students have completed the course, a half of the student group each year.

Jón taught the module and conducted participatory observations for both years. He was thus both a part of the module (course) as a teacher and an organiser, but at the same time researcher, doing observations of the outcome of the course and his own teaching. In that sense, Jón was an insider, part of the context of the classroom, which offered particular opportunities for utilising himself as a key resource of data (see, e.g. Atkinson, 2006; Voloder, 2008). To be an insider can both have its drawbacks and strengths when conducting an ethnographic study (see, e.g. O'Reilly, 2009; Webster and John, 2010). However, in our case, it mainly facilitated the research process and made it easier for Jón to gain the trust of students. It was, however, kept in mind during the fieldwork that being an insider could make the research context problematic. In other words, the position of an insider can be a hindrance in terms of making the familiar strange (and the strange familiar) by, for example, not posing critical questions or not being able to see the field through the lenses of the outsider (see, e.g. Gordon, Holland, and Lahelma, 2000). In order to counter the effects of insider bias, Ingólfur, the second researcher, a university professor, a former history teacher himself, observed four sessions in one of the modules in 2015, and wrote fieldnotes and reflections about the module, but did not participate in class discussions.

Ethnographic data

The ethnographic data used in this study are divided into three parts. First, there are the fieldnotes, taken during observations, and reflective research diaries by both authors, along with Jón's autoethnographic data. Second, each group of students was asked to evaluate individually in writing the seminar after they had attended it. They were asked to tell about how they experienced it, what they learned during that time, what surprised them and what factors influenced them the most. Third, the study is based on interviews, with three boys who self-identified as gay. All of them were eighteen years-old when the interviews were conducted in spring of 2014 after the completion of the course. The main objective of the interviews was to focus on their experience and explore whether they thought of the module as emancipatory. They chose their pseudonyms: Hreinn, Gabríel, and Sævar. All interviews were conducted and transcribed by Jón, who met each participant once for ninety minutes.

Conceptual tools and data analysis

In our analysis of the data we use the concept of counterpublics, coined by Fraser and Warner. In terms of analysing the pedagogy, we draw on the writings of Elizabeth Ellsworth (2005) and other scholars on the pedagogy and the curriculum of teaching about the Holocaust (Morris, 2001; Totten, 2001). For instance, Ellsworth has discussed the pedagogical effects of the United States Holocaust Memorial Museum in New York as such: 'The pedagogy of the exhibit opens the door onto the possibility for something else. It opens the door to the possibility, the paradoxical possibility, of a narrative without closure' (Ellsworth, 2005: 104). Further, we draw on the psychoanalytically based pedagogy developed by Deborah Britzman (1998). These authors all emphasise the importance of troubling rather than transforming the dominant curriculum. *Troubling* in the context of this research also means *queering* the curriculum by not just adding-on queer themes into the curriculum, but indeed engaging with knowledges and sexual and gender categories in a critical way.

When the data had been collected, both authors examined the data in order to define themes that would portray changes of perceptions and the construction of queer counterpublics (Fraser, 1990; Warner, 2002). The themes were selected on the basis of whether they demonstrated any notion of counterpublics or indicated troubling of knowledges and norms. We soon determined different themes and when the module was taught the second time, Ingólfur, the second author, had the opportunity to observe classes to look for further themes to confirm or cast doubt on the themes deduced in the beginning. Moreover, both researchers discussed at length their experiences after each class session, and then drafted the chapter. In the last year of the research we gathered more data and added nuance to the analysis for the complete chapter.

In our analysis, we also used a variety of methodological advice that enlightened our examination of the data. Of such especially useful sources, Silverman (2012), Kvale (2007), and Mills and Morton (2013) were consulted during the processes of data collection and analysis.

A seminar about the Pink Holocaust: A narrative without closure?

As noted before, the three-week module about the Pink Holocaust is part of a larger course about the Holocaust and the racial policy of the Third Reich. In the overall course different texts were used. The main text in the Pink Holocaust module was Heinz Heger's book, *The Men with the Pink Triangle*, available in an Icelandic translation (Heger, 2013). Heger was born in Austria and survived imprisonment in Nazi concentration camps. The autobiography was published in the original language of German in 1972, one year after homosexuality had been decriminalised in Austria (Waaldijk, 2000).

Heger's narrative is both emotional and influential, and his first person account gives students the opportunity to experience these historical events through the personal connections they establish with the narrator. This kind of personal narrative has the potential of changing the perceptions of the reader, transforming his literacy experience. In that sense, 'literacy can be used as a tool for making one's life more bearable but also for making the world a more socially just place' (Blackburn, 2012: 17). In fact, Heger's personal narrative had great impact on most of the students who attended the module as, in a way, it opened their eyes to the injustices of the past and the present. Moreover, when they were asked to rate the book most of them felt that this book should be obligatory in any course about the Holocaust. Some even said that its narrative was sometimes so emotional and unreal, that they did not fully grasp whether they were reading a novel or a true account of events that really took place. One student wrote the following when he was asked to rate the book and how it affected him:

> When I was reading the book I needed to stop many times and watch one good and cheerful Friends episode in order to pacify my mind. How can humans be so cruel? ... Even today there are so many prejudices and what I learnt, both from reading the book and from the seminar was, that one needs to respect everybody, irrespective of how s(he) is or looks like. (Student evaluation, 2014)

Thus, the personal experience of Heger influenced some of the students participating in the module, and thus served as an effective and powerful learning tool in conveying past experiences (see, e.g. Totten, 2001). Moreover, many of students made some connections between the prejudices of the past and the prejudices of the present as the quote above reveals. This was in fact one of the pedagogical aims of the module, to draw attention to the situation today of LGBTIQ people worldwide and to nurture a human rights culture and critical thinking. Thereby, we wanted the students to become more aware of the prejudices still existing in societies worldwide (see, e.g. Petersen, 2010).

However, the goal was not only to nurture pity or sympathy, but also to encourage the students to reflect upon their own privileges and become critical of the dominant discourse of sexuality and gender. In that sense, the module was taught from a queer position, in a double sense.

First, by having the aim of queering the heteronormative discourse within schools and challenge taken for granted assumptions about gender and sexuality. In other words, creating queer counterpublics. This was done in order to encourage critical thinking, address institutionalised heterosexism and homophobia worldwide, and to challenge any heterosexist and homophobic beliefs. During the module, various topics on gender and sexuality were discussed, which were initiated when the students read the book. These discussion were both in small and large groups, and among discussion topics were for example the social construction of sexuality and how sexual behaviour often depended on the context, such as the one described in Heger's narrative. Some students had difficulties understanding how for example straight men could engage in non-heterosexual sex during that time in the concentration camps. Here, the teacher used the opportunity, teachable moment (Martino and Rezai-Rashti, 2012; Martino and Cumming-Potvin, 2014), to introduce to the students the Kinsey scale (Kinsey et al., 1953) and initiate discussion about the fluidity of sexuality.

Second, Jón, who identifies as gay, taught the module. During the teaching of the module he often made references, both direct and indirect, to his experiences and knowledge of LGBTIQ reality. He, however, never *came out* directly in class by declaring at the beginning *I am gay*. Khayatt (1997) has discussed the implications, both pedagogical and political, of disclosure of sexual identity. According to her, declarative statements about one's sexuality, *I am gay or lesbian*, can have some complications and do not always address those assumptions about its effects, such as being a role model for other LGBTIQ students or to unsettle the dominance of heterosexuality. This kind of direct disclosure can even alienate some students, both straight and non-straight. Thus, she argues against 'the notion of coming out in a declarative way' (Khayatt, 1997: 141), mainly on the ground that there might be some pedagogical reasons for teachers not doing so. However, Khayatt is not saying that LGBTIQ teachers should conduct their life in secrecy and hide their identity from the world. She emphasises that in her classes she often gives out some clues about her sexual identity when discussing the topic. Moreover, she stresses that LGBTIQ teachers 'can exercise the right to privacy and still be sensitive and supportive of students who suffer any form of discrimination' (Khayatt, 1997: 142). In that sense, Jón's sexual orientation was assumed by some but not by others, and any references to it, were made in connection to the content of the module.

The focus was on the content, the Pink Holocaust and current homophobia worldwide, rather on Jón as a gay teacher. However, it can be assumed that being openly gay without disclosing it directly, created a *safe space*, for students, both straight and non-heterosexual to discuss these topics. The gay students mentioned this in the interviews as will be discussed later. Moreover, the students seemed also more willing to discuss issues related to sex and sexuality, even referring to their own experience, presuming that the teacher would not judge them and be more likely to understand them. The presumed sexuality of the teacher might also have silenced those students who might have had homophobic views. Here it needs to be emphasised, that any notion of a safe space(s) in schools and classrooms can also be problematic, even in some instances creating a false security, in the sense that some students might be likely to expose themselves more in those spaces, defined as *safe*. Thus, the discussion about a *safe space(s)* in schools and classrooms, particularly in respect to LGBTIQ students, should be directed at the processes and forces that necessitate the construction of such spaces.

One way to do this is to use the classroom as a platform to create a queer counterpublic, where new identities and worldviews can be formed. Thus, being gay and referring to his experience when teaching the module, Jón tried to create a queer counterpublic, teaching the module from a queer position, referring to and including themes of queer lives and culture. He for example felt, during a discussion about various themes in relation to the module, that being gay, gave him the opportunity to gain better rapport with his students, in the sense that they were somehow less afraid of discussing difficult topics and content of the module. Anderson (2009) has suggested that because there are so few openly gay teachers, indicating or referring to your sexuality, not necessarily in a declarative way, can create a more relaxed learning environment and further elicit disclosure and openness among students (see also Kong, Mahoney, and Plummer, 2002). Jón partly felt this, and mentioned it several times in his research diary during the teaching of the module. Thus, for Jón, being gay, the teaching of the module created a counterpublic in two ways.

First, in the sense that it helped Jón to discuss queer issues with the students. In that sense the discussions and the content of the module transformed the classroom into a space where students engaged with the content of the book and interacted with each other. This Jón mentioned in his fieldnotes, adding that most students had read the assigned chapters of Heger's book beforehand and were thus prepared to take part in discussions.

Second, it created a LGBTIQ *niche* within the curriculum of the school under investigation, whereas the content of the module was proposed and organised by Jón, solely because of his interests in the topic.

So far the module had been taught for three years, gradually becoming an established part of the curriculum at that particular school, an indication *per se* of the queer counterpublic nature of the module.

In this context, it is important that when the module was first taught in January to April 2014, three openly gay students attended the course. After the completion of the course Jón interviewed them and asked them how they had experienced the module. When talking about his experience, one of them was *impressed* bt having a gay teacher, stressing indirectly its importance within the heterosexual institution of schools:

> I mean, I was rather impressed when I heard for example that you are gay. You know, wow, it does not occur so often that you have a gay teacher, and it was you know, it was good. (Interview, 2014)

No openly lesbian students or other queer students attended the course. However, it could be interpreted from the responses of the gay students who attended, that it created an atmosphere of diversity, particularly in terms of sexual diversity. In that sense, it could be seen as emancipatory for LGBTIQ students in general, creating a queer counterpublic for diverse discourses on these issues.

We emphasised that Heger's story is only one voice of many victims of the Nazi regime. As Totten argued, 'no single telling can ever hope to provide its complete story' (Totten, 2001: 113), because of the complex nature of the Holocaust. In that sense, we underlined that any *understanding* of the Holocaust would be a narrative without closure (Ellsworth, 2005). This was apparent when students asked if the Holocaust could happen today. Atrocities in Rwanda and Bosnia in the 1990s were mentioned, stressing that a comparison was not a possibility (Fieldnotes, Ingólfur, 2015).

'It was too unreal to be true': A fictitious narrative of true events

In the beginning of the module, the students could hardly believe that the events that Heger described could be true. In the evaluation of the course, one of them wrote: 'I felt that I was in another world, like I was reading a novel or something' (Student evaluation, 2014). In this way, Heger's memoirs initiated a 'crisis of learning' (Ellsworth, 2005), disturbing their previous knowledge about the past.

However, this uncomfortable learning experience, which was according to some of the students, too fictitious to be true (Student evaluation, 2014, 2016), took place within a comfortable space of the classroom, where students had the opportunity to discuss various kinds of doubts and pose different questions on the topic. There, they were able to engage with 'the subjective and emotional dimension' of Heger's narrative about the barbarism of Nazi politics through first-hand account, which objective accounts or interpretations from textbooks on the Holocaust would never be able to convey (Lixl-Purcell, 1994: 237).

Henry Friedlander has advised that when using such first-hand accounts, they should not 'be used as a shock treatment to arouse interest' (Friedlander, 1979: 542), but that it is important to provide ample time for in-depth discussions, where students have the possibility to express their innermost thoughts and feelings. During the module about the Pink Holocaust, we discussed in detail different views, what the students should expect while reading Heger's narrative, their misconceptions and questions. By going through this kind of *briefing* session, working together on the topic through questions and discussion, the students were prepared to listen and think about those details in the narrative that at first seem unbelievable, as some students mentioned in their remarks. Moreover, according to our fieldnotes, during some of the discussions, many of the students became more aware of the situation of gays and lesbians during the twentieth and the twenty-first century. They were also able to make some kind of meaning out of the totality and enormity of the Holocaust and Nazi racial policy as the following quotes from some students demonstrate:

> I am shocked that I did not know that gays experienced so grim fate during WW2 and still today some only think of the Jews as the only victims of the holocaust and Nazi persecution. (Student evaluation, 2014)

> It was so revealing to have the opportunity to get a glimpse into the inner thoughts of Heger and see through his eyes how gays were treated during that time. So little discussion has been about the situation of European gays after WW2, but also of their reality today. (Student evaluation, 2015)

As the above quotes reveal, the module and Heger's memoirs influenced the students' perception of the Holocaust and past struggle of non-heterosexuals. They found it illuminating to learn about the Holocaust and Nazi atrocities from a different perspective, and thereby became more aware of the reality of non-heterosexuals, both in the past and in the present. In that sense, it created a queer counterpublic, troubling their worldview and giving them another aspect of the Holocaust.

LGBTIQ reality in light of invisibility—past and present

The module most often began with drawing attention to the situation of the legal rights of LGBTIQ people in the world today and historically. These students were not even born or they were babies and toddlers when the first same-sex marriage legislation was passed in Iceland in June 1996 so they do not remember the earlier situation in Iceland. They mentioned in their evaluations that before attending the course they did not have any idea about this aspect of history nor that other groups, such as homosexuals or Roma people, were systematically exterminated during the Holocaust. One student said:

> I cannot comprehend why they [the Nazis] were more against homosexuals than for example criminals. Actually I cannot understand why they were against homosexuals at all. (Student evaluation, 2014)

This student referred to *criminals* in his comment and that they had a higher status and got more respect than the gays, who had the lowest status within the hierarchy of the camps. This was commented by most students and nearly all of them found it both strange and perverse. In fact, it offended their moral integrity and righteousness and somehow disturbed their worldviews, initiating some inner conflicts (Ellsworth, 2005). Moreover, the fact that many homosexuals were still considered criminals after the war, even after their imprisonment in concentration camps, was even more disturbing for most of the students. They found this difficult to imagine as the following comment reveals:

> What strikes me the most is how homosexuals were treated after war. They did not get any compensation or like pity and in many countries they were still despised. (Student evaluation, 2014)

The students have been raised in a society where the visibility of LGBTIQ people has been increasing during the last decades, especially after the turn of the millennium (Kjaran and Jóhannesson, 2013). Moreover, LGBTIQ rights have improved and societal attitudes have changed dramatically. This, however, is in stark contrast to schools where in our previous work we have indicated a gap between the more liberal society and conservative schools in respect to sexuality and LGBTIQ students. In many Icelandic upper secondary schools, institutionalised heterosexism, for example in the form of unquestioned assumptions about heterosexuality as the norm, is prevalent (Kjaran and Jóhannesson, 2013).

Thus, reading about the Pink Holocaust through the memoirs of Heger and participating in the module gave these students a new understanding of past struggles and the situation for how LGBTIQ people is in many countries today. The discussion during the module and when reading the book in particular brought these events closer to them in a personalised narrative, which did not close or limit their own interpretation and experiences of these events (Ellsworth, 2005). This was then expanded upon further in order for them to make the connection of current human rights violations towards LGBTIQ people.

In these ways, the module and the book increased the visibility of LGBTIQ people within the curriculum, the school and history teaching in general. For Gabríel, one of the gay students attending the class in 2014, interviewed afterwards, this was somehow liberating:

> I had read the whole book on day two ... it was so interesting to read about this ... you know we are always taught about the reality of heterosexuals. (Interview, 2014)

We discuss this further in the following section on how the module about the Pink Holocaust used available clauses in the new National Curriculum Guide to queer the actual curriculum in practice.

Queering history, queering space: A queer counterpublic?

We wanted to know if the students who attended the module, particularly those who identified as queer, experienced it as liberating and how it created a platform for the making of a queer counterpublic, where new identities and worldviews could be formed. The self-identified gay young men who attended the course, made some positive comments in interviews:

> I have never been in a course or a seminar where one of the topic is this, you know gay issues. I think for me I was maybe more enthusiastic learning about these issues, even more than my classmates. (Hreinn, interview 2014)

> I had never heard about these issues in compulsory school or in any other course at my school until now. You know there have never been any discussions about homosexuality at this school so this was something new ... It was so nice to have finally some kind of cause to stand for ... hearing that my classmates were now talking about this even after class. It was really interesting and nice to hear that. (Sævar, interview 2014)

Both Hreinn and Sævar experienced the module as empowering, as it created a platform to discuss queer history and LGBTIQ lives, breaking the silence surrounding these issues in a way that validated a discussion out of class. So far, neither of them had experienced any education or discussions about these issues in school, so this was apparently something new for them. In that sense, this seems to be a sign of a counterpublic within the heteronormative discourse of the school (Fraser, 1990; Kjaran and Jóhannesson, 2015; Warner, 2002). Thus, the module and the reading of Heger's memoirs worked the cracks of the new curriculum and taught about LGBTIQ issues through the lens of history (Collins, 2000).

For many students, the module included difficult topics, and they experienced some inner conflicts and crisis, which can be used to enhance understanding and empathy. For example, many of them mentioned in their comments that they found it strange that so many men were having sex with men, without even identifying as homosexuals, and despite the fact they despised homosexuals. This often took place under the rubric of giving sexual favours in exchange for food or lighter work. Following are examples of their comments on these issues:

> What surprised the most were all these male lovers and *ladyboys*. I did not know that this kind of behaviour had been practiced in the concentration camps. (Student evaluation, 2014)

> The prisoners hated homosexuals although they themselves had sex with men. (Student evaluation, 2014)

These manifestations of context-based sexuality, sometimes called *men who have sex with men* (MSM), troubled the students' view about sexuality, as many of them had so far perceived sexuality as something fixed and stable over time and context (see, e.g. Seidman, 2008, 2009). They were more used to fixed binary categories of sexuality: either you are straight or gay, allowing for some possibilities of a person to identify as bisexual. Thus, the description of context-based homosexuality, offered the teacher an opportunity to discuss the social construction of sexuality and gender. By drawing attention to these issues and discussing it openly with the students, it could therefore be seen as a way to queer the normative binaries of sexuality. In fact, it destabilised the notion many students had about sexuality and sexual behaviour.

The cruelty of the Nazis and the endurance of the victims was one of the themes that the students mentioned in their comments in the evaluation texts. This they had not realised before nor had they had such a direct confrontation with the terror of the concentration camps, from reading a first-hand or personalised account of the events. One student mentioned that s/he 'felt so small and vulnerable' after reading Heger's memoirs and another one said: 'I was so angry and frustrated when I read the story and I sometimes wanted to throw the book away' (Student evaluation, 2014). Thus, the module and particularly Heger's memoirs disturbed their experience and threw them out of their comfort zone. It gave them a different perspective on the Holocaust and created a kind of a queer counterpublic of what they already knew about it. It not only put them into a crisis of learning as the previous comments reveal but also made some permanent marks on them, changing their perspective in the long run to these events and human rights abuses in general as the following comments indicate:

> The book influenced me greatly, and I am actually just speechless, I do not know what to say. I had never before realised how terrible this was. (Student evaluation, 2014)

Two of boys who self-identified as gay and attended the course mentioned that they could somehow put themselves in the shoes of Heger. Hreinn did that in the quote above, although emphasising that one could never do that to its fullest extent, as each experience is unique. Gabriel also mentioned this and adds to it that he somehow felt surprised and amazed when he read about how Heger *discovered* his sexual identity.[2] Gabriel related to this quite strongly as he expresses:

> It surprised me that when he [Heger] was describing how he came to terms with or discovered his sexuality, and it was exactly as I would have done it, even word by word. It felt a bit strange. (Interview, 2014)

---

2 Heger discusses in his memoirs how he *came out* and *discovered* his sexual identity. He describes that most of his friends at high school were girls and that he gradually noticed that he was not sexually attracted to them, only felt deep friendship towards them. He realized then that he had sexual attractions and feelings towards guys. When he finally decided to *come out*, he only told his mother about his feelings, who told him to be careful and not to reveal his identity to anyone else (see Heger, 2013).

The module about the Pink Holocaust created a queer counterpublic by including the views and the experience of a sexual minority group in the curriculum. It queered the heteronorm and destabilised predetermined sexual identity categories. The self-identified gay students attending the course felt this as empowering, whereas other students experienced some inner conflicts and crisis, influencing their worldviews and perspectives about these issues.

Conclusion

We asked how the module about the Pink Holocaust created a queer counterpublic, and by doing that, whether it troubled the educational cultures at Hilly. In our views it did so in four ways.

First, through the visibility of queer lives and its reality in the classroom and that its content got a space in the school curriculum under investigation. By revolving around Heger's memoirs, the narrative about the Pink Holocaust, which described past experiences, was made contemporary through the literary experience of the students participating in the module. Heger's memoirs had the potential of challenging the present, as they intersected prejudices in the past and the present, revolving around homophobia worldwide, particularly when connected to stringent racial policy and extreme nationalism. The module changed the perceptions of the students, not only about the Holocaust, but also made them more aware about LGBTIQ realities worldwide today.

Second, it created queer counterpublics through the ways the content was presented and taught, relying mostly on queer pedagogy. The students, who attended the course, gained new insights into the reality and history of LGBTIQ people; in other words the module disturbed their preconceived worldviews and engaged them in a kind of 'crisis of learning' that Ellsworth (2005) has described. Gradually, they became aware of the many voices of such a complicated and enormous event as the Holocaust was, nurturing in them an understanding of the Holocaust as a *narrative without closure* which is not easy or in some ways is even impossible to comprehend (Ellsworth, 2005). Thus, our contention is that the module was *troubling* in the way that it engaged the students in critical thinking, by drawing attention to the regime of binary thought, particularly in terms of gender and sexuality, and heterosexist ideology and homophobia, both in the present and the past.

Third, the module created a queer space for the self-identified gay students, who were interviewed. They experienced the module as liberating and talked about how it made them feel more safe, included and welcoming. We as teachers and researchers experienced the module as a space of learning where different voices and narratives were welcomed. Thereby, the module could be understood as a counterpublic, *vis-à-vis* the dominant narrative of the Holocaust and drawing attention to counterstories of other minority groups that were persecuted by the Nazis. In that sense and also because it influenced most of our students profoundly it could be said that the module had some troubling effects, and in that sense queered the hegemonic discourse of gender and sexuality (see, e.g. Jagose, 1996; Warner, 1991) and thus created a queer counterpublic.

Fourth, the course about the Holocaust and the module about the Pink Holocaust in particular, contributed to the transgression of the curriculum and the dominant discourse of gender and (hetero)sexuality at the school under investigation. Approximately forty-five per cent of each graduate class of student for the past three years (2014, 2015 and 2016), or 450 students altogether, attended the course. The fact that queer studies are mentioned in the current national curriculum from 2011 made it feasible to pose *queer* as an organising principle of the module, which opened a space for creation of queer counterpublics within Hilly. Thus the initiative of the history teachers and the curriculum supported each other in that the course was provided.

References

Act on equal status and equal rights of women and men, no 10/2008.

Allen, L., (2009) 'The 5 cm rule': Biopower, sexuality and schooling, *Discourse*, 30(4): 443-456.

Anderson, E., (2009) *Inclusive masculinity: The changing nature of masculinities*, London: Routledge.

Atkinson, P., (2006) Rescuing autoethnography, *Journal of contemporary ethnography*, 35(4): 400-404.

Blackburn, M., (2012) *Interrupting hate: Homophobia in schools and what literacy can do about it*, New York: Teachers College Press.

Britzman, D., (1998) *Lost subjects, contested objects. Toward a psychoanalytic inquiry of learning*, New York: State University of New York Press.

Collins, P. H., (2000) *Black feminist thought: Knowledge, consciousness, and the politics of empowerment*, New York: Routledge.

Dose, R., (2014) *Magnus Hirschfeld: The origins of the gay liberation movement*, New York: Monthly Review Press.

Ellsworth, E., (2005) *Places of learning: Media, architecture, pedagogy*, London: Routledge.

Elman, R. A., (1996) Triangles and tribulations: The politics of Nazi symbols, *Journal of homosexuality*, 30(3): 3-11.

Epstein, D., (ed.) (1994) *Challenging lesbian and gay inequalities in education*, Buckingham: Open University Press.

Ferfolja, T., (2007) Schooling cultures: Institutionalizing heteronormativity and heterosexism, *International journal of inclusive education*, 11(2): 147-162.

Fraser, N., (1990) Rethinking the public sphere: A contribution to the critique of actually existing democracy, *Social text*, 25(26): 56-80.

Friedlander, H., (1979) Toward a methodology of teaching about the Holocaust, *Teachers college record*, 80(5): 519-542.

Gordon, T., Holland, J. and Lahelma, E., (2000) *Making spaces. Citizenship and difference in schools,* London: Macmillan.

Grau, G. and Shoppmann, C., (1995) *The hidden Holocaust? Gay and lesbian persecution in Germany 1933-1945*, London: Routledge.

Heger, H., (2013) *The men with the pink triangle: The true life-and-death story of homosexuals in Nazi death camps*, New York: Alyson Books.

Jagose, A., (1996) *Queer theory: An introduction*, Melbourne: Melbourne University Press.

Jóhannesson, I. Á., (2015) *Does the National Curriculum Guide 2011 in pave way for gender and queer studies in Icelandic schools?* Presentation at the Nordic educational research association conference, Gothenburg 4-6 March.

Khayatt, D., (1997) Sex and the teacher. Should we come out in class? *Harvard educational review*, 67(1): 126-143.

Kinsey, A. C., Pomeroy, W. B., Martin, C. E. and Gebhard, P., (1953) *Sexual behavior in the human female,* Philadelphia: Saunders.

Kjaran, J. I. and Jóhannesson, I. Á., (2013) Manifestations of heterosexism in Icelandic upper secondary schools and the responses of LGBT students, *Journal of LGBT youth*, 10(4): 351-372.

Kjaran, J. I. and Jóhannesson, I. Á., (2015) Inclusion, exclusion and the queering of spaces in two Icelandic upper secondary schools, *Ethnography and education*, 10(1): 42-60.

Kong, T. S., Mahoney, D. and Plummer, K., (2002) Queering the interview, in Gubrium, J. F. and Holstein, J. A., (eds.) *Handbook of interview research*, London: Sage: 91-110.

Kumashiro, K. K., (2002) *Troubling education. Queer activism and anti-oppressive pedagogy,* New York: RoutledgeFalmer.

Kvale, S., (2007) *Doing interviews*, London: Sage.

Lipkin, A., (2004) *Beyond diversity day: A QandA on gay and lesbian issues in schools,* Lanham, Maryland: Rowman and Littlefield.

Lixl-Purcell, A., (1994) Memoirs as history, *Leo Baeck institute yearbook*, 39(1): 227-238.

Martino, W. and Cumming-Potvin, W., (2016) Teaching about sexual minorities and 'princess boys': a queer and trans-infused approach to investigating LGBTQ-themed texts in the elementary school classroom, *Discourse: Studies in the cultural politics of education*, 37(6): 807-827.

Martino, W. and Rezai-Rashti, G., (2012) *Gender, race, and the politics of role modelling. The influence of male teachers,* New York: Routledge.

Mayo, C., (2013) *LGBTQ Youth and education: Policies and practices*, New York: Teachers College Press.

Mills, D. and Morton, M., (2013) *Ethnography in education*, London: Sage.

Ministry of education, science, and culture, (2012) *The national curriculum guide for upper secondary schools*, Reykjavík: Author.

Morris, M., (2001) *Curriculum and the Holocaust*, Mahwah, New Jersey: Lawrence Erlbaum Associates.

O'Reilly, K., (2009) *Key concepts in ethnography*, London: Sage.

Petersen, T., (2010) Moving beyond the toolbox: teaching human rights through teaching the Holocaust in post-apartheid South Africa, *Intercultural education*, 21(1): 27-31.

Plant, R., (1986) *The pink triangle. The Nazi war against homosexuals,* New York: Holt.

Ragnarsdóttir, G. and Jóhannesson, I. Á., (2014) Curriculum, crisis and the work and well-being of Icelandic upper secondary school teachers, *Education inquiry*, 5(1): 43-67.

Seidman, S., (2008) *Contested knowledge. Social theory today*, Malden: Blackwell.

Seidman, S., (2009) *The social construction of sexuality*, New York: W.W. Norton.

Silverman, D., (2012) *Interpreting qualitative data*, London: Sage.

Stümke, H. G., (1989) *Homosexuelle in Deutschland: Eine politische Geschichte*, München: C. H. Beck.

Totten, S., (2001) Incorporating first-person accounts into a study of the Holocaust, in Totten, S. and Feinberg, S., *Teaching and studying the Holocaust,* Boston: Allyn and Bacon, 107-138.

The upper secondary school act, no 92/2008.

Voloder, L., (2008) Autoethnographic challenges: Confronting self, field and home, *The Australian journal of anthropology,* 19(1): 27- 40.

Waaldijk, K., (2000) Civil developments: Patterns of reform in the legal position of same-sex partners in Europe, *Canadian journal of family law*, 17(1): 62-88.

Warner, M., (1991) Introduction: Fear of a queer planet, *Social text*, 9(4): 3-17.

Warner, M., (2002) *Publics and counterpublics*, New York: Zone Books.

Webster, J. P., and John, T. A., (2010) Preserving a space for cross-cultural collaborations: An account of insider/outsider issues, *Ethnography and education,* 5(2): 175-191.

Chapter 8

The little things that matter: Research experiences of challenging heteronormativity in Finnish schools

Riikka Taavetti

In discussions on the experiences of young queer people (or LGBTIQ, i.e. lesbian, gay, bisexual, trans, intergender or intersex and queer or questioning), the first topic that comes up is, almost without exception, schools. As schools are one of the compulsory settings that young people cannot choose, making schools a safe place for all is an urgent task. Furthermore, schools produce and reproduce structures that maintain inequality and norms harmful for queer students. At the same time, though, schools may have the power to change attitudes and they may be a tool for a more equal society. As schools undeniably have a huge impact on young people's lives, there has been a number of initiatives to promote equality and diversity in schools, and, moreover, a number of research projects interested in queer experiences of school.

This chapter analyses the findings of the Wellbeing of LGBTIQ Youth (Hyvinvoiva sateenkaarinuori[1]) research project, especially focusing on experiences of resisting normativity in schools. The project was the first in Finland to cover in depth the experiences of young people in sexual and gender minorities. It consisted of a large web survey, the collection of life writings and the work of peer research groups who discussed the findings. The project was, in the Finnish context, ground-breaking in producing new knowledge on the much-neglected experiences of discrimination, invisibility and resistance of LGBTIQ youth. It gained considerable publicity, and its results have been used to promote equality and diversity.

Although the Wellbeing of LGBTIQ Youth research project certainly has helped to bring forward issues faced by queer youth in schools as well as other walks of life, it naturally had several limitations. A short-term project, focusing on individualised aspects of well-being, sets limits on what kind of modes of resistance can be produced within it. By being critical and acknowledging the

1 This research project, conducted by Finnish Youth Research Society and Seta – LGBTI Rights in Finland from 2012 to 2015, was funded by Finnish Ministry of Education and Culture from the funds for the implementation of the Finnish Government's Child and youth policy programme 2012-2015.

limitations of the project I do not mean to abandon its achievements, on the contrary, my intention is to ask what kind of forms of resistance was it possible to produce within the project and why? Being self-reflective on the limitations of our project, I wish to discuss how research on young LGBTIQ people can be developed so as to tackle normativities, discrimination and other obstacles faced by them.

In this chapter, I claim that while the project, and especially the young peer-researchers participating in it, succeeded in producing novel ways to challenge and resist heteronormative and gender-normative practices in schools, these ways can be seen as rather tame and polite. This, I suggest, is because the resistance produced was shaped by the context of project-formed equality research in particular (Brunila, 2009, 2011, 2014) and the Finnish thinking of equality in general.

The outline of this chapter is as follows. First, I introduce my key concepts and the theoretical framework and then describe the research project on which this chapter is based. Next, I move to the research results on how the normativities of school and possibilities of resistance were depicted by the young people participating in the project. I analyse how these young people describe the production of heteronormative and gender-normative practices in school and, especially, what kind of possibilities they see for challenging these practices. I will scrutinise these findings in the light of Kevin Kumashiro's (2002) four different approaches to an anti-oppressive pedagogy. These approaches are (1) education for the *Other* and (2) about the *Other*, which aim at bringing those who challenge the norms into the teaching, and (3) education that is critical of *Othering* and, finally, (4) education that discusses the oppressive discourses in the society and helps to unlearn the partialities involved in teaching. At the end of the chapter, I draw together the discussion of challenging norms and the limitations of *troubling*.

From heteronormativity to equality

For at least two decades, heteronormativity has been one of the core concepts of queer studies (for early usage, see Warner, 1991). The concept has now penetrated everyday language outside academia, which is also visible in my research, where young people used it to describe the invisibility and exclusion of non-heterosexual and non-gender conforming students at schools. The deployment of the concept of heteronormativity tells of the possibilities that have opened for the young people of today to discuss and to challenge the limitations they face.

Heteronormativity in schools takes the form of exclusion and silencing, in which, also, many non-heterosexual and non-gender conforming students and teachers take part by closeting themselves and keeping the difficult queer issues covered (e.g. Sanders, 2013: 163). Following the thinking of Jukka Lehtonen (2010: 177), who has discussed heteronormativity in Finnish schools, I see heteronormativity as a structure that works to silence and deny other forms of sexuality and gender besides those of binary-gendered, heterosexual man and woman. As Lehtonen points out, silencing needs not to be complete: othered sexualities and genders may become visible, but as marginalised and as less valuable or real than normative heterosexualities (Lehtonen, 2010). In other words, the existence of the othered is needed to support the norm.

In this chapter, I use the term queer to refer to all LGBTIQ youth and other young people who challenge the norms governing sexuality and gender. I also wish to include under the umbrella term queer those young people who are somehow seen as sexually or gender non-conforming but do not identify with any of the identity labels listed above. As one of the key findings in my research was the versatility of identifications among young people when discussing gender and sexuality, and the reluctance many of them felt to use categorising labels, I too refrain from using listings of labels. In this sense, queer can also be seen a verb: it is not a stable identity or a group of identities, but an act of shaking the normativities (for this kind of usage of the word queer, see e.g. Youdell, 2004: 220).

I am aware that queer does not function as an uncontested term for all those concerned–especially so in Finland (on the Finnish translations of queer, see Mizielinska, 2006: 89-92). The Finnish concept used in the research project was neither queer nor any acronym, such as LGBTIQ, but the word *sateenkaari* (*rainbow*), which is sometimes used in Finland to refer to people outside of heterosexual and cisgendered[2] norms.

2 Cisgendered is a term developed in the 1990s in trans communities to refer to those who are not transgendered. The aim of the term is to avoid subscribing to the idea that being non-transgendered would be the norm and trans an exception. The term was introduced into academic discussion by Susan Stryker (2008). While the term certainly is helpful in undoing the uncontested naturality of being cingendered, it has also been criticised for, despite the opposite intentions, maintaining the binary difference between trans and cis and, thus, including only cis on the normative side (on this discussion, see Aultman, 2014).

When discussing school, I refer mostly to the highest classes of comprehensive school and upper secondary schools, as these were the educational institutions described by most participants of the research. The recounted experiences date to the early 2000s or later, when the participants were mostly aged between thirteen and eighteen years-old. The reflections, if they named the type of school, mostly concerned general upper secondary schools.[3]

In my analysis of the ways in which queer students challenge the normativities in school, I use the framework of Kevin Kumashiro's four approaches of anti-oppressive pedagogy (Kumashiro, 2002: 31-71). The first approach is named as *education for the Other*, and in it the teacher acknowledges and takes into account the diversity of the students, trying to also include those in the teaching that do not fit in the norms–in the case of heteronorm and gendernorms this means queer students. The second approach is *teaching about the Other*: telling all students about those who do challenge the norms. Kumashiro sees it as one of the core problems with these approaches that they do not shake the boundaries between the norm and the other but may even work to strengthen them.

The third approach is education that is critical of privileging and Othering. This directs attention to the norm instead of focusing on those othered. Kumashiro notes that this approach not only analyses the oppression but also aims to bring about change. On the other hand he critiques the approach for hiding the diversity of experiences of marginalisation. The fourth approach, education that changes students and society, discusses oppressive discourses that are cited in the society, analysing how these citations can be changed. This, according to Kumashiro, requires both acknowledging the partiality of teaching and adopting *a pedagogy of crisis* (Kumashiro, 2002: 62-64), in which students are on purpose made uncomfortable, in order to *unlearn* the oppressive norms they have grown up with.

It needs to be underlined that Kumashiro sees all these four approaches as essential and states that only by working within all of the modes is it possible to challenge the norms and trouble hegemonies in education. As Kumashiro mainly focuses on the role of the educator, it is left somewhat in the shade what the students can do to support and promote anti-oppressive practices. In my research the focus is on the students, their experiences and inputs and I shift the focus on queer adults or queer educators discussed by Kumashiro to queer youth.

---

3 Upper secondary education in Finland is divided into general upper secondary schools (*lukio*), preparing students for universities, and vocational schools.

What is, then, the equality that is supposed to be promoted in schools? In Finland, equality is most commonly understood as gender equality, that is, equality between men and women. However, other aspects of equality have become increasingly visible through European Union initiatives during the last twenty years. In the Finnish language one word, *tasa-arvo*, is used for gender equality and another, *yhdenvertaisuus*, for other aspects of equality and non-discrimination based on factors such as sexual orientation, ethnicity or (dis) ability. (On the different connotations of these words in Finnish, see Holli, 2003: 8-14.)

It has been seen as a core of Finnish equality work that equality needs to be driven through consensus, not conflict. In addition, equality needs to be made beneficial for all, not only for those suffering from inequality. Furthermore, the idea of achieved equality is an integral part of the self-portrait of the Finnish society. According to Anne Maria Holli, this view of equality in Finland is so strong that gender equality and the promotion of it has been presented in juxtaposition with feminism. Feminism is represented as advancing conflicting interests and a conflict between genders, whereas promotion of gender equality is seen as striving for harmony and gender cooperation (Holli, 2003: 16-19). The same kind of thinking is visible with respect to other aspects of equality and non-discrimination: they should be promoted emphasising the common good of the whole society, rather than differing and possibly conflicting interests.

I analyse both the research project Wellbeing of LGBTIQ Youth and the possibilities for equality work in schools produced in it in the context of Finnish and Nordic equality work. In Finland, the work for equality has been carried out largely through educational projects, which are often short-term and individually oriented, in line with the neoliberal ideas of self-governing subjectivity (see e.g. Brunila, 2009: 35; 2011). As Kristiina Brunila and Charlotta Edström (2013) state, heteronormativity is one core concept of the Nordic equality model. The Nordic equality thinking relies on the unchallenged norm of binary heterosexual gender. Thus, I think is worthwhile to analyse how heteronormativity was contested within the frame of this short-term research project.

Researching experiences of queer youth

Kristiina Brunila (2014) analyses the growing tendency of advancing the equality of *at risk* groups in precarious, short-term development projects, which often have very individual approaches to inequality. According to Brunila (2014: 9), 'development programmes are publicly-funded (e.g. by the EU or Finnish government) short-term efforts that educate, guide and rehabilitate young people'. One could add researching young people in volatile positions to the goals of these efforts–this was done in the Wellbeing of LGBTIQ Youth research project. The duration of the project was, all in all, two years, during which an extensive collection of data was carried out, the data was analysed, and two research publications were published (for a summary of the project, see Taavetti, Alanko and Heikkinen, 2015).

The project was organised by The Finnish Youth Research Society and Seta–LGBTI Rights in Finland. In the first part of the research, a quantitative study based on a web survey was conducted. The survey was the first of its kind in Finland to cover in depth the well-being and social positions of young LGBTIQ people. It reached a high number of participants: 1,619 respondents, aged between fifteen to twenty-five years-old, filled the comprehensive survey, and as the survey was open to everyone regardless of their age, in total it was answered by 2,515 respondents (Alanko, 2014: 12). The questions in the survey covered mental and physical health, social relations, experiences of discrimination and violence, as well as personal evaluations on how sexual and gender identity had affected various aspects in the lives of young queer individuals.[4]

My task in the second phase of the project (Taavetti, 2015) was to deepen the knowledge on queer youth by conducting a qualitative study. As there were already studies depicting the experiences of queer youth (see especially Lehtonen, 2003 on school and Lehtonen, 2004a on working life), I wanted to take a step further and find out how the young queer people act in situations they face in their everyday life. Thus, in addition to studying the data collected from the open-ended questions of the survey conducted in the first part of the research project, we organised a life writings collection campaign in collaboration with the Finnish Folklore Archives.[5] A total of 142 people took part in the collection, and sixty-five of the writings were from young people between the ages fifteen to twenty-five. The call for writings was made mainly online, and it was possible to participate via a web form. Should the participant wish so, it was possible to answer completely anonymously.

In addition to these two forms of written individual accounts, the survey and the life writings, I formed groups to work with the issues raised in the study. I was

4 Katarina Alanko's research findings were published in a research report, first in 2013 in Swedish and in 2014 in Finnish. (Alanko, 2013 and 2014.)

5 Folklore Archives of the Finnish Literature Society is an institution specialised in the gathering and research of folklore, reminiscence writings and life writings.

especially interested in what kind of changes the young queer people themselves would like to see in their lives. The six peer-research groups, which were led by young volunteers (thirty-two young people in total), gathered in spring 2014 to discuss experiences of young queer people. The groups could freely choose the topics they wanted to discuss, and the subjects varied between equality, support needed for queer youth, assumptions and prejudices, family, and experiences of discrimination. One of the groups was planned from the beginning to focus on issues faced by trans youth. The groups were gathered with the help of the young group leaders, and the call to participate was again made over social media. The groups were gathered for the purpose of this research only, and though some of the participants were taking part in LGBTIQ activism, this was not the case with all of them.

The method of peer-research groups was inspired by activist-oriented Participatory Action Research (PAR), in which the aim is to work with the research participants for social change. PAR stresses the reflective nature of the research process both for the professional researcher and peer-researchers. (McIntyre, 2008: 58-59). Participatory research has become especially popular in youth research during approximately the last decade (Heath and Walker, 2012: 7-10). This is partly due to the view that the participation of children and young people is essential in developing policies concerning them–this applies to Finland as well as, for instance, the UK (Heath et al., 2009: 59-62; for Finnish examples, see, e.g., Kaukko, 2013). According to Mervi Kaukko (2013: 201-203), PAR can be seen as a circular process, in which observing, planning, action, and reflection follow each other. In my research, the peer-research groups worked to gather data and partly also to interpret it, using the data collected in the survey.

The peer-research groups could document their work in the form of texts, but also in other forms, such as recordings, drawings or videos. It has been seen as worthwhile to give the young peer-researchers the possibility to choose in which form they wish to document their findings (e.g. Bagnoli, 2012: 78-80), so the peer-researchers have control over the form as well as the content of their work. The two groups that met online provided the whole chat log of their meetings for the research. In two of the other groups, the leaders wrote a memo of the groups' discussions, and in one of these the leader also made a small questionnaire for the group. The last two groups made videos: one recorded interviews of the group members and the other made statements concerning equality on video.

Even as the confidential atmosphere created by research conducted by peers is certainly an asset, as young peers may have better contact to other young people than an adult researcher, this may also involve dangers. Sue Heath and Charlie Walker (2012: 11), for example, have noted that young people working in peer research groups may be too open, revealing things that they would not, in fact, wish to be used in research. Independent work without the presence of an adult researcher may partly reduce this risk. In my research, the groups were not observed, and they could choose how they wanted to present their work for the research. Even though the group leaders were young peers, the methods and topic choice were directed by the need to produce useful material for the research. This pressure was mentioned by some of the group leaders. Confidentiality of the group work was stressed for all the participants. I also made it clear that no-one in the group was required to tell any more of their life than they felt comfortable. This was also underlined by the possibility to discuss the topics described by the survey participants instead of the experiences of the group members, For this purpose, the groups had a selection of the survey answers for their use.

The methods of collecting the data–extensive survey, collection of life writings and peer-group work–all require comparable strengths from the participants. Brunila (2014) states that young people at risk are offered two roles, either coming out of their difficulties as survivors or being socially excluded. According to her, the therapeutic discourse exercised in projects concerning at-risk youth invites young people to address themselves as survivors in order to be heard. In our research project, especially the open-ended questions in the web survey told stories of survivors: often, young people recounted their hard experiences and how they have overcome them. When it comes to life writings, it has been noted (e.g. Kontula and Haavio-Mannila, 1995: 20-21) that commonly those who write have had tough experiences, which they want to share, while those who have been crushed by hardships seldom have the strength to tell. Thus, survivors are often well represented also among the writers. In addition, taking part in participatory research requires both the will to challenge norms, often resulting from experiences of their limitations, and the strength to do so–in other words, being some sort of survivor.

According to Heath and Walker (2012: 10; see also Heath et al., 2009: 14-15), participatory research methods as such may create additional forms of self-governance of young people, as they move the control used in research, at least partly, from the adult researcher to the young peer-researchers. This puts participatory methods, and especially a critical researcher practicing them, in a difficult position. The very same methods that are used to challenge the hierarchies in research and to raise the voices of queer youth, are, in fact, moving the control of the research to the responsibility of the young participants.

In studying the results, I deployed grounded analysis by coding the themes discussed in the data from the survey, life writings and peer-research groups. I analysed the different strategies the participants described, such as hiding one's personal feelings, opposing the normative structures or withdrawing oneself from surroundings that has felt unaccepting. Thus, I studied both the discrimination and support the participants described as well as the ways they had found to challenge the norms and limitations they have faced.

Invisibility, discrimination, and support in schools

In our study, evidence of the importance of schools was that so many participants had experiences to share: in the survey the question about school was the most commonly answered open-ended question about experiences in different walks of life. The experiences described by the respondents, of course, vary greatly and sometimes offer contradictory views of queer youth.

One important way of building heteronormativity in schools is the invisibility of everything that fails to fit this norm. Kumashiro (2002: 32-34) discusses this in his work when he addresses the need of teaching for the *other*, which means acknowledging the diversity of students in the classroom. In fact, it is surprising how detailed the descriptions young queer people can give of the norms in school: it is often very difficult to describe invisibility, as the main aspect of it is that there is nothing to tell.

According to descriptions by the participants, love or sexual relationships between members of the same sex are usually mentioned in school only when discussing different sexual orientations in health education. To connect this to Kumashiro's work (2002: 39-40), these answers tell of the need for teaching about the *Other*, of including the marginalised or othered groups into the curriculum. In the survey, the respondents described that whenever family relations, romantic love or dating were visible in teaching, heterosexuality was the unquestioned norm. This was described by one respondent:

> I feel that upper secondary school teaching does not take sexual minorities into account, and due to that, some situations in school have been extremely awkward. Teaching material and teachers skip sexual

> minorities with only a few sentences, as if homosexuality was extremely rare and in no way central to any student.[6]

Moreover, the example above tells of the need the students have felt to contest the normatives in teaching. To apply Kumashiro's thinking (2002: 44-50), it is not enough that some teaching about homosexuality is included, but the heterosexual norm in itself needs to be addressed.

One of the changes in queer visibility in Finnish schools, during recent years, is the relative growth in the visibility of homosexuality in teaching. The trend has been from complete silence to marginal representation. Even if the current way of representing homosexuality is minoritising, depicting homosexuality as an attribute of a distinct group of people (Sedgwick, 2008), it still opens more possibilities of challenging heteronormativity than complete silence. The same power that marginalises homosexuality also makes it intelligible, a named identity (Foucault, 1990: 42-43). In comparison with a Swedish analysis (Ambjörnsson, 2008: 217-238), it still seems that Finnish queer students have more experiences of exclusion and invisibility than their Swedish peers.

As noted in the excerpt above, even when queer issues were discussed in schools the manner may have been alienating and placed queerness outside the classroom, as not relevant to the students (see also Lehtonen, 2003: 66-67). This may lead to alienating experiences, especially as the few portrayals of other than straight cisgendered people in teaching might not resonate with queer young people's experiences and their views. Many young queers are not interested in labelling themselves with identity-based categories (see also Lehtonen, 1998). They might feel alienated from common terms, such as gay, lesbian or bisexual, and only use them if absolutely necessary. When any queer issues are dealt with in school teaching, it is usually based on strict and categorical identity labels. One respondent of the survey compared the teaching about sexual minorities to familiarising the students with an alien animal species:

> The topic [sexual minorities–RT] is introduced as some new animal species in the biology class: We are shown a wildlife-film-like video on a rainbow family's every-day life. They mean well, but I don't think tolerance is achieved by watching a video and then assuming that the students should tolerate different minorities. If the life of sexual

6 Translations form the original Finnish by the author.

> minorities is completely normal, as it is, why do we need to see a video on it at school? We don't watch videos on straight life either?!

As well as in Kumashiro's approaches (2002: 32-44), it is noted in this example that increasing knowledge about the othered groups or the processes of othering does not automatically mean increasing tolerance, empathy or, even less, will to work for breaking the norms.

While the visibility of homosexuality causes fractures in heteronormativity in schools, gender diversity is still almost invisible in schools. Students who do not feel comfortable in their assigned gender may be unable to find a name for their feelings, let alone knowing what to do in their situation. This was described by a participant in a chat-based peer-research group for trans issues:

> I find it quite unbelievable that a school nurse for example can be so utterly ignorant about trans issues and even more surprising is the fact that an employee (a nurse) in a youth psychiatric polyclinic can "justify" this by saying that there are so few trans youth.

According to this participant, teachers and school nurses seldom have sufficient knowledge of the gender reassignment process, or other services the young people may need. When this ignorance is criticised, trans issues are interpreted as being so marginal that they can be safely ignored in general health care.

In the young participants' descriptions, school is by no means only an arena of exclusion and invisibility. Many young people report encouraging experiences of support from teachers and other adults in school. In the general atmosphere of absence and invisibility, very small changes can make a difference: a supportive teacher, an assignment in which one can touch issues concerning gender and sexuality, or just someone who is willing to discuss queer topics can prove to be of enormous value. For example, a teacher who is willing to use the name chosen by a student to match their gender identity better than their original name, may send a powerful message of acceptance and respect, as illustrated by one of the responders of the survey:

> My music teacher in upper secondary school was a very kind and tolerant person. They accepted everyone as they were, and when I told I wished to be called by a name chosen by myself, rather than my given name, the

> teacher called me by the name of my choice, my own name. Music class and music lessons were a safe place in a difficult life situation in upper secondary school; there I could load my batteries in the middle of school days and my personal troubles. In the classroom I also learned important lessons on being a human and grew enormously as a person. I have always held the teacher as my role model and I appreciate them enormously.

In addition to the huge meaning of the right to use one's own name, this excerpt also demonstrates the impact of seemingly small deeds. One single teacher, in a subject often considered rather marginal in schools, was able to give the student memories of acceptance they recollect after years when answering a survey.

Queer challenges to school

Additionally, young queer people tell about ways of tackling invisibility and heteronormativity in schools. In the survey and personal narratives, writers recount individual ways of challenging school: correcting teachers when they use outdated terms, or speaking in the classroom as part of school assignments of their own sexual or gender identities. Sometimes these fractures on normativity are met with praise and support:

> Once during the second year of high school I held an "effective speech" (title of the assignment) on trans topic. During the speech I also "came out" with the issue. People looked very confused, but afterwards I got comments that the speech was very good. I also got a ten [the highest mark–RT] for it (I wonder if I got it because it actually was so good as a speech, or because of my courage).

Sometimes teachers are not supportive for students who challenge the normativities of school, as described by one of the survey respondents:

> Now in high school homosexuality or trans issues have often just been ignored. I have started to note this to the teachers, and I don't know if they like it. Anyway, I have started to criticise their behaviour.

These courageous individual efforts to bend the norms often fall under the topic of educating for the *Other* or about the *Other* in the Kumashiro's

(2002: 31-75) classification, in which, on one hand, the diversity of students is taken into account in teaching and, on the other hand, all students are taught about those groups that are marginalised in the society. Young queer people are bringing their own views to teaching, thus making the othered visible in the class.

Sometimes just being visibly present can equal challenging norms. Dating gay couples, for instance, may challenge the school norms and regulations, and force them to address the double standard according to which homosexuality is considered as private and thus not suitable for school, unlike heterosexuality (on the contradictory invisibility of dating lesbians in school, see Ambjörnsson, 2008: 235-237). Also, the mere identification of a student as non-straight may queer their actions in the eyes of others and, thus, queer the school space as well, as Deborah Youdell (2004) has suggested. Recent achievements in struggles for equality and diversity have normalised queerness in general and homosexuality in particular. But still, there are examples from recent years of young queers facing limitations due to marginalisation or, for example, oversexualisation of their queerness. According to a survey respondent, born in 1994, when she was in upper secondary school she was told not to hold hands with her girlfriend. This was justified by the teachers as a way of preventing bullying.

The peer-research groups, who discussed the problems faced by queer students at school, hoped to gain more visibility for queer issues and diversity, especially outside sex education. Accommodating queer issues in teaching outside health education can been seen as a drive towards more a universalising view of homosexuality (Sedgwick, 2008), in which homosexuality is not a feature of well-defined *species* (Foucault, 1986: 18-19) but part of everybody's lives. The participants saw it vital that homosexuality and trans issues would be a part of normal, daily teaching starting from an early stage:

> The teaching should be started in elementary school, not as late as in lower secondary school's health education classes. It's been a while since my elementary school days, so it might be different now, but I don't remember that sexual diversity would have been covered in any way there. Of course, we discussed puberty and, along with that, sexual awakening, but even that focused on things like 'it is normal that you start liking boys etc.', so from the straight point of view.

The marginality of trans issues in teaching, however, may be about to change. The new core curriculum of Finnish comprehensive schools that was accepted in 2014, states that teaching should provide understanding of the diversity of gender.

According to Irina Schmitt (2010), even as invisibility is a great problem for queer students, it is also a form of safety, and being visible is often a threat to one's safety and position. Schmitt (2010: 20-21) writes that being visible as queer often means an exhausting need to educate everybody in one's surroundings. In the ideas developed by the peer-researchers, this need was moved, at least partly, from queer students to teachers. Peer-research groups hoped that teachers who are queer could be open about it in school:

> In the discussion, teachers who had spoken openly about their homosexuality were seen as some kind of idols and role models. The group found it great that a teacher, who is often an authority, can show that you can do well in life even if you belong to a sexual minority.

According to Jukka Lehtonen (2004b, 242), support from the school staff is vital for teachers who ponder the possibility of openness about their sexual orientation at school. As participants of the peer-research groups were well aware of the normative pressures, they also demanded that the school should be supportive of the openness of teachers, as exemplified in the report of another peer-research group:

> We would like that non-heterosexual teachers would be able to tell about their lives to students as they like, as heterosexual teachers sometimes tell. The school should stand behind these teachers.

These ideas, too, are in line with teaching about the *Other* or teaching for the *Other* (Kumashiro, 2002: 31-75), although these are more structural than those described above. They direct the focus to the support of teachers and to ways that the curricula should accommodate queer topics, so that they would not be left the responsibility of queer students' activism. In addition, these accounts tell of intergenerational solidarity felt by the students: on the one hand, they need queer teachers for their own support; but on the other hand, they are aware of the difficulties faced by these teachers and express the need for structural support.

One of the peer-research groups suggested a new version of Living Libraries for schools. A Living Library (sometimes called Human Library) is a method in which a Reader can *borrow* a Living Book, a person representing some discriminated minority, for discussion and ask all the questions they have not dared to ask in public. The method is meant to increase knowledge and to lessen prejudices, and thus, to promote anti-discrimination. The method–or at least the variant used in Finland–originates from Denmark, where the first Living Library was arranged in 2000. Although it has spread to many countries, Living Libraries is most popular in the Nordic countries (Little et al., 2011: 10-13).

In the Living Libraries version discussed in the peer-research group, the Library would be part of the teaching in every school, and all students would *borrow* all the Books available in the Library selection. This is because otherwise students might be afraid of stigmatisation and avoid choosing the Living Books most relevant for them. Also, as Finland is a country of long distances and queer people, especially in smaller towns and villages, might feel awkward posing as Books, it was suggested that the loan sessions could be organised via video connections.

One survey respondent, as described earlier, criticised showing a video on queer life in biology class as exoticising sexual minorities like a new animal species. In the light of this criticism, it seems somewhat contradictory that one of the methods to increase queer awareness suggested by the peer-researchers was a version of Living Libraries. There are, though, some notable differences between these methods. From the viewpoint of the students, a video is a passive way of learning, as opposed to actively asking questions from a Living Book. Also, if a Living Book is a young person, a peer in a way, it may be a welcome addition to normal teaching and text-books–or videos–in which queer issues are usually shown only as part of adult life.

Even as both Living Library and a video on a queer family might, as methods of education, fit to the same forms of anti-oppressive pedagogy in Kumashiro's (2002: 31-75) classification, they have significant differences. The main target of Living Libraries is the reduction of prejudices, promotion of empathy and provision of information on those othered in the society (Little et al., 2011: 16), and these could very well also be the goals of showing a video. But fulfilment of these goals might not be the only thing that happens during a Living Book loan. One-on-one or small-group discussion may result in questioning the Loaner's own assumed normalcy in addition to addressing the Loaner's prejudices and the group represented by the Book. For instance, experiences from Australia show that loan sessions in Living Libraries are more complex than just those in the mainstream being the Loaners and those othered being the Books (Dreher and Mowbray, 2012: 56). Contemplating one's own normalcy and diverse differences may cause, on a minor scale and in a positive manner, a crisis in the Reader, which Kumashiro (2002) sees as a condition for a learning process that can truly challenge the normativities of society.

Queering the school, queering the world

To summarise, the suggestions made by the peer-research groups were twofold. First, providing up-to-date information about queer issues, and second, having queer people as role models for the students. These ideas for equality work were also directed towards the whole school and all students, not just to strengthening the queer students by organising peer-support groups or some other targeted actions. Reading these suggestions in the light of Kumashiro's typification, they mostly cover educating for the *Other* and educating about the *Other*. In other words, what the young participants identified as key problems in the schools were the lack of knowledge of queer issues and queer invisibility. They produced ways to tackle these problems, calling for queer topics to be added to the curriculum, as well as promoting queer visibility in schools by demanding support for queer teachers and suggesting that a version of Living Libraries should be arranged in every school. In her article on the narratives of queer youth, Susan Talburt (2004) suggests, that certain very similar approaches adopt the logic of heteronormative mainstream and the queer as an exception. While Talburt is critical of the ways in which adults impose these kind of solutions on young people, I might add that young people themselves produce them as well.

These ways of promoting equality are very well in line with those that, according Kristiina Brunila and Charlotta Edström's (2013) analysis, are the most common ways to work for gender equality in the Nordic countries: in order to achieve equality, the public should be educated about the downsides of discrimination, and especially girls should be offered role models guiding them to male-dominated fields and professions. Also, in Finland as well as in other Nordic countries, equality is seen as important, as it is beneficial for the society as a whole, and it is to be achieved by education for all, not first by emancipating those who suffer from inequality (see e.g. Brunila and Ylöstalo, 2013: 3; 7-9).

Focusing on information, education and role models might seem individualistic. This is very well in line with the neoliberal idea of internalised control, which is seen by Brunila (2009: 27-29) as one core element of contemporary equality work. Even as the ideas for equality work produced by the peer-researchers were geared towards the school as a whole, they did not focus on norms or oppressive discourses, but on educating the assumed majority about the minority. The stress on education and information puts the responsibility to act in an equal manner on the individual being educated instead of addressing the structures that maintain the unequal status quo. Deriving from Finnish discourses on equality, and framed by project-formed individual-based research, this was perhaps the extent to which and the ways in which it was possible to produce challenges for the normativities of school.

Not only do these polite ways of promoting equality as an issue for all fit very well in the Finnish understanding of equality as a common denominator of Finnish society (e.g. Holli, 2003: 10-14), but they are also mature, civilised ways of advancing one's agenda. As Talburt (2004) states, adults may view youth experiences through their current understanding of their identity, which they project upon queer adolescence, failing to remember or see the experiences that are not comprehensible in their adult framework of thinking. In the peer-research groups, as the young participants were involved in an adult-defined research process, they were probably led to think of ways mostly encouraged by adults, that is polite and mature, not of those more rebellious or disturbing.

Interestingly, however, at the same time the young queer people hit what Brunila and Edström (2013) define as the unchallenged core of Nordic gender inequality: heteronormativity. Following Brunila and Edström's thinking, queer visibility as such can be seen as challenging heteronormativity, and thus a very important tool for promoting equality and breaking the structures of inequality. Thus, the young queer participants' views on promoting equality implicitly take a very interesting position on Nordic equality work: they are in line with the dominant methods of Nordic equality work, but, when it comes to the actual content, they manage to employ the very same methods to challenge the heteronorm.

When considering Kumashiro's (2002: 31-75) four approaches to anti-oppressive pedagogy, the productions by the participants of our research project fit into the two forms that do not challenge the boundaries between the norm and the *Other*. However, as the participants' ideas work from down to up, producing student-led and peer-based forms of teaching, all the results may not be the same as in Kumashiro's view. More *troubling*, or more queerness, may be caused when students themselves act as instructors of their peers, as has been depicted in readings of the results of Living Libraries.

The ways that young queer people challenge schools are, still, quite tame and polite, even when the individual deeds might require a great amount of personal courage. The young people mainly want to offer new insights and open new possibilities, instead of openly confronting the discriminatory practices, which might make the majority more uncomfortable. Without the support of teachers and the school in general, and within the Finnish climate of consensus where equality is promoted as beneficial for all, this is perhaps the extent to which one can even think of bending the productive normative power and troubling school. Still, even the tiny fractures in the normativities make a huge difference. Young queer people are creative in thinking of novel ways to cause these breaks and shake the normativities, as they challenge the teacher-centred modes of learning and call for peer-led forms of queering the school.

References

Alanko, K., (2013) *Hur mår HBTIQ-unga i Finland?* Ungdomsforskningsnätverket/ Ungdomsforskningssällskapets nätpublikation 68, Seta-publikationer 21. Helsinki: Nuorisotutkimusseura and Seta.

Alanko, K., (2014) *Mitä kuuluu sateenkaarinuorille Suomessa?* Nuorisotutkimusverkoston/ Nuorisotutkimusseuran verkkojulkaisuja 72. Seta-julkaisuja 23. Helsinki: Nuorisotutkimusseura and Seta.

Ambjörnsson, F., (2008) *I en klass för sig. Genus, klass och sexualitet bland gymnasietjejer,* Stockholm: Ordfront.

Aultman, B., (2014) Cisgender, *TSQ*, 1(1-2): 61-62.

Bagnoli, A., (2012) Making sense of mixed method narratives: Young people's identities, life-plans, and time orientations, in Heath, S. and Walker, C., (eds.) *Innovations in Youth Research,* London: Palgrave Macmillan, 77-100.

Brunila, K., (2009) *Parasta ennen. Tasa-arvotyön projektitapaistuminen,* Kasvatustieteen laitoksen tutkimuksia 222. Helsinki: Helsingin yliopisto.

Brunila, K., (2011) The projectisation, marketisation and therapisation of education, *European Educational Research Journal*, 10(3): 421-432.

Brunila, K., (2014) The rise of the survival discourse in an era of therapisation and neoliberalism, *Education Inquiry*, 5(1): 7-23.

Brunila, K. and Edström, C., (2013) The famous Nordic equality and what's Nordic about it? Gender equality in Finnish and Swedish education, *Nordic Studies in Education,* 33(3): 300-313.

Brunila, K. and Ylöstalo, H., (2013) Challenging gender inequalities in education and in working life - a mission possible? *Journal of Education and Work*, 28(5): 443-460.

Ministry of Education and Culture, (2012) *Child and Youth Policy Programme 2012-2015, Publications of the Ministry of Education and Culture 2012:8*, Helsinki: Ministry of Education and Culture, http://www.minedu.fi/export/sites/default/OPM/Julkaisut/2012/liitteet/OKM8.pdf?lang=en [Accessed 1 June 2015].

Dreher, T. and Mowbray, J., (2012) *The power of one on one. Human Libraries and the challenges of antiracism work,* Sydney: University of Technology Sydney, https://opus.lib.uts.edu.au/research/bitstream/handle/2100/1397/ThePowerofOneonOne_monograph.pdf?sequence=3 [Accessed 3 June 2015].

Foucault, M., (1986) *The use of pleasure. Volume 2 of the History of sexuality,* New York: Vintage Books.

Foucault, M., (1990 [1978]) *History of sexuality. Vol. 1, An introduction,* London: Penguin Books.

Heath, S., Brooks, R., Cleaver, E. and Ireland, E., (2009) *Researching Young People's Lives,* London: Sage.

Heath, S. and Walker, C., (2012) Innovations in youth research: An introduction, in Heath, S. and Walker, C., (eds.) *Innovations in youth research,* London: Palgrave Macmillan, 1-20.

Holli, A. M., (2003) *Discourse and politics for gender equality in late twentieth century Finland,* Acta Politica 23, Helsinki: Department of Political Science, University of Helsinki.

McIntyre, A., (2008) *Participatory Action Research, Qualitative Research Methods Series 52,* Thousand Oaks, California: Sage.

Kaukko, M., (2013) Everyday choices, meaningful activities and reliable adults. Diverse paths to empowerment of unaccompanied asylum-seeking girls, in Törrönen, M., Borodkina, O., Samoylova, V. and Heino, E., (eds.) *Empowering social work: research and practice,* Helsinki: Palmenia Centre for Continuing Education.

Kontula, O. and Haavio-Mannila, E., (1995) *Matkalla intohimoon. Nuoruuden hurma ja kärsimys seksuaalielämäkertojen kuvaamana,* Helsinki: WSOY.

Kumashiro, K., (2002) *Troubling education. Queer activism and antioppressive pedagogy,* New York: RoutledgeFalmer.

Lehtonen, J., (1998) Young people's definitions of their non-heterosexuality, in Helve, H., (ed.) *Unification and Marginalisation of Young People,* Helsinki: Finnish Youth Research Society, 185-192.

Lehtonen, J., (2003) *Seksuaalisuus ja sukupuoli koulussa. Näkökulmana heteronormatiivisuus ja ei-heteroseksuaalisten nuorten kertomukset,* Helsinki: Yliopistopaino and Nuorisotutkimusseura.

Lehtonen, J., (2004a) Lesbian, gay and bisexual youth in the labour market, in Lehtonen, J. and Mustola, K., (eds.) *"Straight people don't tell, do they..." Negotiating the boundaries of sexuality and gender at Work,* Helsinki: Ministry of Labour, 137-153.

Lehtonen, J., (2004b) Lesbian, gay and bisexual teachers—invisible in the mind of the students? In Lehtonen, J. and Mustola, K., (eds.) *"Straight people don't tell, do they..." Negotiating the boundaries of sexuality and gender at Work,* Helsinki: Ministry of Labour, 238-254.

Lehtonen, J., (2010) Gendered post-compulsory educational choices of non-heterosexual youth, *European Educational Research Journal,* 9(2): 177-191.

Little, N., Nemutlu, G., Magic, J. and Molnár, B., (2011) *Don't judge a book by its cover! The Living Library Organiser's Guide 2011,* Budapest: Youth Department of the Council of Europe, https://rm.coe.int/16807023dd [Accessed 3 June 2015].

Mizielinska, J., (2006) Queering Moominland: The problems of translating queer theory into a non-American context, *SQS,* (1): 87-104, https://journal.fi/sqs/article/view/53722 [Accessed 3 June 2015].

Sanders, A., (2013) Safety for K-12 students: United States policy concerning LGBT student safety must provide inclusion, *Confero,* 1(2): 162-172, http://www.confero.ep.liu.se/issues/2013/v1/i2/130822/confero13v1i21c.pdf [Accessed 15 October 2015].

Schmitt, I., (2010) Do you have a boyfriend? Feeling queer in youth and education research, *Lambda Nordica,* 15(3-4): 15-39.

Sedgwick, E. K., (2008) *Epistemology of the closet,* second revised ed., Berkeley: University of California Press.

Stryker, S., (2008) *Transgender History*, Berkeley: Seal.

Taavetti, R., (2015) *"Olis siistiä, jos ei tarttis* määritellä … " Kuriton j*a tavallinen sateenkaarinuoruus,* Helsinki: Nuorisotutkimusseura /Nuorisotutkimusverkosto and Seta, http://www.nuorisotutkimusseura.fi/julkaisuja/hyvinvoiva_sateenkaarinuori.pdf [Accessed 15 October 2015].

Taavetti, R., Alanko, K. and Heikkinen, L., (2015) *Hyvinvoiva sateenkaarinuori - tutkimushanke. Tiivistelmä / Sammandrag / Summary,* Helsinki: Nuorisotutkimusseura /Nuorisotutkimusverkosto and Seta, http://www.nuorisotutkimusseura.fi/images/julkaisuja/hyvinvoiva_sateenkaarinuori_tiivistelma.pdf [Accessed 7 June 2017].

Talburt, S., (2004) Intelligibility and narrating queer youth, in Rasmussen, M. L., Rofes, E. and Talburt, S., (eds.) *Youth and sexualities: Pleasure, subversion, and insubordination in and out of schools*, Gordonsville: Palgrave Macmillan, 17-39.

Warner, M., (1991) Introduction: Fear of a queer planet, *Social Text*, 29: 3-17.

Youdell, D., (2004) Bent as a ballet dancer. The possibilities for and limits of legitimate homomasculinity in school, in Rasmussen, M. L., Rofes, E. and Talburt, S., (eds.) *Youth and sexualities: Pleasure, subversion, and insubordination in and out of schools*, Gordonsville: Palgrave Macmillan: 201-222.

Chapter 9

Using postcolonial discourse analysis in social science education: Troubling hierarchical human relations

Pia Mikander

Social science education is an attempt to make sense of human activity in the world, including its historical and global dimensions. The scope of social science is almost limitless, but the instruction time for the subject is not. This raises important questions such as: What constitutes useful knowledge about the world? Whose perspectives of history or of the present time need to be portrayed? The global information society suggests that more attention should be paid to the concept of knowledge within social science. What knowledge can be considered trustable? Whose versions of reality are to be believed, and why? What kind of knowledge is assumed to be true and relevant?

Postcolonial thinkers have shown how learning about the world has historically been connected to ventures to colonise it (Willinsky, 1998). While the Nordic countries were peripheral to the major colonising projects, they 'participated actively in the production of Europe as the global centre and profited from this experience' (Loftsdóttir and Jensen, 2012: 1). In Finland, school curricula have stated explicitly that education should be based on a number of core values such as human rights, equality and democracy (FNBE, 2004; FNBE, 2014). If these are to be fully taken into account, it is necessary to dismantle the *imperial framework* (Merryfield, 2002) and the hegemony that assumes that Westerners are essentially superior to other people. A truly equal and democratic perspective would suggest that social science not portray anyone in the world as more valuable than another. What would this mean in practice?

In my earlier work (Mikander, 2016) I discuss how textbook material can either strengthen or question the discourse of Western superiority. Textbooks tend to include plenty of information that takes the form of neutral, objective knowledge. Learning to consider these texts critically while at the same time learning about the world is a challenging task for social science students. Here, I develop the idea of postcolonial discourse analysis as a method of analysing school textbooks in social science. The purpose is to consider what postcolonial discourse analysis can bring to the reading of social science textbooks. In practice, the idea is to discuss how postcolonial discourse analysis can be used as an educational tool for social science, as well as to show practical examples of how school textbooks can be analysed.

Theoretical background

The idea of postcolonialism is about challenging colonial domination and the legacies of colonialism (Loomba, 1998; Said, 1978). Even though the world no longer consists of formal colonial powers and colonies, postcolonial analysis can help to explain contemporary human activity such as the current global division of labour. This includes the interrelated material and epistemological dimensions of colonial rule. In *Orientalism* (1978), Said showed how the European and Western portrayal of the world as reflected in academia and culture was linked to economic and administrative control over colonies and other territories. This meant that children and adults even in countries that were not the major players in colonial ventures, such as the Nordic countries, learned to consider people from these places as inferior while simultaneously learning to rationalise the need to dominate them. Textbooks in history and geography in the Nordic countries took part in constructing images of non-Western people as inferior (Paasi, 1998; Isaksson and Jokisalo, 2005; Palmberg, 1987; Ajagán-Lester, 2001; Loftsdóttir, 2010). By portraying these *others* as less intelligent, more static and irrational, readers were encouraged to consider *us* Westerners as more intelligent, dynamic and rational. Education thus provided support for institutions of control over *others* by constructing such hierarchical relations as normal. Through a postcolonial discourse analysis, the construction of this normalising process can be traced and challenged. While the term *postcolonial* should not simply be seen as referring to all kinds of oppression (Tiffin, 1995), postcolonial theory can provide inspiration for developing tools to analyse any hierarchical power relations between humans, including gender and class (see Bracke, 2012; Kilomba, 2015).

Postcolonial analysis highlights the perceived neutrality and objectivity of knowledge, as well as its role in constructing hierarchies between people. Said considered the descriptions of people in colonised countries as inferior to be so common that they could not be attributed only to individual authors. Instead, they had to be seen as products of widespread belief systems (Kumaravadivelu, 1999). Studying these systems, or indeed discourses, is a way of challenging the preconditions for language and actions. What is considered normal or common sense? How do certain kinds of views come to be seen as reasonable while others do not? Postcolonial analysis offers a way to understand how knowledge is and gets constructed as well as how power and knowledge are connected.

Before describing the process of postcolonial discourse analysis further, some words about epistemology are required. Epistemology plays an important role within discourse theory analysis. Laclau and Mouffe (2001) see reality not as something objective that can be discovered, but as something constantly created through words and action. This is an essential part of postcolonial theory as well (Andreotti, 2011). There is no way of establishing a neutral or objective description of reality. For social science teachers, for example, grasping this means having to reconsider old truths about history and geography. It also means that neither teachers nor students are the only neutral spectators of the world–everyone has a set of cultural, ideological glasses through which to observe the world. The good news is that although there might not be many universal, objective truths about the world, and although nobody is watching the world from a neutral perspective, it does not mean there is nothing to be learned about human activity in the world. Quite the opposite: by learning to recognise how discourses work, students can proceed to disrupt hegemonic understandings of, say, the role of Westerners and non-Westerners in the world. This can pave the way for new and different perspectives, building a social science knowledge base that draws on a variety of descriptions.

What can postcolonial theory and discourse analysis bring to education and the study of social science? According to Rizvi, Lingard and Lavia (2006), using the deconstructive and liberatory potential that is essential to postcolonialism can be a way of learning to understand aspects of contemporary globalisation, such as processes of production and the global division of labour. They suggest that postcolonialism makes the history and legacy of European colonialism visible to educational scholars, showing how today's discursive and material global hierarchies are linked to historical power relations. Much social science education is about making meaning of texts. As Kumaravadivelu (1999) suggests, the way a text is deconstructed within the context of the classroom might be more important than the content of the text itself. A critical, reflective perspective can be considered the first requirement. Lozic (2011) takes the analysis of texts within social science a step further and proposes discourse analysis as a model of teaching history in the twenty-first century. He shows, through the example of the history of migration, how students can be encouraged to view texts and images in history textbooks from a discursive perspective. Challenging, for example, how the word *we* is used, and deconstructing explanations that are considered common sense, are ways to approach the textbook practically.

In *Pedagogy of the other*, Burney (2012) draws on Said's postcolonial theory to suggest practical implications for postcolonial teaching practices. These include questioning hegemonic interpretations of the world. For social studies education, she offers a range of things to challenge, such as the Mercator map, which places Europe at the top centre. Burney shows how seemingly objective images such as maps can be considered ideological. A closer look reveals that textbooks and other teaching materials used for history, geography and social studies are filled with concepts, texts and images that would benefit from postcolonial discourse analysis. They include, for instance, names of places or of historical events (such as *journeys of discovery*, see Mikander, 2015).

The critical global citizenship education initiative (Andreotti and Pashby, 2013) emphasises the need to historicise and contextualise education about the world. The concern is that conventional global citizenship education is overly focused on the given moment, and neglects the historical power inequalities that are embedded in today's global issues and relations (Andreotti and de Souza, 2012). Because of this, they see a need within education to examine the processes of knowledge production and their role in the continuing construction of inequalities and violence (Andreotti, 2011). Andreotti and Pashby (2013) list practical, critical questions to ask of educational material, such as:

> What creates poverty? How do different lives have different value? How are these two things connected? What are the relationships between social groups that are over-exploited and social groups that are over-exploiting? How are these relationships maintained? How do people justify inequalities? What are the roles of schooling in the reproduction and contestation of inequalities in society? What possibilities and problems are created by different stories about what is real and ideal in society? (pp. 423-424)

Questions such as these can be modified to fit the topic of the material. Obviously, textbooks and other teaching materials have a limited scope, and compiling them is largely about making choices about what to include and exclude. My research has shown that certain descriptions and understandings that have been disproved by modern science still prevail in textbooks, perhaps because they have been considered commonsensical, or because they are part of a common understanding of how the world works. There are many examples of this, ranging from the myth that non-Western populations are exploding (Mikander and Holm, 2014), to regarding Columbus a hero (Mikander, 2015). In order to challenge such common misconceptions, I propose some further questions to focus on, questions that could help disrupt the idea that neutral knowledge exists in social science. These include: From what perspectives are the events described? Whose voice is being heard? What is portrayed as natural or commonsensical? What practices are considered neutral or sensible? When events are described, what information is included and what is not?

For teachers, asking these questions can mean having to leave the *safe* environment that teaching has traditionally meant (Leonardo and Porter, 2010). However, the fact that education has never been *neutral* points to the need to focus on the silenced voices within social science. As has been suggested by Walsh (2012), while education can either hide or expose how domination and alienation works, this is something that has not been reflected upon enough within social science education.

The textbooks that are quoted in the following sections are part of the material for a research project (Mikander, 2016). They include Finnish textbooks on geography, history and social studies for grades 5 to 9 (eleven to sixteen year-olds). The research covers all textbooks published on these subjects in Finnish and Swedish by the six major publishing companies in Finland between 2005 and 2010. The textbooks were analysed using discourse theory analysis, focusing on descriptions of Westerners and others.

People, places, power and privileges: Challenging seemingly neutral descriptions

Many topics in social science, as described in school textbooks, relate to human interactions, often between different social groups. In history textbooks, wars, peace agreements, revolutions and reforms, for example, are all fundamentally about how groups of people relate to one another. Social studies topics such as human rights, globalisation, trade, crime and political action can also be viewed as examples. Geography textbooks contain descriptions of human interactions, for instance relating to traveling. Countries with a large tourism industry might feature descriptions such as the following, which make the privileged position of tourists visible:

> Many travel to Thailand to admire the nature of the country: the landscapes of the coastline, the lush vegetation and the animals. More and more people are interested in nature traveling, and because of this, it pays off for tourist countries like Thailand to protect their environment. In a tightly inhabited country this is especially important, since there otherwise is the danger that habitation spreads everywhere, leaving no room for animals living in the forest. (Cantell et al., 2008: 67)

This geography textbook quote implies that because of their interest in nature, tourists are saving the nature of Thailand, including wildlife. The last part of the quote specifies what the nature is being preserved from; however, it does not mention the hotel developers but rather the Thai people who might otherwise choose to live there. Using the word *habitation* to refer to people can be considered dehumanising (see Mikander and Holm, 2014) since it turns the focus away from the people who actually live in the houses and who might not have anywhere to live if not for these dwellings. Instead, the focus is on the animals whose space is being restricted. The areas that are built for tourists are not mentioned as harmful or threatening to nature. Postcolonial discourse analytical questions could be used to challenge the assumptions made here, for example that tourists help save the environment by travelling across the world, or that the main reason for Thai people to protect the environment would be because it attracts tourists.

The text shows that plenty can be discussed on the basis of simply a few lines in a geography book. For the teacher, it is important to consider texts such as this as objects of enquiry to be analysed together with students. Textbooks have traditionally held a position of unquestioned authority. In order to teach critical thinking, they, too, benefit from being viewed critically. The analytical questions suggested can help students realise that there are always several perspectives to every story. Generally, when approaching texts, teachers can ask the students to focus on how different people are described, how their actions are described, which practices are considered commonsensical and which are not (such as in the above-mentioned example, building a house for one's family).

Also worth considering in social science teaching is that to understand the social world, one's own position in it needs to be recognised. Many students in the Nordic countries are privileged, due to owning a passport that allows travel to practically all countries (even though not all students come from families that can afford travel). There are good reasons for students to learn to recognise and reflect on their own positions (see Mikander, 2016). This is not always encouraged in textbooks. One Finnish social studies assignment textbook (Honkanen, Marjomäki and Rajala, 2009: 182) encourages students to circle places in the world that they would like to visit, live in, and not live in. While it is easy to understand why this sort of activity would be attractive to students, since it is engaging and encourages them to think about the circumstances in these places in a cross-disciplinary way, it can be considered problematic. These kinds of assignments disregard the position of the Finnish student by not considering that few people in the world can travel freely. The privileges are not made explicit and thereby taken for granted.

Simultaneously, the textbook implies that not everyone can be allowed to move around freely. On the following page (183) of the same social studies book are two follow-up questions:

> 2. Imagine that we are living in a future where the world consists of one supranational state, where moving about and spreading information occurs freely. a) What problems can this situation bring? b) How could these problems be pre-empted?

The first question can be understood to mean: 'Why cannot everyone in the world be allowed to move around and spread information freely?' That way, it could spark discussions about who has the right to decide over other people's mobility and information, perhaps questioning the reader's position. The questions in the book are posed in such a way that they do not challenge the notion that it makes sense to restrict the mobility of certain people (most likely non-Westerners). For a teacher working through this chapter, guiding the discussions towards a more critical analysis would be difficult the way the questions are expressed. However, turning them around and looking at the implicit assumptions behind them, reminding the students of the privileged positions of Westerners and the idea of universal human rights, for instance, might lead to a different kind of learning.

On a broader scale, analysing implicit values and ideologies in social science textbooks could spark discussions about the nature of geographical or historical knowledge. What has traditionally been considered valuable knowledge about the world? How has this changed? What ideologies are reflected in the curriculum? What values in society can be seen to have an impact on what we consider valuable knowledge about the world? What kinds of alternative views could be imagined? These are questions that teachers could elaborate on together with colleagues or with student groups.

The need for intersectional thinking

The analytical method that is proposed in this chapter is about analysing descriptions of social groups as well as challenging hierarchical human relations that might seem commonsensical. Disrupting the *common sense* behind such assumptions requires some effort. Often, much of the textbook material might not raise many eyebrows upon first reading, since most people are familiar with statements that suggest hierarchical relations. We are simply used to a discourse that sees some people as more meaningful than others. This includes media reporting about deaths, for instance: white, Western victims of war or violence are lamented in a different way than non-Western people (Kotilainen, 2016). When the textbooks echo such statements, there is a need for the teacher to keep an observant mindset. Are the textbooks in line with the core values of the curriculum? What would be required from the text for it to truly reflect values such as equality, democracy and human rights? Furthermore, it is important to consider the different intersections of hierarchical relations. Focusing solely on gender, race, class or sexual orientation, for instance, might be needed in the early process of learning to conduct such an analysis; however, learning that unequal human relations are most likely intersected in texts is an important second step.

As an example of this, consider how the following history textbook assignments approach the relation between Europeans and Chinese (question 4), and between the reader and Chinese women (question 5).

> 4. Look at the English soap advertisement. A. How are the Chinese pictured in the advertisement? B. What does the image say about the attitudes of the Europeans towards the Chinese?
> 5. Read the story on the next page about the status of Chinese women and answer question A. What injustices did the Chinese women face in their lives? B. Construct a four-step program to improve the status of Chinese women.
>
> (Rinta-aho, Siltala-Keinänen, Lehtonen and Niemi, 2010: 86)

The first part of this assignment is a form of discourse analysis in itself. Students are asked to examine how a Chinese person is portrayed in an English soap advertisement, most likely from the nineteenth century. The man, who has the face of a monkey, is standing in a dancing pose, and the soap that is being advertised is called *Monkey brand*. The students would likely answer that the image shows Europeans belittling the Chinese. The text on the next page tells how Chinese families used to wish only for boys, and how baby girls were still killed during the twentieth century. It also talks about how Chinese girls had their feet tied and how European missionaries fought hard to have the Chinese give up this tradition. Chinese girls were not allowed to choose their partners, and could end up as the second or third wife of much older men, the text says. It concludes by discussing how difficult it has been to improve the status of Chinese women, since girls were not allowed to go to school. The last sentence, however, suggests that 'Trips that upper-class Chinese women made to the U.S. and to Europe gradually led to Chinese women beginning to demand improvements in their lives, too.' The point is fairly clear: any advantages that the Chinese women received were due to interventions by Westerners. After reading the text, the students are not asked to discuss how differently Westerners are portrayed in relations to the Chinese: both as oppressors and as liberators of women. The analytical element from the first part of the question that is asked reaches only so far as analysing the image. Instead of continuing the discussion about the relations between Westerners and Chinese, the students are asked to first recount the injustices that Chinese women faced, and secondly to construct a program to improve their lives.

From a postcolonial feminist point of view, this assignment can be considered controversial (Mohanty, 1988; Spivak, 1993). It does not challenge but rather confirms the idea that any improvement in the women's situation would necessarily come from the West. Even though it is likely that the textbook authors have intended that the questions be an exercise in critical, independent thinking, since the text also includes several critical points about what the Europeans did to China, there are problems with the assignments. It can be assumed that the answer to the initial question is that Europeans saw the Chinese as inferior, immature, and in need of guidance or protection. The questions that follow the text are, however, a continuation of that very attitude. The analytic take that is presented in the initial question does not carry through the following one; instead, it becomes an arena for students to reproduce hierarchical, colonialist understandings of relations between humans. This should not be considered to mean that studying China or the situation of women in historic or present-day China would not be important—quite the contrary. However, when the frame of mind is that the student in Finland can provide some kind of neutral answers, there is a need to rethink the impact of these kinds of assignments.

Apart from showing the need to analyse the position of Westerners, this assignment shows how strongly different categories of inequality can intersect. The students are asked to critically assess both the Western/non-Western aspect (4b) and the gender aspect (5a, 5b). In the question that focuses on gender, however, the Western/non-Western aspect is considered irrelevant. These aspects are veiled unless the whole set of questions is analysed, keeping different intersections in mind.

Class relations, too, can be analysed by questioning the portrayed perspective. One aspect to focus on in history textbooks is how slavery is described. Quotes such as the following tend to be fairly frequent: 'However, the Iron Age was also a cruel time. Then, people had slaves.' (Aarras-Saari et al., 2006: 43). This is an example of a text written from the perspective of the slave owners. It tells about the lives of both slave owners and slaves, but focuses primarily on the former. A text stating that 'in those times, people were slaves' would be no less accurate than 'in those times, people had slaves.' In my opinion, one rarely comes across the first option in history books. This suggests that the reader is expected to identify with the slave owner, not the slave. I see these descriptions more commonly in textbook passages that only mention slavery, not focusing on the phenomenon in particular. When the topic of slavery is focused on, the textbooks might turn the perspective, such as in the following quote: 'Being a slave meant being owned by another person, just like any object.' (Ahlskog and Sandholm, 2008: 180). Analysing the perspective from which history textbooks approach the concept of slavery is a task that even young students can be expected to be able to do together with social science teachers.

As a slightly more complex example, consider how the following history textbook describes the lives of women in Athens:

> The girls in Athens were brought up differently than in Sparta. They learned needlework, spinning, weaving and embroidery, and to manage the household. At the age of fifteen they were usually married off and got to command servants as well as male and female slaves in their new home. They were not allowed to be concerned with governing the state: that was something the men took care of.
>
> (Snellman and Tötterman-Engström, 2008: 50)

The quote requires an analysis of both gender and class. It refers to the difference between the ancient Greek city-states of Athens and Sparta. There is a triumphant twist to the description of the women's lives at the end of the quote. They had to learn to do chores but were rewarded for this. Suggesting that they got to command servants and slaves means that they rose on the social ladder. The quote could be analysed focusing on the gender and class norms that are suggested in it. It serves as another example of how tightly woven the intersecting gender and class perspectives can be. They should be analysed by looking at the larger concept of hierarchical human relations.

The ordinary: Challenging the norms of implied middle class and whiteness

Apart from descriptions of historical events, there is a need to analyse hierarchical human relations in textbooks dealing with the present day as well. In its description of contemporary America, one history textbook includes the following description:

> In the big cities, there are areas where ordinary citizens are not safe to move around in even during daytime. Steel reinforcements are installed on the doors and windows of apartments. Schools are surrounded by high fences, and metal detectors are installed at the gates. Fear has driven many Americans to more easily take to arms. Ever since the 1990s, the USA has had to pay more attention to its swelling social problems.
>
> (Lähteenmäki and Troberg, 2007: 195)

Several parts of this quote would benefit from a postcolonial discourse analysis. First, the concept of *ordinary citizens* needs to be considered. Who is being portrayed as ordinary? If the cities are not safe for ordinary citizens, who are the ones that can be considered safe? It could be assumed that here, *ordinary* means people who are not (very) poor. Mentioning the concept of *social problems* anchors the quote to class. As argued by Juva and Vaahtera (Chapter 3), normality is constructed through the ideal citizen who fits the social system, and the poor thus become a threatening exception. Mentioning the *fear* experienced by *ordinary* people suggests that those who make up the exception are the source of it, that it is they who pose the threat. Who are the people that are not counted as *ordinary citizens* and who are not afraid to move about? What is the opposite of *ordinary citizens*? Are they all criminals? Are they all poor? Are they people of colour? Race is not mentioned in the passage; however, it can be argued that the above text brings it to mind. It is likely that the concept of *ordinary citizens* implies whiteness. It must be remembered that these kinds of statements do not exist in a vacuum. Moreover, statements like this continue to construct and reconstruct such understandings among students. It is, however, possible to change the perspective and actually question what *ordinary* means.

Concluding remarks

The aim of this chapter was to discuss how postcolonial discourse analysis can be used as a tool for social science education. I have suggested that it can open up different perspectives and enable a questioning of social explanations that do not challenge inequalities. The need for a reflective attitude with respect to one's own privileged status has been emphasised, as well as the potentially difficult task of keeping in mind the intersections of human hierarchies.

The textbook examples shown here might not be particularly shocking. Anyone who has studied social science has probably come across similar formulations. Many of these also echo a language that has become known to readers through the media or non-fiction literature. As an example, the saying,'in those times, people had slaves', would probably not be upsetting to many people. We have heard these kinds of statements before. However, and importantly, the role of social science, including history, geography and social studies, is not to reproduce common understandings of the world: it is to encourage students to become critically aware of human activities in the surrounding world, including its chronological and global dimensions. It is understandable that a teacher would be tempted to approach social science topics by focusing on the familiar, even if it only concerns the history of the winners, colonialism from the perspective of the colonisers, economic history from the perspective of slave owners, or geography from the perspective of tourists (Mikander and Zilliacus, 2016). However, instead of this, as teachers and students, we would benefit from learning to sensitise ourselves to other voices, stories and versions of the past, the present, the local and the global, always bearing power relations in mind. There is much to be gained and little to be lost by switching the perspective and questioning society's hegemonic accounts of the world.

The concept of critical thinking in social science is a relevant part of the Finnish curriculum. As Hyytinen (2015) has suggested, critical thinking involves not just a method but also a critical mindset, and a willingness to put this mindset to use. I argue that despite the frequent references to criticality and critical thinking in the educational curricula, few concrete tools exist for teachers to use in order to teach or promote criticality in the classroom. In this regard, the postcolonial discourse-analytic method presented here could provide some guidance for teaching critical thinking. The textbook quotes analysed in this chapter are used in grades five to nine in Finnish basic education. Students in this age group could learn to question the material in their own textbooks while they are using them as sources of information.

It would be fair to ask: Does this not involve risks? Can students at such a young age (as young as eleven years old) use a textbook as a source and at the same time develop a critical mindset towards it? By way of response, I would suggest conveying to students the message that the textbook in question is but one of many voices. As opposed to other types of texts, school textbooks go through plenty of editing by knowledgeable people. Yet the need for them to be evaluated remains. As I see it, the argument is not that students should become cynical, thinking that no information can be trusted. It is simply to suggest that no story about the world can be considered neutral or universal.

As I have shown above, using postcolonial discourse analysis as a method in social science would broaden the perspectives of students and sensitise them to the idea that there are different versions of reality. This has implications for the idea of social science knowledge, for students, and also for teachers and teacher education.

Quoted textbooks

Aarras-Saari, R., Edgren, H., Edgren, T., Hanste, T., Juutinen, J. and Probst, I., (2006) *Kauan sitten. Matka Suomen historiaan* [Long ago. A journey to the history of Finland], Helsinki: WSOY.

Ahlskog, H. and Sandholm, S., (2008) *Vår Historia 3. 1800-talets historia* [Our history 3. The history of the 19th century], Borgå: Söderströms.

Cantell, H., Jutila, H., Laiho, H., Lavonen, J., Pekkala, E., and Saari, H., (2008) *Pisara 6* [Drop 6], Helsinki: WSOY.

Honkanen, T., Marjomäki, H. and Rajala, K., (2009) *Yhteiskunnan tuulet 9. Tehtäväkirja* [Winds of society 9. Assignment book], Helsinki: Otava.

Lähteenmäki, M. and Troberg, M., (2007) *Kronikka 8* [Chronicle 8], Helsinki: Edita.

Rinta-aho, H., Siltala-Keinänen, P., Lehtonen, O. and Niemi, M., (2010) *Historian Tuulet 7. Tehtäväkirja. Ranskan suuresta vallankumouksesta ensimmäisen maailmansodan loppuun* [Winds of History 7. Assignment book. From the French Revolution to the end of the First World War], Helsinki: Otava.

Snellman, A.M. and Tötterman-Engström, T., (2008) *Vår historia 2* [Our history 2], Borgå: Söderströms.

References

Ajagán-Lester, L., (2001) *'De andra' i pedagogiska texter. Afrikaner i svenska skoltexter 1768-1920*. Lunds universitet, Institutionen för nordiska språk, nr 13.

Andreotti, V., (2011) *Actionable postcolonial theory in education*, New York: Palgrave Macmillan.

Andreotti, V. and de Souza, L., (2012) *Postcolonial perspectives on global citizenship education*, New York: Routledge.

Andreotti, V. and Pashby, K., (2013) Digital democracy and global citizenship education: mutually compatible or mutually complicit? *The educational forum*, 77(4): 422-437.

Bracke, S., (2012) From 'saving women' to 'saving gays': Rescue narratives and their dis/continuities, *European journal of women's studies*, 19(2): 237-252.

Burney, S., (2012) *Pedagogy of the other. Edward Said, postcolonial theory, and strategies for critique*, New York: Peter Lang.

Finnish National Board of Education (FNBE), (2004) *National core curriculum for basic education 2004,* http://www.oph.fi/download/47671_core_curricula_basic_education_1.pdf [Accessed 22 September 2015].

Finnish National Board of Education (FNBE) (2014). *OPS 2016: Esi - ja perusopetuksen opetussuunnitelman perusteiden uudistaminen,* http://www.oph.fi/ops2016 [Accessed 22 September 2015].

Hyytinen, H., (2015) *Looking beyond the obvious: Theoretical, empirical and methodological insights into critical thinking*, Thesis (PhD), University of Helsinki.

Isaksson, P. and Jokisalo, J., (2005) *Historian lisälehtiä. Suvaitsevaisuuden ongelma ja vähemmistöt kansallisessa historiassa*, Helsinki: Like.

Kilomba, G., (2015) *Decolonizing knowledge. A lecture performance*, http://www.goethe.de/mmo/priv/15259714-STANDARD.pdf [Accessed 6 June 2017].

Kotilainen, N., (2016) *Visual theatres of humanity. Constituting the western spectator in the age of the humanitarian world politics*. Thesis (PhD), University of Helsinki.

Kumaravadivelu, B., (1999) Critical classroom discourse analysis, *TESOL quarterly*, 33(3): 453-484.

Laclau, E. and Mouffe, C., (2001) *Hegemony and socialist strategy. Towards a radical democratic poitics,* London: Verso.

Leonardo, Z. and Porter, R. K., (2010) Pedagogy of fear: toward a Fanonian theory of 'safety' in race dialogue, *Race, ethnicity and education*, 13(2): 139-157.

Loftsdóttir, K., (2010) Encountering others in Icelandic textbooks: Imperialism and racial diversity in the era of nationalism, in Helgason, T. and Lässig, S., (eds.) *Opening the mind or drawing boundaries? History texts in Nordic schools*, Göttingen: VandR unipress, 81-98.

Loftsdóttir, K. and Jensen, L., (2012) Nordic exceptionalism and the Nordic 'others'. Introduction, in Loftsdóttir, K. and Jensen, L., (eds.) *Whiteness and postcolonialism in the Nordic region. Exceptionalism, migrant others and national identities*, Farnham: Ashgate.

Loomba, A., (1998) *Colonialism/Postcolonialism*, London: Routledge.

Lozic, V., (2011) *Historieundervisningens utmaningar. Historiedidaktik för 2000-talet*, Malmö: Gleerups.

Merryfield, M. M., (2002) Rethinking our framework for understanding the world, *Theory and research in social education*, 30(1): 148-151.

Mikander, P., (2015) Colonialist ‘discoveries’ in Finnish school textbooks, *Nordidactica - journal of humanities and social science education,* (4): 48-65.

Mikander, P., (2016) *Westerners and others in Finnish school textbooks*, Thesis (PhD), University of Helsinki.

Mikander, P. and Holm, G., (2014) Constructing threats and a need for control: textbook descriptions of a growing, moving world population, *Review of international geographical education*, 4(1): 7-25.

Mikander P. and Zilliacus, H., A postcolonial discourse analysis of Finnish school textbooks: learning about the world from a tourist perspective, *Journal of International Social Studies*, 6(2): 96-108.

Mohanty, C., (1988) Under Western eyes: Feminist scholarship and colonial discourses, *Feminist review*, 30(1): 61-88.

Paasi, A., (1998) Koulutus kansallisena projektina: ‘Me’ ja muut suomalaisissa maantiedon oppikirjoissa, in Alasuutari, P. and Ruuska, P., (eds.) *Elävänä Euroopassa: muuttuva suomalainen identiteetti*, Tampere: Vastapaino.

Palmberg, M., (1987) *Afrika i de svenska skolböckerna*, Uppsala: Nordiska Afrikainstitutet.

Rizvi, F., Lingard, B. and Lavia, J., (2006) Postcolonialism and education: negotiating a contested terrain, *Pedagogy, culture and society*, 14(3): 249-262.

Said, E., (1978) *Orientalism*, New York: Vintage Books.

Spivak, G., (1993) Can the subaltern speak? In Williams, P. and Christman, L., (eds.) *Colonial discourse and post-colonial theory: A reader*, London: Harvester Wheatsheaf, 66-111.

Tiffin, H., (1995) *Postcolonial literatures and counter-discourse,* in Ashcroft, B., Griffiths, G. and Tiffin, H., (eds.) *The post-colonial studies reader,* New York: Routledge.

Walsh, C., (2012) ‘Other’ knowledges, ‘other’ critiques: Reflections on the politics and practices of philosophy and decoloniality in the ‘other’ America, *Transmodernity: Journal of peripheral cultural production of the Luso-Hispanic world,* 1(3): 11-27.

Willinsky, J., (1998) *Learning to divide the world. Education at empire’s end*, Minneapolis: University of Minnesota Press.

Ethnography and Education publications

Titles in the series include›

Creative learning: European experiences, edited by Bob Jeffrey;

Researching education policy: Ethnographic experiences, Geoff Troman, Bob Jeffrey and Dennis Beach;

The commodification of teaching and learning, Dennis Beach and Marianne Dovemark;

Performing English with a postcolonial accent: Ethnographic narratives from Mexico, Angeles Clemente and Michael J. Higgins.

How to do Educational Ethnography, edited by Geoffrey Walford

Ritual and Identity; The staging and performing of rituals in the lives of young people, Christoph Wulf et al.

Young people's influence and democratic education: Ethnographic studies in upper secondary schools, edited by Elisabet Öhrn, Lisbeth Lundahl and Dennis Beach

Learner biographies and learning cultures: Identity and apprenticeship in England and Germany, Michaela Brockmann

Learning care lessons: Literacy, love, care and solidarity, by Maggie Feeley

Identity and social interaction in a multi-ethnic classroom, by Ruth Barley

The postmodern professional: Contemporary learning practices, dilemmas and perspectives, edited by Karen Borgnakke, Marianne Dovemark and Sofia Marques da Silva

Further information available at

www.tufnellpress.co.uk

or

www.ethnographyandeducation.org

www.ingramcontent.com/pod-product-compliance
Ingram Content Group UK Ltd.
Pitfield, Milton Keynes, MK11 3LW, UK
UKHW021053270726
13967UKWH00012B/819

9 781872 767598